Learning to Govern

Billy
The Best!
P.A. Vallone

Learning to Govern

My Life in New York Politics, From Hell Gate to City Hall

by

Peter F. Vallone

CHAUCER PRESS
Published by Richard Altschuler & Associates, Inc.
New York

 For information contact the publisher, Richard Altschuler & Associates, Inc., 100 West 57th Street, New York, NY 10019, RAltschuler@rcn.com or (212) 397-7233.

Library of Congress Control Number: 2005931304
CIP data for this book is available from the Library of Congress

ISBN: 1-884092-07-1

Chaucer Press is an imprint of Richard Altschuler & Associates, Inc.

A portion of Chapter 7, "The Creator," was published in somewhat different form in the July 1980 edition of *Guideposts* magazine.

Editor: Paul De Angelis

Text and Cover Design: Natalie Kelly

Printed in the United States of America

To my beautiful Tena Marie
my partner in life

You were there for me when I ran for Governor,
    The same for Mayor, for I needed no other
So I am there for you for now and for all time,
    As God so has blessed me by making you mine;
Yea, the elections are gone and I do not fear,
    For the victory is mine because you are here.

—Excerpt from a poem, February 14, 2002

Contents

Foreword

- *Telling the truth is one of the foremost principles of good government.*
- *The moment you are elected you are supposed to serve the public, not the other way around.*
- *Credibility and honesty really do count in politics, government, and most assuredly in life.*

After three decades of public service within the contentious world of New York City politics, Peter Vallone seems to have learned a lot more than simply how to govern.

Flip through the pages of this book, and you'll find observations on public life that provide a refreshing antidote to the cynicism that so often seems ready to engulf politics in America. As the former New York City Council Speaker makes clear in the fascinating stories that follow, the lure of public service was, for him, the chance it offered to make a positive difference in the future of the city he loves. Indeed, for Vallone such service is a responsibility. As he says in his preface, "What a waste our lives would be if we neglected the opportunity to make our world a better place, or never even tried."

That sentiment perfectly expresses the Peter Vallone I know: passionate, sincere, energetic, optimistic—and a fighter. As he recounts his early years in borough politics in Queens and his work on the City Council through three mayoral administrations, one begins to understand that public service married his love of New Yorkers' causes and clashes to his sense of idealism and justice, bringing together compassion and fairness, compromise and conviction, power and humility. He reminds us that, in the end, politics should be about people, the values they hold, and, always, the importance of telling the truth.

His embrace of this city began with a nearly idyllic boyhood in Astoria, and his recounting of those roots—family dinners, public schools, summer jobs—resonates with all of us who have grown up with parents grateful for the chance to find the American dream in America's greatest city. He tells *our* stories even as he tells his, and we can follow the direct line he draws from that history to his fervent commitment to the city's public schools, parks, libraries, and neighborhoods—and, most important, to the immigrants who developed and continue to nurture this city. His remembrances are most passionate and poignant when they recall his father (the man who taught him the most about politics) and the faith that was nurtured in those early years, a faith that has sustained him and has led to his deep respect for the mosaic of religious beliefs in New York City. It is in his most personal recollections that we see vividly the earnest optimism that is at the heart of any great civic leader.

But the pragmatist is never far behind. Peter understands New York City politics as few people do, and his store of detail makes the very human drama of elections, budgets, and governance come alive. In these pages, we are able to sit across from someone who has been a key player in behind-the-scenes discussions and decisions and hear frank talk about the relationships, principles, and personalities that have shaped the city for the past few decades. Who else could speak as directly and knowledgeably about the battle to eliminate the Board of Estimate, the soothing of racial tensions in Brooklyn, and the efforts to lower crime on subways and in neighborhoods? He has had a unique vantage point from which to view the style and substance of three New York City mayors, Ed Koch, David Dinkins, and Rudy Giuliani, and his insights are as revealing as they are judicious.

Because of Peter's deep belief in the power of public education, it was inevitable that our paths would cross. My work with him on behalf of The City University of New York (CUNY) disclosed the same man whose personality leaps from the pages of this book: decent, funny, practical, strategic, tenacious, and absolutely committed to the best possible future for all New Yorkers. Today, thanks to the New York City Council and its leadership, nearly 34,000 CUNY students with "B" averages or better have benefited from the council's Peter F. Vallone Academic Scholarship Program. It is indicative of the forward-thinking, community-based work for which Peter is celebrated.

Peter Vallone has secured a place in New York City history—one can't imagine the city without him—and his plea for civic involvement and responsibility should be heeded by all of us who hope for a bright future for the city and, indeed, the country. His is the authentic voice of a New Yorker who loves this city and its people and who cherishes New York's role as a beacon of hope to those still seeking the American dream. His contributions to the city make for a remarkable read, to be sure, but perhaps even more important, they restore our faith that in the right hands, public service is, as he says, "a noble profession."

— *Matthew Goldstein*
Chancellor
The City University of New York
July 2005

Preface

I am continually dismayed by Americans' lack of knowledge of the basics of our system of government in Washington, D.C., a lack made worse by their general lack of interest in their state and municipal governments. Thankfully, we are now the only superpower on Earth, and we do not have to worry about losing a war by force of arms from an outside power. Today we must concentrate on protecting ourselves from the terrorists who, on September 11, 2001, were able to plan and execute the most despicable single act of terror in recorded history. To do that, the more we know about our democracy, the better our chances are of preserving, protecting, and improving it. If malcontents are willing to die for a nefarious cause, how much more important is it for us to live out the most worthy of all causes?

If we wish to maintain our democratic freedoms—a system made possible by a balanced system of government in which the people rule—we better take the time to learn more about it and attract good people into it. Our enemies are willing to blow themselves up and kill thousands of innocent people while they do it because they believe in a distorted idea of government where death and subjugation, not life and freedom, are their ultimate goals. Now is the time for Americans to take a greater interest in our governing system. There can be no better way of doing so than by studying America's greatest city, especially during the last thirty years, when New York City's system of governance evolved from an unbalanced intermingling of executive and legislative powers to a prototype of good municipal government.

It seems to me that certain principles are essential if you wish to be successful in both life and politics. Politics should be viewed as a perfectly acceptable way of getting into government, but never as an end in itself. Success can never be measured in simply winning an election, because in the long run it is how you get there that counts. If you do not build a solid foundation and make friends along the way, the quicker you rise to the top, the surer you are to fall. Credibility and honesty really do count in politics, government, and most assuredly in life.

My purpose in writing this book is to share the experiences I have had over three decades of public service. I have kept a short daily diary since 1953 and will intersperse references and events throughout my recollections in an attempt to tell a truthful story. I will be as accurate as possible without unnecessarily revealing any confidences or hurting anyone along the way.

Public service is a noble profession, and in this country it is the noblest of all because the bedrock of our system of government is our "Creator."

By that I am not suggesting that our citizenry ought to practice or believe in one religion or another, but rather that our rights flow from a higher authority than whoever holds office at any particular time. I hope to prove that "doing the right thing" will serve as the best policy for any aspiring officeholder to follow, even if not the politically correct thing to do at the moment. I hope my experiences will serve as a road map for others to follow. I hope further that they illustrate why people should never get discouraged by a few bumps along the way. Politics and principles of government need not be at odds, but can and should work in harmony with each other.

In the end, I am convinced that we will all be accountable to the one who created us in the beginning, our "Creator." What a waste our lives would be if we neglected the opportunity to make our world a better place, or never even tried.

Acknowledgments

Besides my family, which has stood beside me every step of the way in the writing, re-writing and discussion of this book, several associates from my public life as well as publishing professionals have been of inestimable assistance in seeing this work through to completion. My first thanks must go to Dr. Matthew Goldstein, Chancellor of The City University of New York, for encouraging me to round out the first draft with more details of my personal life, and to persevere beyond that second draft to create a full narrative that might be of interest to both students and the general public. Next I would like to salute my brilliant editor, prodder, and prompter, Paul De Angelis, who worked with me to shape both sentences and story into a readable whole. Gary Altman, that incredible trove of City Council history, proved invaluable in providing the facts when memory and diary proved incomplete. Richard Weinberg provided valuable interpretive context for many of the incidents portrayed in the book. Arden Melick provided welcome encouragement at the midpoint of the final composition. Peg Breen, Ralph Miles, Joe Strasburg, Richard Emery, Gail Benjamin, and *New York Times* reporter Alan Finder all provided assistance at key moments in preparation of the text. Jack Rudin has provided guidance and advice through the years. My office staff, including Teresa Jarnick and Christine Kukunis, were there at every moment when I needed them. In the final stages of preparing and publicizing the book, I have been fortunate to have found publisher Richard Altschuler and reconnected with public relations guru Howard Rubenstein. My heartfelt thanks to all of these, and the many others who have helped over the last several years.

Learning to Govern

Prologue

On the Sunday evening of Labor Day weekend, 1990, twenty-two-year-old Brian Watkins and his family were waiting for a train in the subway station at 53rd Street and Seventh Avenue in Manhattan. The Watkins family, tennis enthusiasts, had come to New York from Provo, Utah, to attend the United States Tennis Open in Flushing Meadows, Queens. Brian, his parents, his brother, and sister-in-law were on their way to have dinner at Tavern on the Green. A roving band of thugs entered the station in high spirits and spotted the tourist family. They surrounded the Watkinses and demanded money. There was a struggle. The young men had a box cutter. They slashed up the trousers pockets and buttocks of Sherwin Watkins, the father, and took his money and credit cards. When Mrs. Watkins objected she was kicked and thrown down. Brian and his brother tried to defend their parents, and Brian was stabbed in the chest. That didn't stop him from chasing the hoodlums down the subway platform as they fled the scene. Brian collapsed on the platform stairs and died on the way to the hospital. The murderers used their plunder to go dancing at the nearby ballroom disco, Roseland. Most were arrested there, shortly before dawn the next morning.

Young Brian became the eighteenth person slain in the subway that year: one of a record 2,262 homicides in the city overall. Worse yet, the killing was only the latest in a series of well-publicized incidents involving gang violence against apparently random victims. The year before a group of youngsters roaming Central Park had attacked and nearly killed a young woman jogger there in what was called an episode of "wilding." In Bensonhurst, Brooklyn, a young African-American named Yusef Hawkins had been murdered by a group of Italian-Americans in a case of mistaken identity. Over the summer of 1990 many taxi and livery car drivers had been assaulted and twenty-one killed, while dozens of young children had been hit by stray bullets, six of them fatally—one while lying in her own bed in her family's Brooklyn apartment.

The reputation of New York City, which had struggled so hard to put behind it the budget and crime crises of the 1970s, was being tarnished. Worldwide publicity about the earlier attacks had already led many tourists to cancel their plans to visit New York. Immediately following the Labor Day subway attack, bewildered visitors worried about losing their lives "like the man in the subway," and some residents talked about finding another place to live. The *New York Times* of September 5 declared: "The stabbing . . . underscored . . . the perception that almost anyone could become a crime victim almost anywhere in the city, at almost anytime."

For me, it was very hard going back to work after that Labor Day weekend. In September of 1990, I had just been elected the first Speaker of the New York City Council, a body that had been known in the days of the infamous Boss Tweed as "The Forty Thieves" and more recently as a legislature that did nothing more than rename streets and pry a few pennies out of the mayor's budget for local pet projects. Only days earlier, all that had changed for good. On August 27 the Board of Estimate, a panel of executives dominated by the mayor that had wielded broad budgetary and other powers for over a century, had passed into history, and its legislative powers had devolved onto the City Council I now led. For several months my top staff and I had been struggling to reconcile the pressing social and safety needs of the city with the dismal economic facts of life.

The Watkinses had had no idea that the vaunted New York City police force had been so severely decimated by budget cuts that many of the subways and streets were in fact no longer safe. I *knew* that my city was not doing enough to protect both its citizens and visitors like the Watkins family. I had no idea at the time, however, that such a horrible crime was going to be the first test of whether the City Council was capable of sharing real power in the world's most important city. Unlike many who wrung their hands in despair while deploring the tragedy of Brian Watkins's slaying, I knew we had to do something dramatically different, and I anxiously awaited my four closest advisors as I did every morning at about 8 A.M.

My chief of staff Joe Strasburg arrived first, closely followed by budget director Marc Shaw and communications director Peg Breen. As we began discussing the outrageous killing of Brian, Richard Weinberg , counsel to the Speaker, came storming in, angrily threw his jacket on my sofa, and exclaimed furiously, "We've got to do something *now!*"

"We all agree with that, Rich," I said, "but the question is, *how*? The city's broke and the mayor is focusing on social services, which are also decimated. You're my advisors, and I've told you my highest priority is to make the city safe. This town is already overtaxed. But if we don't do our job, no one who can afford it will stay. We've got to start by rebuilding our criminal justice system. So you tell me—*how?*"

For years the City Council had been putting money into the budget for more cops, only to see the Mayor's Office of Management and Budget and the Board of Estimate defer, delay, or refuse to hire them. Their battle cry: "Not hiring a thousand cops saves the city a hundred million dollars!" The same basically held true for fire and sanitation officers. This savings was realized because at the time uniformed services were paid for entirely with New York City taxes. There was no loss of matching state and federal dollars, as there was with most other city programs, including many of the Board of Estimate's priority programs. Thus it was far easier to cut cops and fire and sanitation officers than social service workers. If you cut or refused to hire in non-uniformed areas, the city would lose two-thirds of the funding and save only one-third of our budget, meaning that you had to cut three times the number of workers at the same salary level to save the same $100 million. This was the real reason mayors had gone along with the dramatic decrease in the number of cops on the street.

The decision to cut back on cops was traceable to the city's terrible financial crisis of the '70s, when the city finally faced up to its habit of paying for programs with fictitious revenue. In those years, Mayors Beame and Koch had balanced the budget because they were required by law to do so, even though it had meant cutting back significantly on police, fire, and sanitation. The police force, in particular, which had numbered above 30,000 before the '70s fiscal crisis, had dropped to 26,000. Perhaps inevitably, crime and lawlessness had increased, though the deterioration was checked in the mid-1980s by the stock market boom and a robust economy. That bubble burst near the end of the decade, and we now faced the consequences.

Joe Strasburg, my chief of staff, agreed with Rich that we needed to do something, and quickly, to restore public confidence. A clear signal had to be sent that rampages like this would not be tolerated in our city. "It's all over the national airwaves: tourists leaving town, others canceling trips. . . . Did you know about Japan? I hear they issued a travel advisory to all their tourists."

"Another senseless subway slaying. Just what New York City needs!" I lamented. "It was bad enough with the Central Park jogger, but at least then people said, 'Oh, it was a distant corner of the park, she was alone, I would never go out in the park alone like that. . . .' But here they had the impunity to go after a whole family."

"Our mayor says New York City is as safe or safer than most other American cities," Rich reminded us sarcastically.

"That approach misses the whole point," argued Joe. "The fact is, the headlines accurately reflect what each of us in this room feels—that no one is really secure boarding a subway train alone at eleven at night. And if we don't feel secure about our own safety in public places in this city, how can we expect the general public to feel safe? It doesn't matter what the statistics say, it's what we believe that matters."

Over my years in government I had learned the hard way that perception is often just as important as reality. Even if New York was "objectively" a safe city, the subjective perception of many if not most visitors and even residents was that it was unsafe. "As long as people think that you've got crime packs out there willing to attack a family, and no one to stop them, things will only get worse," I said. "What can we do to calm people, to make people feel more safe now?"

More cops, was the unanimous response. Yet we all realized we could not realistically put cops on the streets that we did not yet have.

How about guaranteeing that there would be more? That seemed a good start. But how many? To most of us at the strategic meeting that began on September 4 and carried over into the next day, it was clear that nothing less than a full restoration of New York City's traditional level of police staffing—five thousand additional cops on the streets—would send the necessary signal to the city, national, and international community that New York City was going to crack down on the apparent wave of lawlessness. That was the number that Mayor Koch had proclaimed as his target throughout his twelve years in office, only to have the actual numbers always fall well below it. The question remained, how? If Ed Koch had been unable to do it during the go-go '80s, what made us think we could do it in today's stagnant economy?

We would have to do what any real legislature does: pass a law. Thanks to the United States Supreme Court, we on the City Council would no longer have to triangulate between the mayor's office and an unsympathetic Board of Estimate. And with the right public relations campaign, the mayor would almost certainly respond to our initiative.

My staff and I devoted the rest of that day and the next defining the basic legislation and the parameters of possible compromise. We then brainstormed every possible legal, financial, political, and publicity angle. It was a bold and risky plan. No City Council, no City Council leader had ever taken such an initiative—or, indeed, been in a position to do so. Exactly one week earlier, the Board of Estimate had gone out of business forever after nearly one hundred years holding the reins of power in Gotham. Because of the institutional revolution in the way New York City was governed, we were making the rules up as we went along—and everyone was watching. Certainly we risked the wrath of voters tired of empty promises and higher taxes. But the very survival of the city was at stake. We simply had to convince people that it was safe to come back to New York.

Our staff planning paid off over the next week. We kicked off the next morning with a crowded news conference in my newly painted, rosé-colored office: myself, flanked by the council's Steering Group along with the chair of Public Safety. We announced the outlines of our proposal for mandating an increase in cop levels of 5,000 and thus dramatically shifting the dynamics on the streets. Anticipating criticism from those who thought we were somehow trampling on the mayor's prerogative, I declared: "We have to do something to take back the streets. We don't think we can wait even a day. Far from stealing the mayor's thunder, we'd like to see both sides of City Hall strike lightning together."

Coincidentally, on the same day in Provo, Utah, Brian Watkins's brother Todd appeared before the press to "challenge the people of New York City to get involved," and "to take the risk." Fighting back tears, Todd Watkins declared that he and his family, as devout Mormons, had fought back their bitterness and "chosen to take the more difficult path of faith and patience." All the family was asking from New Yorkers was not to let "Brian die in vain."

Over the next few days Peg Breen arranged for me to talk with the editorial boards of all the major newspapers. The media coverage was intense and mostly favorable to our initiative. A year earlier, the press would have laughed off our proposal to mandate an increase of 5,000 police officers as so much posturing. Now the media was saying: "Hey, the new charter gave these guys the power to do something. What if they're for real?" We got the front page of the *New York Times* and editorials on radio, television, and the dailies. "Mr. Vallone Stands Up to Crime," declared the *Times*, while a prominent newscaster admitted: "Now I know why they changed the city charter!"

The political support that pushed us over the edge, however, came the following Tuesday, when Governor Cuomo delivered a speech before the Citizens Crime Commission, a civilian watchdog group, and endorsed our target of 5,000 new police officers. As if to cement the healing of a few years of estrangement from one of my earliest political associates, Mario came over to me a few days later at a celebration in honor of an Italian World War II hero by the Italian-American Coalition—and kissed me on the forehead!

In my opinion, the genesis of New York City as the safest big city in America lies in the intense discussion among that small group of my closest advisors on September 4 and 5, 1990. The reclaiming of our streets and subways that began in the Dinkins years and accelerated under Mayor Rudy Giuliani first took shape in this chamber. By 2003 homicides in our city had fallen from 2,300 to less than 700, and as of this writing are still falling. The year 1990 also began a new era of balanced and accountable government in a safer New York. Since 1986 I had been the leader of the New York City Council, and I was about to begin my twelve years as the council's Speaker, second in power only to the mayor.

The end for me as an elected official came on December 31, 2001, the day that term limits legislation forced me and Rudy Giuliani out of City Hall. Three years earlier I had lost my race as Democratic gubernatorial candidate against Republican George Pataki, and three months before, had lost my own quest to become mayor in a complex, interrupted Democratic primary.

I have had the unique opportunity to serve on a daily one-to-one basis with three very different mayors. The office they occupied is arguably second in difficulty and prestige only to that of the presidency of the United States. If I had to pick a word to describe each of the mayors I served with as Speaker, I would call Edward I. Koch the "Spirit," David N. Dinkins the "Heart," and Rudolph F. Giuliani the "Brain" of the Big Apple. They were dedicated to helping their beloved city and I was equally committed to their succeeding, no matter what our political or governmental disagreements might have been at the time.

The man from whom I learned the most about politics, however, was neither a mayor nor a legislator, but a judge: my father, Charles J. Vallone. What he and my mother taught us about tolerance, life, God, and love formed the bedrock on which I constructed my political career, for better or worse. Before I look over that career, therefore, let me take a brief look at its youthful foundations.

PART I

Starting Out

1

Tell the Truth

I love this country. For the twenty-seven years I had the privilege of serving as an elected official in the City of New York, sixteen as second in power only to the mayor, I finally understood why I love being an American so much. It all started for me when I was born in a soon-to-be rent-controlled apartment house in Astoria in 1934. It seems that the Board of Aldermen, then the governing body of the city, passed a law in 1932 requiring every apartment to have a bathroom. My grandfather had immigrated from Sicily in 1904 with $21 in his pocket, and my grandmother arrived shortly thereafter, carrying my two-year-old father with the rest of the Vallone clan in hand. All eleven moved into an apartment at 337 East 14th Street and shared a bathroom with three other apartments on the same floor. This was the typical tenement house that millions of new immigrants moved into at the turn of the century. The New York City Council in which I served memorialized this part of our history by funding and creating the Tenement Museum, located at 97 Orchard Street on the Lower East Side of Manhattan. After viewing it, you come to realize what sacrifices these hardy new Americans made.

The new bathroom ordinance spurred a great migration out of Manhattan into the "suburbs." Many landlords were forced to close their buildings to residential use because they could not afford the cost of upgrading. This was also the time of the Great Depression, and it was hard for my father, a young lawyer, to find work. Since my parents couldn't afford their own house, they elected to move into an apartment building in a neighborhood of Astoria, Queens, which was mostly single- or two-family homes. The apartment consisted of five rooms, a virtual palace compared to what they were leaving on the Lower East Side, and it was here that my older brother Buddy (Charles J. Vallone Jr.) and I grew up. Our building was called The Tips, and was located at 22-07 19th Street. It fronted on Astoria Park, and when I was young, I used to sit out on the fire escape and look out over "my country": the park, the Triborough and Hell Gate bridges, the river, and the great city of New York just on the other side of it. The park and the Triborough were in the process of being completed the year I was born. I still live only one block away, in a two-family house.

In 1932 my family may not have been able to afford their own house or car, but my father, who was thirty, had been lucky enough to find a job at J. P. Morgan's Bank in Manhattan just before moving to Astoria. Within a year or two he opened his own law office in Astoria, across from the elevated subway line, on 31st Street, one of the area's commercial thoroughfares. He also started the Astoria Civic Association, the forerunner of many civic and community action groups.

I learned a lot about principles and politics from my father, about faith in God, country, and family, and about loyalty and ecumenicism. He was deeply in love with my mother, Leah, and would not even think of having breakfast or dinner with anyone but her and their two sons. She was exceptionally beautiful, intelligent, and loved her job as special assistant to the principal of Julia Richman High School on Manhattan's East Side, where she also served as teacher. Dad always rang the downstairs doorbell three times at about six in the evening, our fixed dinnertime. Mom, who had come home only a few hours earlier, would hasten to have Buddy and me greet him at the door with a kiss. I will never forget the joy and happiness we shared during these formative years.

We all looked forward to Saturday nights because that was when the Sunday papers came out, and it was a special time for the four of us to read together. Dad would buy every newspaper, including the *New York Times, Daily News, Daily Mirror, Journal American, Post,* and *World-Telegram,* and Mom nearly every magazine—*Life, Cosmopolitan,* and *Reader's Digest,* to name a few. Every week Buddy and I could purchase one Classics comic book each. Saturday night was our reading marathon: we would discuss the day's, week's, and world events with each other, always with the admonition, "Don't believe everything you read, but read everything you can."

Mom loved to read novels, and enrolled us in the Children's Book-of-the-Month Club, where for the first time I could enjoy the adventures of the world by simply reading a book for pleasure, and not because I had to for school. To this day, I have never stopped buying and reading every New York newspaper daily, as well as many magazines. I still love to read adventure novels of all kinds, and usually have three or four books at my bedside that I dip into before retiring. Mom brought me to our local public library for my first library card at the age of five, and at the tender age of seventy I still carry one from the same library. Is it any wonder that one of my first priorities after being elected leader of the New York City Council was to reopen and strengthen libraries, and register every child in his or her local library?

Saturday night was also the time Dad would cook to give Mom a break, and whenever possible it would be a three-steak dinner. Buddy and I always marveled how Dad would so tenderly cut the filet off his huge T-bone steak to give to his beloved Leah, and invariably say, "The best part always goes to your mom because she is the best part of my life."

As Dad's law practice grew, so did the Astoria Civic Association he had founded. It was one of the first, and flourished under his leadership, no doubt because of the numerous new Italians in the neighborhood, as well as the many Irish friends he made. The main goals of the group were to help improve the area, increase police protection, and fight juvenile delinquency. He started a Queens Boys Club a few blocks from his office, and later, the Astoria Youth Auxiliary sponsored baseball and football teams that gave a start to such future stars as Yankee pitcher Whitey Ford and Dodger pitcher Billy Lowes. It is no coincidence that some of the best farm teams in professional sports came out of Astoria.

When World War II broke out Dad was too old to serve in the military, so he became an air raid warden and the western Queens zone commander of civil defense. Astoria—with its huge generating plant, newly opened airport and, most important, the largest railroad bridge in the country—was an extremely sensitive area. I remember nights as a kid watching the stark profile of tanks on open railroad cars being transported across the steel spans of Hell Gate Bridge. Huge searchlights pierced the sky from Astoria Park. An army barracks and recruiting station could be found in a big undeveloped field north of the park, which was also used for Victory Gardens. They didn't build there until after the war, and, in fact, my uncle James had his Victory Garden right next to where my home is today.

On occasion, the army would move their antiaircraft guns right into Astoria Park to provide more protection to Hell Gate Bridge. We kids loved these maneuvers and played "guns" incessantly, running through the barracks and backyards looking for "Japs" and "Nazis" to kill. During air raids, which happened almost every night, we would have to pull down the black shades on the windows and turn off all lights and appliances except the radio. The wardens would come around and bang on the door, while my mother and brother and I would sit by the radio listening to the war news. Things were not going well for the Allies in the early '40s, and we were particularly fearful for all of our relatives serving in the war effort overseas.

During the war Dad used to lead so-called Brotherhood Day parades up Ditmars Boulevard—Astoria's main drag. We were practicing Catholics deeply immersed in our faith (I still am). Both my brother Buddy and I wanted to attend the local Catholic school where most of our friends went, but we were rejected. As preschoolers I vividly recall my brother and me walking behind Dad as he marched arm in arm with a Protestant minister and a rabbi. There were certain misguided elements of the Catholic Church at the time who believed that the way to salvation could come only through the Roman Catholic Church and that everyone else was going to hell; we were not to socialize or give credence of any kind to another clergyman. Of course, my father rejected this un-Jesus-like theory, but unfortunately the local monsignor and pastor did not. So as we marched past our local church the good monsignor called out, "Vallone, you should be ashamed of yourself. You are going to be excommunicated!" Dad would merely tip his hat in respect and keep marching—and never missed mass on Sunday. Since we were not let in to the local parochial school, I spent eight of the best years of my life attending our local public school, PS 122.

Queens had become the new home of a huge number of Italian immigrants, and the United States was then at war with Italy. My father was fluent in both Italian and English and he relished speaking at civic meetings, war bond rallies, or wherever more than a few Italian-speaking people were gathered. I remember going around with my father to Civic Association meetings, and meetings sponsored by them, in big halls and movie theaters. I loved to listen to him, even though when he mangled a joke it sometimes proved embarrassing. He would say, in both Italian and English:

"Remember why you came to this great country called America. This is the only country in the world where our rights do not come from a ruler called a dictator, a king or queen, a general, or even a president or a congress. In this country our rights come from our Creator, our God." Then he would read the Declaration of Independence and close with this flourish: "In this country God, country, and family come first. That is why we are fighting the Fascist alliance and why we will prevail. You are not Italian-Americans! You are Americans of Italian descent! Be proud of your Italian roots, but be willing to die for what this country stands for, 'one nation, under God, with liberty and justice for all.'"

This "melting pot" ideal was more than just words for my father, and I still maintain it is the secret of America's strength. Dad had a deep and abiding faith in God and country and practiced what he preached. In The Tips, we lived the melting pot every day—and endured the resentments stirred by war. There was a Polish family above us, a Greek one under us,

Hungarians next to us, and Maltese, Romanians, and Lithuanians on the other side of the building. The native countries of every one of these families seemed to be allied with the United States—except for ours. Although Italians kept moving into Astoria, we were one of the few Italians in the building, and in the neighborhood the dominant groups were still Irish and German, who mostly owned their own homes.

My full name—Peter Fortunate Vallone—comes from my grandfather's name, "Pietro Fortunato" Vallone. Though my parents had thoughtfully anglicized both my given names, my teacher always liked to call out "Fortunato!" when she came to me. That quickly got transformed into "Footy!" and led to innumerable fistfights. I was a little kid anyway, unlike my brother, and a little on the heavy side. One day Paul, the six-foot boy from the Polish family upstairs, called me a "guinea bastard," punched me in the stomach, and sent me bouncing down the marble staircase. My dad went up to talk to his family and lay down the law: 1) don't ever have him touch my son again, and 2) don't ever use that word again. He had absolutely no tolerance for ethnic insults: he once decked an Irish guy in the audience who made fun of his Italian background.

Because or in spite of Italy's role in the war, the most patriotic group seemed to be the Italians. In fact, more New Yorkers of Italian descent died for their country than those from any other ethnic group. The bad part of it was that we never learned to speak Italian, because the language was dropped from the classrooms and our grandparents and parents would not speak the language at home. They wanted us to be Americans first, last, and always.

All of my cousins and uncles were in the uniformed services, mostly in the Pacific. My uncle George, who later became a flamboyant Fifth Avenue beautician (George V of 5th Ave) was attached to a navy unit on an island in the Pacific that served as an ammunition storage area. Somehow he arranged it so that all of the Vallones in the Pacific met on that island for a reunion in the middle of the war. One of my cousins, Carl, took part in many of the U.S. Army's island invasions. On one particular island his entire unit was wiped out when the Japanese, who had dug themselves into hidden caves when the marines took it over, emerged again in a suicide ambush attack as soon as the army moved in. The only reason Carl survived was that he was in the hospital with malaria.

As we grew older and my cousins and I became more physically able to defend ourselves—and the neighborhood itself became increasingly Italian—we weren't beaten up anymore. Also, by then I had learned a thing or two about defending myself. My older brother Buddy and I were only twenty-two months apart. We had a good relationship, but we fought all the time. I can't list all the things we either broke playing around or fighting in the apartment. My first recollection of Buddy is of him giving me a bloody nose and my knocking his tooth out. I was three and a half years old. After that my father gave us boxing gloves, and I learned how to fight for real. Later on my fighting skills would often save me.

When the war ended in 1945 I was almost eleven years old, and Dad would let me help in his law office. Since my mom still worked and taught in Manhattan, his office also served as a safe haven for me and a great place to do my homework. There I would spend hours reading from his classic book library, which included everything from Cicero to summaries of United States federal court decisions.

We still lived in The Tips, which by now was a rent-controlled apartment house, but after the war Dad became serious about buying a vacation home about sixty miles north in the Catskills. It was called Mountain Lodge Park, and was situated between Washingtonville and Monroe in Orange County, New York. To me and my brother it was the Garden of Eden come to life: a brand-new bungalow on top of the world, on half an acre, with all kinds of adventure waiting.

Dad took me to what was supposed to be the closing as his "law assistant." Instead of a joyful event, it was a disaster. Halfway through, my father's usually cheerful face reddened with anger. It seems they wanted him to sign a restrictive covenant that would prohibit him from reselling the property to "Hebroids or Negroids," two terms I was thoroughly unfamiliar with. Dad stormed out, saying he would never sign something that belittled everything this country stood for: "Don't you know how many Jews and Negroes have died just so that bungalows like this can be freely bought and sold?"

Back home on my fire escape, I cried my eyes out. It seemed we had just lost our dream house over a technicality. Well, as things turned out, we didn't lose the bungalow. My dad decided to mount a campaign to remove the offensive covenant from all Mountain Lodge deeds, and once he succeeded, the closing took place. We spent every summer thereafter in our little piece of paradise. For me it was really heaven on earth. Some years later, after my father died, a man I recognized as a former neighbor in Mountain Lodge joined one of my campaigns as a volunteer. "I am doing it for your dad," he told me. "I was the first Jew to buy in Mountain Lodge Park."

As far as my family was concerned, I never met anyone busier than my dad. He was a busy trial attorney, a schooled pianist by age seventeen, head of a large civic association, a checkers champ, and an avid pinochle player. But he was always home by six for dinner every day, and all day Sunday. There were to be no controversial subjects during dinner, but after dinner all grievances could be aired. The golden rule of self-discipline was that as long as we told him the truth, he would stick by us and help us out of any jam. Dad's admonition to always tell the truth—or to remain silent rather than tell a falsehood—turned out to be one of the best ways to succeed in both politics and in life. Telling the truth is one of the foremost principles of good government. It is the one principle that I have tried hardest to keep all through my years of government service. In his book *Leadership,* Rudy Giuliani had this to say about the relationship between him and me: "City Council Speaker Peter Vallone [and I] had major disagreements of a substantive nature. We even went to court and sued each other. But we became and remained good friends because I knew I could trust him to tell me the truth."

It is common knowledge that the media reports on what the public likes to hear and see, and usually this means on what is going wrong. Thus, far from following the prophet Micah's admonition to "do the right thing," most of what the newspapers print and the radio and TV promote are "the wrong thing." This translates into front-page coverage of the most sensational crimes and events. If you need proof, just look at the headline news coverage the day you read this chapter. Why not more good news? One of the best answers I know was given by Jim Jensen, the late anchor of WCBS-TV, at a meeting of the Astoria Civic Association I was chairing back in the 1980s. Jim was the guest speaker, and when some people in the audience said they were sick of all the bad news, Jim replied, "It really is your fault. You only want to hear about the cat that was trapped in a tree, and not the thousands still safely on the ground." That simple statement quieted the crowd.

The media, he explained, is in the business of making a profit. If they don't do whatever it takes "to sell newspapers," they go out of business. The media supplies what the public "buys." This is also pretty much the story of how a candidate gets elected. You have to "sell" yourself to the electorate. The bigger the office sought, the more important the media becomes, as well as the cost involved. Obviously you cannot hope to become president, governor, or mayor of a large city unless you spend millions on television, radio, direct mailings, and advertisements in the newspapers.

There are ways, however, of getting free exposure without spending a dime, before and after obtaining public office. In addition to the latest violent crimes and wrongdoings, the media are always thirsty for human interest stories. As I mentioned, my dad was a community activist as well as civic leader. I remember him getting very upset once in the late 1940s because a child was run over and seriously injured at 29th Street and 23rd Avenue in Astoria—a very busy intersection near his law office where he had long been asking the traffic department to install a stop sign.

The *Long Island Star-Journal* was then our local newspaper and I was still attending PS 122. I distinctly remember witnessing Dad venting his frustrations at the lack of action by the traffic department to George Douris, a young reporter for the paper and later the founder of HANAC (the Hellenic American Neighborhood Action Committee), one of the premier nonprofit, government-funded service organizations in the city. The conversation in his law office went something like this:

> **DAD:** What do I have to do, George, to get the attention of the traffic department before some innocent child gets killed? I have tried calling, sending letters, getting hundreds of citizens to sign petitions, and even threatened a lawsuit. Do I have to move my desk into the street and block all the traffic?
>
> **GEORGE:** Sounds like a good idea to me, Charlie!

The next thing I knew Dad got together a few members of the Astoria Civic Association to help him move his desk right into the middle of the 29th street intersection. I'll never forget it, because I was terribly worried that Dad would either get run over or be arrested, leaving me, my brother, and Mom out on the streets, too. Soon hundreds of people had joined in the protest, and the traffic department's representative had to rush to the scene. Dad made page one of the *Star-Journal,* his desk was carried back to his office, and soon thereafter the stop sign was installed and has been there ever since.

2

Youth

Accountability. That is a key word in life, as well as in government. At my public grammar school I was extremely fortunate to have an eighth-grade teacher by the name of Miss Flynn who came in an hour early every morning to coach students like me who wanted to attend private or specialized schools where entrance examinations were required. Because of her, I passed the exam, which enabled me to attend Power Memorial Academy, a Catholic private school in Manhattan. This turned out to be another pivotal event in my life, because only two kids in my eighth-grade class were going to Power. Most of the rest were going to Long Island City High School.

Since Catholic schools graduated only in June and at that time public schools graduated in June and January, my classmate and I came into a class that was six months ahead of us. We had to work twice as hard to keep up. We wore uniforms and carried at least six books back and forth from Manhattan every day. Coming home we would take the train to Queens Plaza from 59th Street and then board the bus that took us to 21st Street and Ditmars Boulevard, a block from where we both lived.

Unfortunately, we took the bus at the same time all the students emptied out from Long Island City High. In our brisk new uniforms with solid-color ties and blue jackets and loaded down with textbooks, my classmate and I stood out like sore thumbs. On the day in question, at least twenty rowdy students boarded the bus, led by a huge ringleader by the name of Harry. They began to taunt us with every imaginable name: "Look at the sissies in their pretty mommy uniforms," etc., etc. I knew Harry from the neighborhood. It seemed he was born weighing two hundred pounds; as he grew heavier he became more aggressive. The twenty-minute ride seemed to last forever. My classmate took off his tie and jacket and left me to go sit with Harry, the first betrayal in my fourteen years, and a foretaste of what was to come in politics. This egged on my tormenters to the point where Harry left his seat and began yelling in my ear. The whole bus seemed to chant "Petey-boy's a scared little sissy, going home to mommy to cry." As far as I was concerned that seemed like a very good idea. Somehow I held back the tears and was the first off the bus when we finally reached our stop. But Harry leaped off, too, pushed me and blocked my path home, screaming, "Chicken! Chicken!"

All seemed lost. Fortunately, my dad had taught my brother and me how to box, under supervision, with boxing gloves. Somehow I found the courage to take a swing at the taunting, pushing Harry. With all my might I hit him, square on his huge jaw. He fell right over the fence behind him. Although I didn't yet know it, this was truly the luckiest punch of my life. At the moment all I wanted to do was run home as fast as I could, but my feet seemed glued to the ground. I figured Harry would simply get up and kill me. Instead he got up, climbed over the fence, and ran away, crying and screaming like a hysterical baby. Meanwhile my tormenters, including the classmate who had deserted me, gathered round in congratulations. I never had trouble with Harry or any other local bullies again. That lesson was so important for me (or anyone else who wants to succeed in politics, or in life): never run away from a bully!

Growing up in Astoria in a loving home, attending an excellent public school during World War II where virtually all the students were released one afternoon each week for religious instruction, I soon became interested in whether there was really a Creator, a God up there somewhere. While I was in eighth grade, my mother developed a malignant tumor and had to stay in Mount Sinai Hospital, on upper Fifth Avenue in Manhattan, for two or three months. This was a traumatic episode for the entire family. I remember, shortly after my mother first went into the hospital, hearing my father crying in bed behind the closed French doors. This was very unusual. In public, even with my mother fighting for her life, he was always upbeat and positive. Hearing him sobbing, and not seeing it, frightened the life out of me.

On my afternoons for religious instruction, I would attend catechism class at Immaculate Conception, the parochial school my brother and I had not been admitted to years before. My instructor, Sister John Alicia, who had a very beautiful face, saw that I wasn't paying attention and asked to see me after class.

"Sister," I told her, "I have to hurry to see my mother."

"Where is your mother?" she asked me.

I told her about the tumor and the hospital.

"You come with me," she said, and took me into the convent that was attached to the school. I had never been inside a convent, and I thought, "This is serious." I didn't know what to expect. She brought me to a statue of Our Lady and said, "We're going to say a prayer for your mother."

We kneeled and prayed. "You have to say a prayer every day, and say the rosary every day, and your mother will be fine."

And she was fine. The operation was successful, the malignancy was taken out, and my mother came home. My father returned to his old self with a new vigor. After that episode, I started to go to mass every day, and to say the rosary daily. Since that time I've rarely missed. After I started going to Power Memorial, I wanted to know more about the Creator. I thought very much about possibly becoming a priest.

While I was going to church every day, my brother Buddy was going in the opposite direction. He almost lost his faith altogether during my mother's illness, and he began to ask himself "How can things like this happen?" In our teens, Buddy had developed into a good-looking version of Victor Mature, a popular actor of the day. He was very athletic, and a muscular weight lifter. When we were younger he had always towered over me, but he stopped growing at five foot eight, while I continued on to six feet—an accomplishment he never forgave me. His IQ was thirty points higher than mine, and he could absorb things just by sitting in class, while I had to work for everything. As a youngster he was also physically ahead of me. He could jump right over a johnny pump, while I would stumble. The problem with Buddy was he was so good-looking that girls would call him up; I never saw him open a schoolbook.

Sometimes when I was upstairs in the apartment with my head stuck in books, Buddy probably wondered about me. He would come up and say, "Peter, I have some girls waiting for us down in the park." And I would say, "Can't you see I'm studying?" Well, I wasn't as direct as my brother, and sometimes I really envied him. The only thing that really stopped me from becoming a priest was my sexual attraction to girls: there was no way I was going to give up being with women. By the time Buddy and I were both in Power Memorial, they threw Buddy out in his junior year because he couldn't pass the required Latin Regents exam. So he went back to the public high school.

I learned to swim when my father threw me into the water, either at Astoria Pool or the Rockaways when we went to the beach there. My father wasn't much of a swimmer, but would do the best he could. Astoria Pool was right in the park in front of our apartment building. My friends and I would go there every day all summer from its opening on Memorial Day through Labor Day. Peer pressure was a big thing and I learned quickly how to handle myself in the water. Most of the time we would climb over the fence and use our ten-cents admission to get hot dogs instead.

Sometimes we would simply go for a swim in the adjacent East River between the Triborough and Hell Gate bridges.

When I was sixteen I took a lifesaving course at the East 69th Street Pool in Manhattan so I'd be able to work as a lifeguard. Then, when we bought the bungalow upstate, I planned to become a lifeguard in Mountain Lodge Park; only I didn't right away because I got a job as a laborer with Moschella Contractors, a construction company run by a client of my dad's and a neighbor, making three times as much money as I would have as a lifeguard. They would pick me up every day and I'd do all sorts of heavy lifting, hauling bricks, that kind of thing.

In 1952, when I was seventeen, I started Fordham College. In midsummer after my third year there I got a call at 3 A.M. from my aunt Pauline, who was up at the bungalow at Mountain Lodge. During the summer I was still working days for Moschella, going up to Mountain Lodge weekends only. "How are you?" she asked, as if it were perfectly normal to wake me up in the middle of the night.

"What are you doing, what's going on?" I asked.

She said, "Well, your dad."

"What's the matter?"

"They say he had a heart attack. He's in St. Luke's Hospital, in Newburgh."

I got there around seven in the morning. He was smoking a cigar next to an oxygen tank in bed. "Get me outta here, Peter. All I have is a little indigestion from some finocchio."

"Dad," I warned him, "you're gonna blow the place up!" Then I looked at his EKG, and I saw the lines going all over the place. There was no question he'd had an infarct. My father was a very active man—he even walked fast, and it was no easy matter keeping him shut up in St. Luke's Hospital for six weeks recovering from the heart attack. The local heart specialist was a certain Dr. Stein, and my father drove him crazy. The poor doctor himself died of a heart attack right after Dad was released.

I had come up on a Friday, so I decided to stay at the bungalow over the weekend. I had a date with a beautiful blonde in Brooklyn named Barbara. I called and told her that if she wanted to take a bus upstate I would put her up in a motel nearby. That Saturday night we all went to the Inn, the only place in town. I was sitting there with this girl and my two cousins, Peter and Larry, who had also rushed up to see Dad. Alice Doumas, a striking Greek blonde I knew from weekends up there, who was also Miss Greek Independence, walked in then. I used to drive Alice and a group of other girls to the moviehouse in nearby Monroe, since they didn't like to go without male accompaniment. Along with Alice was a beautiful Italian girl named Tena, who immediately struck my fancy. "Alice," I said, "come over. Sit down and have some pizza."

Later I learned that Tena had seen me the day before and asked Alice, "Who is that guy?" Of course I took an immediate liking to her. After talking and bonding and realizing how alike we were, including our remarkably similar Sicilian families, ideals, and goals, the pizza arrived. I tenderly picked up the first piece, wrapped it in a napkin, and gave it to her. According to Tena it was at that point, when I offered her the first piece of pizza, that she decided to marry me—obviously a case of love at first bite! (When I heard about this later from Tena I fully understood for the first time why Dad always gave Mom the first cut of filet mignon. Thanks again, Dad.)

I decided to tell Barbara that, after all, my dad was not doing well, and maybe it would be better if she didn't spend the night at the motel. Soon blond Barbara was back on the bus to Brooklyn, I returned to the Inn, and we began talking seriously. I quickly learned it was the last night of Tena's vacation, that she lived in Jersey City, and was going into her sophomore year at Montclair State Teachers College. We danced once or twice to the jukebox. I then escorted Tena and Alice back to their bungalow and promised to call Tena as soon as I figured out a time I might come see her in New Jersey. It took me three full weeks, because for the rest of August I stayed with Dad and became the lifeguard at Mountain Lodge.

If it weren't for Tena, I would never have succeeded in politics, government, or life. She has been, and remains, the best part of my whole life. We dated during the school year after that first summer when I was a lifeguard and she was a camp counselor, but it was mostly a phone romance. She was living in Jersey City and going to school in Montclair, while I was a student prosecutor at Fordham and playing football. It seemed like a very expensive trip going to Jersey; even phoning cost a dollar's worth of nickels. We were lucky if we got to see each other once every three weeks.

The following summer, when I was going to be a freshman in law school and she a junior in Montclair, she stayed the whole season with her best friend Alice, the Greek girl who introduced me to her. My father and I drove up to open the bungalow sometime in the middle of June. We arrived with all of the family's luggage for the season, since my mother and brother planned to come up later. It was pouring buckets when we arrived.

Dad and I had just dropped all the luggage in the middle of the bungalow and started playing canasta when I heard Tena and Alice at the locked gate. I went running out in the rain and declared: "Girls, let me and my dad teach you canasta!" The four of us played for hours, and from that moment we saw each other every evening or when we were off work.

Eventually I became the lifeguard and swimming instructor for the whole park. Working as a lifeguard not only enabled me to know Tena, but also to spend the most wonderful five summers as I attended college and law school. Learning how to save a human being's life in a pool or in the ocean is an incredibly rewarding experience. In 1957, my last year as a lifeguard and just prior to my graduation from Fordham Law, eleven youngsters that I saved and their families threw a surprise party for me. The *Washingtonville Post* actually came and took a picture of me that was published the next day.

I could not have been any more full of myself than at the time this picture was taken. Besides lifeguarding, I was playing semiprofessional football and had recently been chosen Most Valuable Player. Originally I was supposed to play football for Fordham, but the year I entered they dropped down to club football and discontinued the scholarship program. They wanted me to practice four hours a day without tuition aid, so I said forget it and used those hours for my part-time job, as assistant credit manager in a chain of stores. Still, I kept playing football with the same group of friends who had been playing together since I was ten or eleven as the Astoria Buccaneers. We decided to go semipro, so my father changed the name to the Astoria Sportsmen, and we played in the Queens Nassau Pop Warner League Unlimited Division. I played football with them until I graduated college. People would pay a few bucks to watch us play on Friday nights and Sundays. We got no income from it ourselves, but used the money to pay the rent for the Eintracht Oval, where we played, and to buy equipment. There were forty-two of us Buccaneers/Sportsmen. We still get together, to this day. While most of the other guys were all-around athletes, I was not: in softball I once earned a jockstrap as Least Valuable Player.

While in college, I was always on the lookout for good after-school jobs. Somehow I found out that the city was going to open night schools for teenagers in community centers and the Board of Education was hiring people to work there. You needed at least two years of education credits, which I didn't have since I was at an academic college. Instead I brought in a book that one of my instructors in philosophical psychology, Father

Donceel, had written. It had a chapter in it on education, so I convinced them it was an education course. The instructor they were trying to replace had been knifed, and they were so desperate that they gave me the job.

I split my time between PS 112, which was all white, and PS 111, five blocks farther south, which was the all-black school. A gang problem had developed between whites and blacks, so they opened up a youth center with the idea of getting the whites and blacks together playing sports. My first night on the job, while I was playing Ping Pong with some kids, a six-foot-seven white guy broke a bottle on the table and started chasing the guy I was playing with around the table. I blocked the guy with the jagged bottle with a hip lock and pinned him to the floor. "If you want me to let you up," I told him, " you've got to promise me you'll never do that again. Otherwise I'll call the police." The fellow gave in, and later became a good friend of mine and one of my protectors. Meanwhile I was playing Ping Pong every night, and I became really good at it. I even ended up training the guy, who came in third place in Ping Pong in New York State.

If it wasn't Ping Pong, I got the gangs to turn their attention to basketball or other outdoor activities. The most important thing was to get the kids into a healthy setting. I brought one street gang in and got them to form their own clubhouse and even arranged for my father to incorporate them as the Pionetians—all on the model of our own Astoria Buccaneers. To this day I have a friend from that group.

I married Tena less than three years after we met, in 1958, at the end of my second year of law school. She graduated from Montclair State Teachers College on June 8, and we married on June 21. We moved into an apartment house in Astoria, and she taught at St. Lucy's Roman Catholic School in East Harlem on East 94th Street. I was in morning session at Fordham Law, which finished every afternoon at 1:30. Afterward I would clerk for four hours a day at Dewey Ballantine, in Manhattan, come home by 6:15, and go out to my evenings with restless teenagers from 7 to 10 at night. At 10:30 I would come home and type up my law school notes.

Tena became pregnant the first year of our marriage, but went on teaching until school was out. The following July we lost the baby, Christopher. It was a horror. My father-in-law had recommended a general physician to us, not an obstetrician. The doctor knew perfectly well that the baby was due on July 25—it happened to be Tena's birthday, for one thing—but still he went on vacation, and assigned us an eighty-year-old obstetrician. When the baby was due we went to Margaret Hague Hospital, in Jersey City, as planned; I was staying with my in-laws in anticipation of the baby. Unfortunately, fathers weren't allowed into the delivery room in those days. The baby was stillborn. The doctor told me it was a rare disease and we would probably never be able to have healthy babies. Tena developed a serious urinary and bladder infection.

I was twenty-four, Tena twenty-three. My wife was sick and her situation looked touch-and-go, so when they asked if I wanted to see the baby I said, "No, I want to see my wife."

Tena spent an extra week in the hospital. It was the same time I was taking the bar exam. I only went through the motions, and I flunked the "Practice" half of the exam by one point. Despite my emotional upset, I couldn't understand how I had flunked, since I had prepped a fellow for the exam who passed. Somebody told me it might be therapeutic for Tena if she helped me do something about the failed bar exam. So I made an appointment and booked a hotel in Albany and drove up there with Tena to look over the exam and samples of "correct" answers. Tena compared my exam with the sample answers and pointed out that on the very first question the graders had accidentally taken off eight points instead of two: I should not have flunked at all! I could have filed a formal protest, but was told that kind of appeal would have taken an entire year. Instead, a few months later I took the exam again, and passed.

At least getting me over the hump of the bar exam took our minds off the loss of Christopher. Eventually Tena and I saw a qualified obstetrician and learned that our doctors had failed to follow proper medical procedures during his birth. Because they did not do a cesarean, the baby had developed pneumonia in the eighteen hours his head was exposed during delivery. The good news, however, was that we could have children. I did not sue; the last thing I wanted to do was perpetuate the memory. For the same reason, we did not want to have a funeral. Instead we made sure that the baby was buried in what they call an "angel's grave." As we grew older and our three boys were born and everyone was healthy, we went back to the funeral parlor that handled it to determine exactly where the baby was buried. They said he had been buried together with a lot of other babies, with only a marker. By that time we had a family plot in Calvary Cemetery in Astoria. In 1999, we put a stone up there for Christopher Peter.

At Fordham Law, one of the exercises I most enjoyed was Moot Court Proceedings. Partly through my father's influence, we were allowed to use the New York State Civil Courthouse, which was located only a few blocks away from the school. My interest in prosecutorial law was further aroused when, by my third year of law school, I was chosen by Fordham Law's dean to become a special assistant to the Attorney General of New York State, Louis Lefkowitz. By this time I wanted to become an assistant DA, so my father took me to see the Queens district attorney, Frank O'Connor. O'Connor was a well-respected prosecutor who later went on to run and lose for governor of New York against Nelson Rockefeller. O'Connor's star was particularly high with me because of *The Wrong Man*, an Alfred Hitchcock movie that starred Henry Fonda and was based on an episode in O'Connor's career in which he prevented the conviction of a man falsely accused of armed robbery. Coming with a sterling recommendation from both my dad and the New York State attorney general, I expected smooth sailing from O'Connor. I quickly learned better. Although my father was no longer active in politics—and as a civil court judge could no longer be expected to be—O'Connor pointed out to him that I was appearing before him without the personal recommendation of the Democratic Party leader. In other words, O'Connor expected my dad to call in his political favors with Democratic district leaders before I could be appointed an assistant DA.

I was mortified. Frank O'Connor was the last person in the world I expected to play politics with public office. I remember thinking, "How dare you ask my dad to do that!" I was bitterly disappointed, and decided I'd rather give up the idea of becoming district attorney than go through those kind of hiring procedures. My father, though, never got angry. Soon he was telling me: "Son, you know there's a small firm in Far Rockaway that's been asking me for some time about you."

"Dad," I complained, " I gotta go to Rockaway?" It was the last thing I wanted to do, but just to please him I agreed to check it out. I was so convinced the interview would not last more than five minutes that I put my bathing suit on underneath my suit, intending to take a quick swim in the ocean afterward. When after the long car ride I at last walked into the office of Weinberg & Jacobowitz I was met by a rotund little man—Milton Jacobowitz—who immediately handed me a file and announced that we would soon be leaving to attend the Rotary luncheon. I never had a chance to say no. Soon he had me going along with him to every court in Queens. I loved the action and excitement so much that I couldn't wait to be admitted to the bar.

Once that happened, I tried cases in what seemed like every court and city in the State of New York. "Mr. J" had a mind like a steel trap: he never took a note, never consulted a file, but registered every word you said for future reference. He was wonderful and crazy to try to keep up with. One morning he called me up at seven in the morning, "Buy the *Daily Mirror*, turn to page four, and take care of it!" he announced, and hung up. Once I got hold of the paper I discovered that an attractive young woman whose negligence case I was handling at our office had been arrested in Far Rockaway for an alleged swindle. From the big picture and a huge headline that trumpeted "The Love Triangle!" I learned that she and her boyfriend had been accused of wangling money and jewelry out of a dimwitted "prospective fiancé" in a scam that was playing itself out in the media from coast to coast.

My first task was to appear in criminal court as this girl's defense counsel. When I arrived in Ridgewood, Queens, where she was being arraigned, dozens of cameras focused on the notorious plotters and the DA, and of course completely bypassed me. The cameras were allowed into the courtroom, and I had no opportunity to interview my client before the proceedings began. Marty Baron, the district attorney, immediately whipped himself up with indignation: "Your honor, this is an outrage! The girl took this poor innocent man's ring and money, with no intention whatsoever of fulfilling their wedding plans!"

"If your honor please," I interrupted, seemingly out of nowhere, "the law firm of Weinberg and Jacobowitz represents the defendant. You will soon find out, your honor, that there's much more to this case than meets the eye, and I know that when you have all the facts before you, you will understand that my client is innocent." Little did I know that this sound bite would appear on television news around the country. Later that day my wife's aunt called from Florida to say she had seen me on television. The case went on for over a year and half, and my client and I finally accepted a plea in which she paid back every cent of the poor guy's money, and she was left without a criminal record.

By this time, 1960, my wife was pregnant again. I was the only Christian in my law firm, but the people who worked at Weinberg & Jacobowitz were the best examples of Christian love I ever met. They knew about us losing our first baby, and they knew we were expecting a second one. I had started out making $60 a week, which was raised to $100 when I got admitted to the bar. Shortly after Tena had stopped teaching and the baby was about to be born, the law firm, without telling me, made arrangements to hire a nurse to be in my apartment to greet Tena when she came home from the hospital. Luckily, I found out a day or two beforehand. My first reaction was first to politely insist that such a thing was far too expensive.

"No, son," Mr. J insisted, "we always do this when one of our partners' wives gives birth. It's not going to cost you anything."

In the end I had to convince him that, among Italians, hiring someone from outside the family to come in after childbirth was just not done. "My mother is there, and my mother-in-law," I explained. "And my wife will divorce me if she finds another woman in the house." In the end I talked him out of it. They had been prepared to pay every penny.

When I finally left the firm in 1962 to open my own law office, Mr. J was so concerned about whether or not I would be able to pay the rent that he wanted to put me on a monthly retainer. I took it for one month before saying thank you, I no longer needed it. In fact, I had so many neighborhood clients happy to no longer trek out to Rockaway that my practice grew quickly.

In May of 1955, shortly before my dad's first heart attack, Mayor Robert Wagner had appointed him a judge of the civil court. The swearing-in ceremony occurred in the Board of Estimate's ornate chambers in City Hall. I recall vividly how thrilled I was as a college student to be participating in my dad's inauguration in this historic capitol building of the greatest city in the world. My brother got a day's pass from the U.S. Army to attend in uniform. My mother, who had retired by this time, and my brother and I were all bursting with pride as we stood next to Dad and watched the mayor swear him in. Gone was the disappointment of Mayor Wagner taking more than nine months from the time his aides had first approached my dad about filling the vacancy to his actual appointment. (Dad had long since disposed of his busy law office in anticipation.) Later we learned that nobody rushed Mayor Wagner. A standing joke around City Hall decades later was that some of the committees he had appointed were still waiting to report. Little did I suspect that Mayor Wagner's son Bobby and I would both be elected to the City Council in 1974, become good friends, and work together to make the council a meaningful partner in government.

Less than twelve years after his first heart attack, Dad had a massive second one, on March 15, 1967. He died immediately in the civil courthouse he loved so much, having just put to rest a war among family members involved in a bitter lawsuit. He had accomplished this by bringing all parties into his chambers, hammering out the terms for a settlement, and suggesting they have lunch together and report back to him afterward. When his law secretary announced a while later that the parties were happily reconciled and wanted to thank him, my father beamed his usual smile. As he put on his robe to greet them, God took him in an instant. He literally died with his boots on, doing what he loved best.

Dad had loved being a judge. Lawyers loved to try cases before him because of his reputation for fairness and courtesy. Once when one of my Weinberg & Jacobowitz cases came up in Dad's courtroom I said to him, "Your honor, as you know, you must recuse yourself from this proceeding."

"I object," retorted the opposing lawyer heatedly, "I want to try this case before you!"

With a big smile, Dad immediately went off the record, called us both up to the bench, and patiently explained to the disappointed attorney why the case had to be sent to another judge.

Some twenty years after his death, PS 85, the elementary school closest to my dad's law office, was renamed the Judge Charles J. Vallone School in honor of the support he always provided education in the community. Then, in 1996, the new Queens Civil Courthouse on Sutphin Boulevard was dedicated in his memory. There is a bust of him in the entrance. The plaque hanging near it reads:

> In memory of the Honorable Charles J. Vallone. Respected jurist, prominent civil leader, and brotherhood advocate. Born in Italy in 1902. Immigrated to the United States in 1904. Graduated from Columbia College of Banking and Finance and Fordham Law School. Appointed to the New York City Municipal Court by Mayor Wagner in 1955 and elected and served as a senior New York Civil Court Judge until his death in 1967 in the Queens County Civil Courthouse that he loved.

3

Politics and Principles

"Politics is the science of government." That is the definition given to me by a very powerful Democratic district leader named Frank McGlynn. I was a sophomore at Fordham College at the time (1954) and my assignment in my first political science course was to interview a local political leader. I was very much impressed with the imposing Mr. McGlynn and the many people who were greeting him respectfully during my ten-minute interview at his clubhouse in Astoria. I learned a lot about political power that evening.

The problem is, Mr. McGlynn was wrong. Politics is anything but a science. I have since learned that there is nothing exact about politics. It is simply a means to an end, and luck is one of the most important ingredients in obtaining that end. The desired end is usually getting elected to public office. But getting elected alone is not enough. The moment you are elected you are supposed to serve the public—not the other way around. In the Book of the Prophet Micah written three millennia ago, the people turned to Micah and asked, "What does God want from us? What does He expect us to do?" And Micah answered, "All that God requires of you is to do the right thing, to love goodness and to walk humbly with your God" (Micah 6: 6–8).

Winning is not everything. Grantland Rice was right in his admonition, "When the great recorder comes to write against your name, he remembers not whether you won or lost, but how you played the game." In November of 1955, a year or so after my interview with Frank McGlynn, his regular organization Democratic club, known as the Steinway Democratic Club, was beaten by the Taminent Democratic Club headed by Ralph DeMarco. The Democratic Party is so strong in New York City because it organizes its district leadership on the basis of assembly districts and directly elects its district leaders in the Democratic primaries that precede the general election. During my lifetime there have always been both male and female district leaders in each Queens district, because the Democratic Party in each county has the right to make up its districts any way it chooses, as long as there's only one county leader. This applies only to the Democratic Party; the Republican, the Conservative, and the Liberal Party each sets its own rules the way it wants.

Because of this party structure, it was not unusual for the same person, or members of the same family, to hold both Party and government positions. In the mid-1950s in my Astoria district, then called the "Fighting 4th," McGlynn's group had been running the whole show for some time: he was male district leader, and his son Frank McGlynn Jr. was assemblyman. The demise of McGlynn's club at the hands of DeMarco was due to a number of factors: McGlynn's imperious style, the changing ethnic makeup of Astoria, and an ever-growing rival Democratic club. McGlynn was a well-dressed man, distinguished-looking—and very Irish, like most members of his club.

Ralph DeMarco, on the other hand, represented the rising Italian, and later Greek power in the district. An energetic businessman who owned a dress factory, he established the Taminent club as a strong rival to the Steinway, even if its clubhouse was little more than a shack under the Triborough Bridge abutments (it's still a miracle to make it in there without the pigeons getting you). Although the rivalry was largely ethnic, my father was in McGlynn's club, and my mother was a state committeewoman. In fact, Dad kept trying to talk the DeMarco people to abandon their rival club and join the Steinway. Once he became judge, however, he had to get out of day-to-day politics, and it was then that the DeMarco club was able to knock off McGlynn's.

They did it by running a strong, largely Italian ticket consisting of DeMarco, Jules Sabbatino, and Adele Broderick during the Democratic primary. In the district leader race, DeMarco and Broderick beat McGlynn Sr. and his co-leader. In the assembly primary race, Sabbatino beat McGlynn Jr. by just one vote. McGlynn's people challenged the results in court, but Sabbatino's victory was upheld. After the results were in, my father said we needed to stick with the power of the vote, and urged us to switch allegiances. As far as he was concerned, Taminent had become the regular organization club and that was the club I should join. Most of the Steinway members joined the Taminent, and McGlynn's club shriveled up.

I joined the Taminent while still in college and have been a member ever since. It became a very powerful club and I rose to become its counsel as well as the chair of its Journal Committee, the main fund-raising activity of the club, while at the same time I was developing a flourishing law practice. My mother happily got out of politics altogether while Dad stayed on the sidelines, though he still had many friends and supporters in the club.

The Taminent club met three times a month; once for the men, once for the women, and once for a joint meeting. They still do. The club was the place where community and politics met on the local level. People would come in and report a pothole on 33rd Street, or complain about a "strange noise over at the Con Edison plant last night," or to look at getting their son or daughter into West Point. It was the party base for the district leaders who hung out there, and it wasn't uncommon to see your city council member, or state assemblyman or senator there. As long as you registered as a Democrat, you were welcome to the meetings. Because many people in Astoria own their own homes and are, generally, serious blue-collar working people from a wide variety of ethnic backgrounds, they are a heavy voting bloc and the people they elect to office tend to be powerful ones. Ralph DeMarco went on to become a legend as one of the most powerful Democratic district leaders in the city.

In the early 1960s a vacancy occurred in our district for state senate. I was in my late twenties, my new law practice was humming, and I was dying to run. I called Dad, who was vacationing in the summer bungalow at the time. The conversation went something like this: "Dad, a vacancy just happened in our area for senate and I'm dying to run. I have a lot of friends in and out of the club who will support me even if I have to run as an insurgent. Dad, I can win this seat!"

"You probably can win, son, but it's not your turn. As you know, the club has a very able assistant district attorney, Nick Ferraro. He has been patiently waiting his turn, and he deserves the seat. I love you, son, but I will vote for Nick."

So much for my plan to become a state senator. After Dad died suddenly in 1967, I thought my turn had finally come in 1968 when the local City Council seat became vacant. A council member runs in a district larger than an assembly district—say 170,000 rather than 120,000. The one in my neighborhood takes in all of Astoria plus a little of Long Island City and at that time took in parts of Jackson Heights and College Point as well. The district leaders involved promised to vote for me, but at the last second decided instead to give their endorsement to a loyal club member named Joe DiMonte who needed two more years on the city payroll "for his retirement pension." In two years, they claimed, the seat would be mine. So I stepped aside again. What I hadn't reckoned with is a young police officer by the name of Tom Manton who had just retired from the force to become an attorney and was desperate to run, with or without club endorsement. Tom came to see me at my law office and said he would support me in my run if I wanted the council seat, because I deserved it, but he would definitely challenge DiMonte in the primary if the leaders picked him instead. I told Tom I would never forget his graciousness for being willing to step aside for me, but I could not support his challenge. By the luck of the draw, Tom went on to win the primary and the council seat. In 1984 our congresswoman Geraldine Ferraro became the first woman of any major party to become the vice presidential candidate, and Tom then went on to take her place as congressman and today still serves as Democratic county leader of Queens.

After I had stepped aside for Joe DiMonte, I went to see Ralph DeMarco for advice. "Sure you want to run," he told me, and rattled off fifteen names ahead of me for any office I could imagine. "If you want to run, you have very little chance of winning . . . unless you get the Astoria Civic Association going again. Because right now, you're not known."

The Astoria Civic Association was the citizens' group my father founded in 1933. It had become moribund after he became a judge. It still existed on paper, but there were no meetings. We re-formed the group under my leadership by gathering together my old teammates from the Astoria Buccaneers/Sportsmen and other people I played sports with, friends of my father, and interested citizens. Eighty-eight people came into my office, and we had a huge meeting at Riccardo's, the big catering hall off Ditmars Boulevard. We took pictures of crowds waiting on the elevated platform and publicized them in order to improve train service; we put pressure on the city parks people to get the fountains in the park working again. Soon we had a membership of 1,200, and were very active.

Astoria is wedged between perhaps the two most vital installations in New York City: La Guardia Airport and the Con Edison plant, the largest fossil fuel plant in the world. An electrical generating facility has been located on that spit of Hell Gate since1953 (before that it was a manufactured gas facility), while La Guardia Airport started operating shortly after I was born. The story is that on one of his flights back from Washington when he had to land yet again in Newark, Mayor La Guardia decided the city needed another municipal airport. It's located on a stretch of land that used to be a beach. We call the airport and the generating plant our "major necessaries and our major nuisances." Whenever someone proposes adding flights, there's an uproar. Whenever someone proposes building yet another generator, there's another outrage.

One of the biggest demonstrations I ever organized happened shortly after I restarted the Astoria Civic Association. It was the late 1960s, and Mayor John Lindsay had announced he was going to allow Con Edison to double its coal-burning capacity at "Big Alice" in Long Island City and in Astoria. Both are located about a half-mile from the two-family home that Tena and I purchased in 1962. Our house was already full of soot from the Astoria plant only two blocks away, and neither we nor the rest of the community were about to allow Con Ed to double its coal-burning capacity. So I organized a protest at City Hall, rented buses to take people there, and traveled by train with hundreds of others to make our voices heard. We were heard—and to his great credit Mayor Lindsay not only blocked Con Ed from doubling its coal-burning capacity, but stopped the coal burning altogether and instead forced this giant producer of energy to switch to the much cleaner low sulphur oil! You cannot imagine the difference it made to the environment in our community, and I'm sure in the city as a whole. The covering of soot disappeared, all kinds of birds returned to our backyard, and the asthma rate in our community, one of the highest, began to decline. I never forgot Mayor Lindsay, and when I became Speaker of the New York City Council I had the chance to become friendly with him. I was shocked to learn in the late 1990s that he was ill and had no medical coverage, so Mayor Giuliani and I corrected that oversight with special legislation.

As luck would have it, redistricting occurred again in my neighborhood in 1970—this time in the national congressional district—when Astoria's 80,000 people were thrown into a brand new "Triboro" district along with 100,000 residents of East Harlem and 300,000 in the South Bronx. When I expressed interest in running, Ralph DeMarco told me, "Sure, nobody else from the club wants it." That wasn't surprising, since the race would clearly be skewed in favor of someone from the Bronx. Six candidates entered the primary, headed by the former Bronx borough president Herman Badillo, who had just finished second to Mario Procaccino in the Democratic primary for mayor.

The county leaders of Manhattan and Bronx were solidly behind Herman, but the hundreds of volunteers working for me, and their enthusiasm, made this uphill race closer than anyone expected. Even if the Taminent club gave me support, my only valuable political endorsement came from Nick Ferraro, the man I'd once stepped aside for, who had gone on from the state senate to become Queens district attorney and was also running again in 1970. It turned out that Dad was right about Nick, because he literally took me under his wing, put me on his campaign literature, took me everywhere he went, and was a tremendous help to me. Of course, in Astoria I was well-known, and campaigning there was like a triumphal parade—in fact, we did have a parade! In the Bronx and East Harlem, on the other hand, I didn't know a soul. Worse, the campaign headquarters I had opened in East Harlem was firebombed, and I was starting to get threats.

Besides Herman and me, the other principal candidates in the race were Ramon Velez, a Puerto Rican like Badillo; a black fellow named Dennis Coleman; and another Italian-American, Father Louis Gigante. Velez kept thousands of people on a payroll for "community development," earning himself the nickname of "Poverty Pimp." Gigante was a priest well-known in the South Bronx for building low-rent housing. Perhaps he was even better known for being the brother of Vincent "Chin" Gigante, the alleged head of the Gambino crime family. The Gigantes had long had a base in East Harlem. I figured my East Harlem campaign office had been bombed by the Puerto Ricans, but the police told me it was the Mafia. Anyway, even if I'm pretty much fearless I started going around with friends who were off-duty cops. On the first day I went to campaign in Harlem, I was walking around feeling out of place when I literally ran into a black woman standing in the doorway in front of me and looking very grim. "Hello, I'm Peter Vallone, and I'm running for Congress!" I greeted her with the warmest smile I could muster.

"Brother," she said, as her grim expression opened up into a wide grin, "With a smile like that, you can't lose." That kind of greeting became typical of the one-on-one campaigning I did with black and Puerto Rican voters in Harlem and the Bronx. I honestly believed that I won the vote of nearly everyone whose hand I shook. I had gone in thinking there would be hostility because they were black and I was white, but there was none whatsoever.

It was one of the turning points in my career, and in the end I got a very good vote out of the Bronx and Manhattan. On primary night the first unofficial count declared me the winner by 900 votes. My supporters were jubilant. But not for long. A few hours later, the second count showed me losing to Herman Badillo by 497 votes out of the more than 20,000 cast. The third-place runner-up was Father Gigante. Given the multiple names and the poor design of the ballot (all six names appeared at the bottom of the ballot) I felt that at the very least there should be a runoff.

With all this on my mind on the morning after the primary, I went to the 6 A.M. mass in my local church and sat in the same pew as always. An elderly woman who always sat near me and greeted me with a cheery smile offered the following words of encouragement in her fine Irish accent: "I am so sorry you lost, but I do want you to know that I voted for you and will keep praying for you, Father Gigante." I didn't have the heart to tell her that just because I went to mass every morning, I wasn't the priest who had just run for Congress. Once again I learned not to assume that anyone even knows your name, not even the person who says hello to you every morning.

Later, Father Gigante went on to become the first priest elected to the New York City Council. When I told him this story about the lady in church, he got a big kick out of it and said, "I need her prayers more than you do anyway." I always valued Lou's friendship and dedication to the poor and needy. As for his brother Chin, he was convicted of racketeering and is now serving time in prison.

I was a practicing lawyer, so we impounded the voting machines and brought the contest to court after laboriously examining the votes cast in each machine in the three boroughs. We found over 1,500 votes counted for Herman in the Bronx that were not even cast or registered on the voting machines. The New York Supreme Court set the results aside and ordered a new election, but the court of appeals reversed that decision, and Herman Badillo became the first Puerto Rican representative in the United States Congress. Some years later I ran into a retired court of appeals judge who said to me, "Son, you understand that it just had to be": that is, Badillo had to win, because electing a Puerto Rican congressman was the real reason the Triboro district had been created in the first place.

Some of my football friends who knew I had been the arm wrestling champ on our old team suggested I challenge Herman to an arm wrestling match "and forget all this court crap!" I thought about asking Herman to do just that—as a joke to pass the time and provide our volunteers with some entertainment—until one morning when I opened the front door to the appellate division's magnificent paneled courtroom and saw Herman there, alone in the room, balancing his body on a brass railing one hand a time, with his feet straight up in the air. And here I had been thinking I would have to go easy on him!

Despite this electoral disappointment, the race had been an eye-opening experience for me. Herman Badillo went on to become an excellent congressman and deputy mayor and he and I remain friends to this day. Considering the next years under the Nixon administration, I'm thankful I did not go to Washington. Finally, as I said before, winning an election is not as important as how you run the campaign. In the course of this congressional race I became known not only in the three counties, but throughout the city. I made friends, learned not to burn any bridges, and to avoid negative campaigning and personal insults. I knew that other opportunities would come my way.

Sure enough, a few years later the then county leader of Queens, Matthew Troy, promised me that I would become the Democratic county candidate for councilman-at-large because of my "great showing for Congress." I did not even have to come to the district leaders' meeting, he said. Only problem was, he promised the same thing to Eugene Mastropieri, a district leader who had just lost his race for state senate. Mastropieri won Troy's endorsement for councilman-at-large. I was stunned, but not really surprised, because by then I knew that promises in politics have more to do with power than principle. Poor Mastropieri later was indicted, convicted, and served time for laundering money. I did not challenge Gene or the organization because I decided that prudence was the better part of valor and it would be a costly county-wide race—campaign financing matching funds were not yet in existence. As luck would have it, the office of councilman-at-large was later abolished as unconstitutional anyway.

Electoral luck finally came my way in 1974 when a new council seat was created in Astoria in line with the 1970 census. With the full support of current political leaders—including critical support again from Nick Ferraro—I went on to win the primary against Jules Sabbatino, the state assemblyman who had once helped Ralph DeMarco unseat Frank McGlynn's organization but had since alienated Ralph by starting up a rival political club. I then won the general election by overwhelming margins. I had not burned any political bridges and had proven myself to be "a good soldier" in the regular Democratic organization.

PART II

Rubber Stamp Council

4

The Council of 1974

"Be careful or you will fall! Balance yourself!" That was and remains the admonition parents give their children when they first try to ride a two-wheel bike, or put on a pair of skates. Every one of us talks about not going to extremes, and of our hope to lead a "balanced life." A government too will fall if it does not balance the rights and expectations of the governed. History is replete with the stories of nations that rise and fall because of this imbalance. The most recent telling example is the fall of the Communist regime in Russia after seventy years of dominating hundreds of millions of people. As of mid-2005 Saddam Hussein was about to go on trial, Iraq was still in turmoil, and Kim Jong Il of North Korea was the new "baddest guy" on the face of the earth. But this is nothing new. For thousands of years people have tried to figure out how to get along with one another and live in relative peace.

It wasn't until the eighteenth century that a group of dedicated volunteers gathered together and drafted a document called the Declaration of Independence, which I believe comes as close as possible to laying the groundwork for our system of government, one that fulfills Micah's prophecy of "do the right thing." Every American should stop and take a really good look at this remarkable manifesto of what this country of ours stands for. I have been a guest teacher at many schools as well as a professor at Fordham University and Baruch College I always tell the students, "If you memorize one thing in your life, memorize the Declaration of Independence." Whenever I recite it, it always reminds me of my father addressing Americans of Italian descent during World War II:

> We hold these truths to be self-evident, that all men are created equal, that they are endowed by their Creator with certain unalienable rights, that among these are life, liberty, and the pursuit of happiness. That to secure these rights, governments are instituted among men, deriving their just powers from the consent of the governed.

The brave American leaders went on to dissolve their allegiance to the Crown and declare their native lands "free and independent states" and to close this incredible document with these beautifully written words:

> And for the support of this declaration, with a firm reliance on the protection of Divine Providence, we mutually pledge to each other our lives, our fortunes and our sacred honor.

This magnificent "declaration" is a primer on what this country is all about. It tells us eloquently where our rights come from. It is the foundation upon which our Constitution rests. The authors and framers of the Constitution had to figure out a way to embody and bring to life principles of just government that had never been defined before. They knew firsthand that the power of governing could not rest with a king, queen, emperor, and a royal class of a favored few—not if "all men are created equal." It certainly could not rest with a military general or benevolent dictator because that is not "with the consent of the governed," and certainly not if our "unalienable rights" come not from men, but from our "Creator."

After the failed experiment with the Articles of Confederation and much pondering and debate, in 1787 they came up with the new notion of balance in government consisting of three branches that would be separate but equal in power and different in jurisdiction. They called this document the Constitution of the United States of America. The ultimate power would be "the consent of the governed," which would be vested in the power to vote. The executive branch would be headed by the president, who would carry out the laws of the land enacted by the legislative branch called the Congress, which in turn would be interpreted by the judicial branch, headed by the Supreme Court. If and when the executive and legislative branches clashed, they would no longer have to go to war to determine the outcome—but simply go to court. The all-important principle of balanced government has served us well and has been amended only twenty-seven times since it became the law of the land, including the first ten amendments which were adopted four years later and aptly called the Bill of Rights.

Today the City of New York serves as an excellent example of balanced government in action, but it took almost four centuries to get there. The first "Common Council" was organized in or about 1625 by the Dutch at a time when the city was called New Amsterdam. A true empowered and balanced council did not come into existence, however, until the charter change of 1989. From 1898 to 1989 the city was ruled by the mayor and an outfit called the Board of Estimate. All members of the Board were executives, yet they exercised legislative power, in violation of the one-person, one-vote principle that applies to the legislative branch of government. The Declaration of Independence said that we were all created equal, so every citizen over the age of eighteen must have an equal right to vote. That once all-powerful Board of Estimate is now a relic, alongside the Articles of Confederation, because it violated the bedrock principle upon which the Constitution was formulated, that government cannot work without the "consent of the governed." What a difference! Starting in 1990 the council exercised real budgetary power and the final say over the use of land located anywhere within the five boroughs. Today fifty-one council members distribute much more fairly both the benefits and the burdens of living out the dreams of life, liberty, and the pursuit of happiness in the five boroughs of New York City.

The 1989 charter change also got rid of one of the last vestiges of the Common Council of 1625, the title of "Vice Chairman," an offshoot of the Dutch title "Viceroy," and changed it to Speaker, the title I enjoyed from 1990 through 2001. The joke going around City Hall prior to the name change was that I was either "the chairman of vice" or second-in-command to some mystery chairman lost somewhere in the chain of command.

Back in 1974, I was elated and overwhelmed with the idea of being an elected official. What a thrill I got walking up the steps of City Hall—I was as close as you can get to heaven on earth. The "Vice Chair" in those days was Tom Cuite. According to the *Daily News,* he "ruled the council with an iron hand." Cuite was almost as old as my father, and in the early days he seemed a kind of god to me. He was a prototypical Irish gentleman-politician, always immaculately dressed in a dark blue suit. I never saw him raise his voice. He never gave a press conference, and was never quoted anywhere. His door was always closed and if you tried to see him you would be told he was "too busy." In fact, we never did see him except at stated meetings or on the day of settlement of the budget. The city was run by the Board of Estimate and the mayor (who was on the Board). Compared to the council, the Board was all powerful, and Cuite was to the mayor like a prime minister of old was to the king: they never had a public dispute. When Tom Cuite needed to hold an important vote, he would call the Democratic county leaders of Brooklyn, Queens, and the Bronx, and the county leader would instruct his council members how to vote. When I first took office I needed to walk no further than the office down the hall to find out how my county leader was voting, since at the time the Queens leader was Matty Troy, a powerful council member from

Queens Village who also held the second most significant post in the council, chair of the Finance Committee. Matty was a funny, lovable guy and a good lawyer who also happened to be an extroverted, colorful character. Once at a veterans' parade, for example, he shimmied up the flagpole on top of a building and put up the red-white-and-blue.

I quickly discovered just how wily this ebullient Irishman was. Shortly after I came to City Hall Matty announced that he was going to make me "whip" of the Queens delegation.

"What does that mean?" I asked.

"That means you're responsible for seeing how the rest of the Queens delegation is going to vote. For instance, we're in a big financial crisis, and on today's agenda we have to vote on an auto use tax that the mayor wants, as well as an increase in the real estate tax. I want to find out how the other members are voting."

There were nine council members from Queens, and the first one I went to see was the most senior member of the council, Arthur Katzman. "Mr. Katzman," I said after introducing myself, "Matt has appointed me whip. You know what we have on the agenda. Would you please tell me how you intend to vote?'

Katzman's reaction was immediate and furious. "What! How dare you ask me such a question!"

I quickly beat a path back to the Finance chair's office, where I declared I was never ever going to ask Arthur Katzman another question. Matty reassured me that Katzman was simply the odd man out, and it would be fine to go to all the others. Indeed, all the other councilmen—except for Walter Ward—declared themselves in favor of both taxes (Ward said he would never vote for the real estate tax). When it came time for the roll call I voted for both. I was such a neophyte, I thought the real estate tax might be a political problem, but not the car tax. And since everyone else was for it except Ward . . . But no—Matty Troy, who had reserved his vote until the end, also voted no on the auto use tax.

Furious, I immediately went over and confronted him: "You made me vote yes!"

"What do you mean?" Matty smiled. "I never told you how I was going to vote."

When I returned home to Astoria the next day, someone had tacked to the front door of my house a notice that read: "Traitor! You will regret betraying us on the auto use tax!" That was just the beginning of the phone calls and letters to my home and office. Apparently it wasn't a man's home that was sacrosanct, but his automobile!

I was so confused that soon I found myself trying to introduce a bill to repeal the auto use tax. Before it got very far, Tom Cuite suggested I talk to Mayor Beame. Now, Abe Beame was so short that when he was sitting behind a desk you could barely see him, an impression that was amplified by his ever-present, huge Irish aide, Jim Cavanaugh.

"Your honor," began Cuite, "council member Vallone wants to talk to you."

I proceeded to tell Mayor Beame the Matty Troy story, and pointing out that the auto use tax was having a negative effect in my district in Astoria, and that I was going to introduce a bill to repeal it—

"You're gonna do what?"

"I'm going to try to repeal the auto use tax."

"Young man, are you surprised that people are mad about a tax?"

"Well, they didn't protest the real estate tax."

"Yeah, so what did you think was gonna happen?"

"I didn't think this was going to happen."

"All right, I'll think about it."

Needless to say, my repeal bill never went anywhere. The local automobile club that had organized the protest soon found other causes to agitate for or against, the letters died down, and the auto tax stayed.

Cuite delegated everything he possibly could. Almost all the work was done by the chair of the Finance Committee, Ed Sadowsky, the council member from Jackson Heights. Sadowsky, like some of us newer members, took the work of the Council seriously, and Sadowsky's work became even more important toward the end of Cuite's reign, when Tom had early Alzheimer's and didn't even recognize people. The way the Vice-Chair, the mayor, and the Board of Estimate worked—"the system," so to speak—wasn't inherently corrupt, but it easily could lead to corruption. Cuite's chief of staff was a bright, likable lawyer from the Bronx, Stanley Friedman, who was the person you had to see if you wanted a bill introduced or anything involved with the budget or problems in your district. If you were lucky enough to catch Tom in the hallway, he would simply pat you on the back and refer you to Stanley, saying with a smile, "We'll touch base again."

Stanley Friedman always seemed to have everything under control, but he overlapped with me only about four months before he was replaced by another Stanley—an excellent lawyer, also from the Bronx, named Stanley Schlein. Schlein had served as counsel to the Housing Committee and was liked and respected by the members.

In 1974 I was one of seventeen newly elected members in a body that consisted of thirty-five locally elected members as well as ten members-at-large. Included in the seventeen were other reform-minded members such as Henry Stern and Robert Wagner Jr., son of the man who appointed my father judge. One of Stern's quotable phrases from the time grew out of the comparison he made between the New York City Council and a rubber stamp: "At least a rubber stamp leaves an impression."

On my very first day I discovered that the council was literally run by proxy. I was told that all I would have to do to have my salary raised from $10,000 to $20,000 was sign a proxy vote—and after that I need not even show up for a committee or a stated meeting. Henry, Bobby Wagner, and I led a successful movement to abolish proxy voting altogether, require the physical presence of members for committee votes or at stated council meetings of which there would have to be at least two a month, and require that each member serve on at least three committees that would also have to meet at least twice a month. With these procedural changes the council would have the tools, if not the power, to make an impression a little deeper than a rubber stamp.

When I first came to the City Council in 1974, it was as a young lawyer who wanted to codify the laws of the city called the Administrative Code. It was almost impossible to find the law that you were looking for in the code of that time, and some of the laws were obviously archaic or unconstitutional. I quickly learned, however, that while the council could pass local laws, it had absolutely no power over land use, and virtually no power over the budget without getting the consent of the Board of Estimate, that infamous body composed of the mayor, the council president (whose only real power was as successor to the mayor), the comptroller, and the five borough presidents—executives all.

One of the first resolutions I attempted to introduce after becoming a council member was one proposing to abolish the Board of Estimate. I saw no need for this albatross of executive interference. Some people liked to consider the Board of Estimate a form of senate or "upper house" that was there to "check" the parochial prejudices of the City Council, the "lower house." That was patent nonsense to me: whoever heard of a senate composed of cabinet officers and county executives?

It would have been pure common sense for my fellow council members to support me in curtailing or getting rid of the "B of E," as it was not so affectionately called, and to empower the council to become an equal power in government, the way it was supposed to be. Alas, fighting this fight was a case of David and Goliath. When I mentioned the resolution to my fellow council members Howard Golden of Brooklyn and Stanley Simon, from the Bronx, they chuckled and said, "Are you kidding?" I went to see council leader Cuite, but he was never available. When I passed him in the hall he would say nothing but "Catch up with you later," and keep on walking. When I went to see Cuite's chief of staff, Stanley Friedman, or other of Cuite's advisors, they all nodded knowingly, a flicker of amusement in their eyes, and suggested I submit my legislative proposal to the Bill Drafting Office. Of course, nothing ever emerged from that bureaucratic bailiwick, and my resolution died unloved and formally unsubmitted. What I remember best about the episode is the disbelief and the soft echo of laughter whenever I brought it up. It's true I had the last laugh sixteen years later, but then it took the third branch of government to do the job.

A joke I tell pretty much sums up what the council was like in 1974:

A new councilman excitedly drove his car right up the steps of City Hall. Ecstatic that he finally had a parking space in this crowded city all to himself, he bounded up the historic steps two at a time. As he reached the top, a voice called up to him, "Hey, Buddy, is this your car?"

"Yes indeed, it is," the councilman answered.

"Good, I'm double-parked in front of you," the man said. "Would you mind watching my car for a minute? I'll be right back."

"What do you mean?" declares the councilman, taken aback. "I have a job to do here. Don't you realize I'm a council member?'

"That's okay," says the man. "I trust you anyway."

It turned out that the most serious problem facing the city in 1974 was not reforming government, but keeping the city solvent. It seemed to me as if the city had just waited for my arrival to go bankrupt. For a number of years the city had been relying on real estate tax revenue that hadn't been collected for decades. This and other budgetary gimmicks caught up with New York's empty coffers at the same time. Poor Abe Beame, a certified public accountant and former comptroller, tried desperately to pull us out of the financial disaster, but we were billions of dollars in debt and it soon became obvious we needed state and federal help. A screaming headline in the *Daily News* from those years carried a special greeting from the president of the United States—"Ford to City: Drop Dead."

Finally a coalition of government and city leaders emerged to create the Emergency Financial Control Board (EFCB) and the Municipal Assistance Corporation (Big Mac), financial oversight groups meant to put the city back on a sound financial basis. So began a new era of public/private partnership that brought together great New Yorkers like Governor Hugh Carey (probably the most underrated governor in our history) and private financier Felix Rohaytn to work together with the city administration.

I was the Queens representative as well as a member of the council's Finance Committee. Over long, late-night hours of deliberation I became fascinated with the brilliance and patience of the people who put together the EFCB and Big Mac. In the end the U.S. Congress backed us up with federal guarantees, and the Feds never lost a penny because of it. The city refinanced all its debt by issuing long-term "Big Mac" bonds, and the city put itself on Generally Accepted Accounting Principles (GAAP). I learned at the feet of the masters, and in the sixteen years I was council leader we never spent more than we had and always passed a balanced budget on time. Of course, there is never any certainty when dealing with any budget, especially when you have to predict revenues from economically sensitive taxes such as the income and sales taxes. Year after year we were on the conservative side, always underestimating revenues.

Redrafting the New York City legal code was one of the largest codifications in history: a daunting task that proved far less difficult than getting rid of the all-powerful board. As a newcomer, I had some learning to do about the interaction between the media and political leadership. In 1974 the council shared a large conference room with overflow from the City Hall press corps that occupied Room 9, a few feet away. One afternoon two important radio correspondents, Doug Edelson of WINS and Steve Flanders of WCBS, were sitting around in the conference room as I entered weighted down with voluminous copies of the Administrative Code that I was trying to codify. Luckily it was a quiet news day and I happened to be on the scene. Doug and Steve asked me if what I was carrying was newsworthy. Enthusiastically I began my spiel: there had been no codification since 1898, the laws were out of order and hard to find, and in many cases unconstitutional. Politely they interrupted: "How about something interesting, in fifteen seconds or less? We have to be on the air by three."

At that I showed them a one-page bill I was introducing that would make it illegal to use one- or two-family homes for prostitution. There happened to be just such a house of ill repute in my district. The police had told me they were powerless to close it down because the law prohibiting such use only covered "multiple dwellings." All I was proposing was to delete the word *multiple* from the original law. It had taken me less than seven minutes to draft that bill; it would take me more than seven years to finish updating the Administrative Code. Well, Doug and Steve just loved the idea of closing the single-family loophole and the following morning I was on every radio and TV program and in every newspaper. Even my relatives in Florida saw me. Besides the importance of timing and luck, these two wonderful newscasters had shown a cub member of the council how important it was to "sell" my ideas if I wanted to accomplish anything at City Hall. I was only a freshman lawmaker, but my bill swiftly passed through committee and the full council.

As far as the Administrative Code was concerned, I was a quick learner. I soon convinced Tom Cuite to appoint me to the unsalaried position of Subcommittee Chair for the Recodification of the Administrative Code. Soon stories started to appear about ridiculous sections of the code that were still in effect. With two bright and patient colleagues, Archie Spigner from Queens and Abraham Gerges from Brooklyn, I now had the forum to "market" my product. Archie, who wasn't a lawyer, was absolutely correct when he said, "I want to simplify the code so that the average person can understand it." Abe, who was a brilliant lawyer, studied every detail. The three of us worked together with the invaluable assistance of first assistant corporation counsel Jeffrey Friedlander, assistant corporation counsel Ellen Schroeder, and my committee counsel Gary Altman, spending hours and eventually years revising this tedious set of rules and regulations.

On one occasion I drew lots of laughs (and press) when I walked into Room 9 and sternly announced, "You will no longer be allowed to quarter your horses on the steps of City Hall!" On another I issued a stern warning to all "pullers-in": a reference to the section of the code that had been designed to stop overzealous merchants from literally "pulling in" hapless passersby to try to make their sale. Soon various merchant associations and chambers of commerce asked me to be their guest speaker, and I again appeared on radio and TV, explaining in short segments both the comic and serious part of my work. The most serious revision needed as far as I was concerned was not the code, but the part of the 1898 charter that had brought into existence the Board of Estimate.

One day in 1974, returning from City Hall to my council and law offices in Astoria, I exited the subway amazed to see about a dozen people dressed in Nazi uniforms, complete with helmets and bootstraps, giving out literature and using a bullhorn right in front of the subway entrance. The "Nazis" were so obnoxious that at first I thought it was a movie set and stopped to see who the actors were. They weren't acting. Police officers were on the scene. I was handed a leaflet calling for loyal Aryan Americans to finish the work of Adolph Hitler and "exterminate the kikes and the niggers."

I was outraged. I tore up the leaflet, ran up the stairs to my office, and called the captain of the local police precinct to demand an explanation. The captain advised me that his hands were tied because the group had a permit and had caused no disturbance thus far. I told him to come by in twenty minutes. I knew they were not allowed to incite a riot, but as far as I was concerned, their hate campaign already constituted one.

I then called members of the Astoria Civic Association and other civic groups such as the Greek American Homeowners, Hellenic American Action Group, Italian-American Federation, and local chapters of the Catholic and Jewish war veterans. Before long, a dozen or so demonstrators and friends arrived, some in VFW hats. There was shouting, a little pushing and shoving—and enough of a disturbance to justify the police in revoking the Nazis' permit and removing them from the public space. The incident was written up in the papers in articles that described my objections to their "demonstration."

Within weeks I began to receive hate mail, threatening letters and calls. Every few months another letter would arrive. Foolishly, I tore them all up. I was a former football player and had no fear of physical violence, certainly not from these fools. Besides, public office invited criticism, and even if I didn't like it, at the time I believed I just had to grin and bear it. The threats were spaced, and there did not seem any immediate reason to be concerned. That is, until February 24, 1977.

In the wee hours of the morning on that day, customers at the bar a few doors down from my offices on 31st Street heard a loud explosion. When they rushed out on the street they saw the windows popping from my office, and the upper floor of the two-story building engulfed in flames. Firefighters spent about two hours bringing the blaze under control. At first when the police called I dismissed it. "Oh come on, it's two in the morning," I groaned, thinking that for the umpteenth time some idiot in the billiard parlor downstairs had set off the smoke alarm by burning a few papers in a wastebasket.

"Councilman Vallone," the officer insisted, "this is serious, you better come over."

I called up Dom Calabrese, my law partner, and ran over to our office. It was an inferno. Scraps of my office were flying out into the street. It was as if somebody had kicked me in the stomach. Dom arrived shortly after in his travel outfit, suitcase packed and ready for a trip to Florida he was planning in the morning.

Instead of a trip, the two of us spent the next weeks sorting through charred bits of paper in an effort to reconstruct whatever was left of our office. Nearly everything inside had been destroyed—all the records in both my council and legal offices were gone, including personal and financial files. Not even the floor in my private office remained. We recovered about six inches from what had been yards and yards of file papers. I cried at the devastation caused by this apparently deliberate firebombing. The only saving grace was that it happened at two in the morning when no one was around to be hurt. Even so, the nearby stores, offices, and billiard parlor were also damaged by smoke and water.

Despite extensive investigations by the city's arson and bomb squads, the perpetrators were never found. I was convinced the Nazi nuts were behind the arson, but since I was constantly involved in public business that some people found objectionable—drug dealers, prostitution rings, operators of illegal car lots—it's possible it could have been someone else. I was less interested in determining who was responsible than just wanting to make sure these people didn't come to my home or in any way harm my family. I changed my home phone to an unlisted number, moved my offices to a more secure building, and became much more security conscious. I also introduced and had legislation passed that amended the city disclosure laws so that elected and appointed city officials no longer had to make public their home addresses unless the person asking for the information filled out a form stating the reason why. I have nothing but the greatest admiration for public officials who serve in countries throughout the world and are subject to constant threats of assassination and, in many cases, are indeed assassinated. No matter how brave you are, no one wants to endanger those near and dear to you, and certainly not invite troublemakers to your home.

5

Family

When asked, "How do you know if you are really in love and want to marry and live together for the rest of your lives?" I answer, "Only when you can truly say you would rather be with the person more than anyone else in the world." This is still how I feel about Tena as we approach the half-century marriage mark, with the exception that I love her more now than ever before. There really are no words that can adequately define love, but actions speak the clearest. Like my folks did, my wife and I enjoy having breakfast and dinner together and invariably do so joyfully. The media always made fun of me for what they thought was an easy schedule. I started at 8 A.M. at City Hall, and the reporters weren't there until 10 A.M. And even if I was home for an hour for dinner every evening, usually by six, I had to go out afterward for political dinners or other engagements—where, thanks to my wife's good cooking and a little common sense, I knew enough not to eat or drink.

Dinners and breakfasts at home are far more filling for my soul than for my body, even though Tena is a superb cook. I admonish everyone who ever worked for me never to forget their first duty is to themselves and their families. If you cannot be good to yourself and your family then you cannot be good to anyone else. God, country, family—and only then work. To me this is the first and most important principle if you expect to become a success in anything you do. Love lasts forever, and giving has a lot to do with what to expect in building a love relationship.

The only arguments I ever have with my wife today arise from my own impatience with other things and people (as when the red light is slow to change, or a conversation with fellow shoppers goes on for more than five minutes), and are never about her. My wife retired as a teacher upon the arrival of our seventh grandchild. Since then she has spent most of her days babysitting, teaching children to play the flute at our local Boys and Girls Club, and volunteering at an animal shelter. There she cleans cages and tends to unwanted and abandoned cats. Through her work, I've learned a little about the dire situation created by cat and dog overpopulation: that if you don't spay or neuter a pair of cats, thousands of cats can emanate from just those two and the end result is a lot of unwanted and unloved cats. In 2000 that education led me to introduce and have passed by the City Council the Spaying and

Neutering Bill, the first of its kind in the country. There was a lot of opposition to the measure, partly because of the cost, but my star witness, Tena Marie herself, was crucial to its eventual passage. According to City Clerk Victor Robles: "When Tena talks, it's like E. F. Hutton—the council listens." She did so well that three months after her testimony Mayor Giuliani wanted her to speak at the signing ceremony. It was a cuddly occasion, with enough kissing puppies to provide smooches for Rudy, Tena, my son Peter, and me.

Shortly after Christmas 1999, Tena was bitten by a cat and came down with a serious and near-fatal infection. Her arm turned ominously purple and she had to spend the last four days of 1999 on intravenous antibiotics in Mount Sinai Western Queens Hospital—proving once again that no good deed goes unpunished. Since I wasn't about to allow her hospital stay to interfere with our being together as the year 2000 dawned, I moved in with her on New Year's Eve and brought with me a candle-lit Italian feast to celebrate. To please me, she started eating . . . the last thing she should have done. Now, how many other men can honestly say they celebrated the advent of the New Millennium in the hospital trying to kiss their wife while she was throwing up?

Tena's selflessness rescued me over and over again early in our lives together, especially during the tough times, like when my father died, and later when my brother Buddy was killed. When we were kids, and then for a while as teenagers, Buddy was a protector to me. But he had an eye for the ladies, and they for him, and somehow after he came back from the service, he never achieved what he should have. He got married, but things didn't work out, and soon after he separated from his wife. He became a nightclub owner. His place was called Buddy's Duplex Lounge, and it was on busy 30th Avenue in Astoria.

Now, being a ladies' man, Buddy hired only the most beautiful barmaids in his club. He was also conservative when it came to money—he considered me a spendthrift. One day he discovered that someone was stealing money from the bar's till. Buddy suspected a particular girl, but rather than accusing her outright he told all six barmaids he was going to find out which one had done it and then fire her.

Of course, I didn't know the first thing about all this until one afternoon when this knockout of a barmaid came to see me. I was a young lawyer, and I never fooled around. Which was a lucky thing for me.

"Someone is stealing out of the bar at Buddy's, " she said to me.

"I'm sorry, that's something I know nothing about," I told her.

"He hasn't said so yet, but I know he suspects me."

"Look, it's my brother's bar. It's none of my business."

"You've got to help me. He's so unreasonable."

"You know, I think you're going to have to help yourself. I can't do it for you. He's the boss. Can't you talk to him?"

"I can tell you're not against me. He's so prejudiced, I just can't get through."

"Look," I finally said to the girl, to get her out my office, "I can talk to him, but he's a very stubborn guy."

The next day I called Buddy to tell him this particular barmaid had been to see me.

"Yeah, I know," he said. "I just fired her. She came back here and said she'd been to see you and you made a play for her. I knew then for sure that she was the one stealing from the bar. Because you would never do that. Not my brother!"

Not long afterward, Buddy was run over. It was Pearl Harbor Day, December 7, 1975. He'd left his own club and was heading out for the nightclub part of Riccardo's, which faces Astoria Park. He loved to wear black, and he was dressed in it top to bottom. It was about midnight. He was crossing the street from the park and, as luck would have it, the street-light on the corner was out. A car without lights came down the street and knocked him down. The driver stopped, then panicked and drove off. My brother was down in the street and rolling, and two other cars were behind the first one. They saw nothing, went right over him. Someone at Riccardo's called the police and the police called me at home, which was only three blocks away. I went running over. There were tire tracks all over him. A priest came and gave him the last rites.

I waited till six or seven in the morning to go tell my mother. It was the hardest thing I'd ever done. "Hi, Peter," she said as soon as I walked in the door, "want to have breakfast?"

"No, Mom, I have to sit down and go over something with you." And I told her.

That same day, after I left, she fainted in the house, fell, and broke her ankle. From the moment of that fall she had a limp. She also started slipping mentally. A little over a year had gone by since I had become embroiled in the dispute with the neo-Nazis, and I had been getting a lot of death threats. I felt I had to warn her not to answer the doorbell when unknown people came calling. Well, she then became convinced that the people who ran over Buddy had actually been looking for me.

In fact, even the police assumed that my brother's death was a hit on me. Not such a bad assumption, given the bomb planted in my office a little more than a year later. Still, it did not make sense to me that anybody out to get me would go looking at midnight in a bar. I decided I had to hire a private investigator to look into what had happened to Buddy. About six months later the P.I. narrowed the possible suspects down to a college kid who had stopped to tell the police he had seen the accident. I told the P.I. to promise the kid I would not go after him if he told the truth. He had been necking with a girl, he confessed to the P.I., and forgot to turn on his lights after he started driving. After feeling the impact of the hit he panicked and drove off. The police were still carrying the accident as an unsolved vehicular homicide. I could have sued, but that would not have brought Buddy back, and I was grateful to know it was not deliberate. So I let the whole thing drop.

With Buddy's death, and the bombing of my office, my mother started deteriorating. Every ailment you could have, she seemed to have. She wanted to live alone, but I stopped in to see her every day. Buddy's passing was worse than my father's death, which at his age and after his first heart attack we were all somewhat prepared for. But Buddy's sudden disappearance when he was only forty-two was something she could not accept. In 1980 she was diagnosed with Alzheimer's disease. I arranged for around-the-clock care for her so she could stay in the home she loved so much. Four years later, in January 1985, she died.

I have always found it disappointing that none of my three sons ever got to really know my father. Peter Jr. was born in 1961, Perry in 1963, and Paul, after Tena had a miscarriage in 1965, in 1967. Dad would have been as proud as Tena and I are of our three sons, who followed his lead as outstanding lawyers, patriots, gentlemen, and fathers, and who love our country and Creator as much as he did, and I do. My eldest son Peter, however, who was not particularly outgoing as a young man, and always told the bare truth even when it hurt, had a special relationship with my mother. Toward the end, when she no longer recognized anyone else, not even necessarily me, she always recognized Peter Jr. No matter what the state of her health, my mother would always sit and stare at the television, even when it was off; but when Peter came in with his cheerful "Hey Gram!" it always brought a big smile to her face. I think, actually, that his demeanor reminded her of Buddy.

At the time my mother died, Peter Jr. was in the middle of taking law school exams and was living at home with us. The morning it happened

Maria, the Spanish woman hired to look after her, called me up to tell me my mother had stopped breathing. A few minutes later when I arrived I started giving my mother mouth-to-mouth resuscitation, but nothing helped. She was clearly dead, and I burst into tears of anguish. All of a sudden, Peter came running in. I had left him back home sound asleep. "Dad, Dad," he called to me, still only half-dressed, "the strangest thing just happened. I was sleeping, and I could swear that Gram came to see me. I saw her standing on a castle, I couldn't understand how she could walk up there, with her bad ankle. She was jumping off, and she said to tell everybody, 'I'm all right!'"

I am so lucky to have had parents who passed along to me strong family patterns. Tena Marie and I were more than happy to continue those patterns with our own family. This meant that my sons and I developed a close relationship, as my brother and I had before with our dad. Ever since they were young, I've always called them Squirts No. 1, 2, and 3. When they were real squirts, I liked to hold them up over my head as if each were Superman (I used to call Perry, who was a natural, the "human fly"). With a little more expertise than my own dad, I taught them how to swim at the Boys and Girls Club and at the Astoria Pool, and like me, every one of my boys also worked summers as a lifeguard. Like me, they all started out at PS 122, but after kindergarten they all transferred to Immaculate Conception, which had a new open-door policy in the spirit of Vatican II. For secondary school they went on to Mater Christi High School in Astoria, now called St. John's Prep. I taught them Ping Pong as well as tennis. In Ping Pong they've long since outclassed me, possibly because it became such a competitive thing among the three of them. They all became school champions and Peter was even asked to represent the U.S. against China on *Wide World of Sports.* Now, tennis is a different story. In tennis, they're not as cunning as I am. They try to kill with every shot, while I place my shots carefully and make them run from side to side and wear them down. And even though they all got to the level of first singles on their high school teams, they still can't beat me. To me it's a lesson I apply whenever there's a tough contest in life. Before you go for the kill, wear them out. Before you adopt a budget, wear them down with all the information you have. Don't let anybody say you're holding anything back.

My wife started teaching again once all three boys were in school, about the same time that I was first elected to the New York City Council. She taught social studies and reading to the sixth grade at Immaculate Conception, the same school our boys attended, and I became head of the Parent School Association for what seemed like forever.

Not only is my wife the most beautiful woman in the world to me, but she and her family together fulfilled for me a dream that I had long feared was unrealizable: the dream of unselfishness. From around the time my brother was killed, there was hardly a Vallone family left for my sons and me. Miraculously, my wife's family stepped into this vacuum, and in the best possible way.

Sometimes I like to tell this story: Thousands of years ago, my tribe, the Vallones, would go around conquering people because we loved them. One of the tribes we conquered was my wife's tribe, the Buttigheri tribe. The Buttigheris smiled and greeted us and offered no resistance. "What a strange tribe," we Vallones thought to ourselves. After we conquered them, they began to show us things. Things like the wheel, which makes things move; and fire, which allows us to cook and warm ourselves. Most important, they taught the Vallones the real meaning of love. What makes the Buttigheris different is their unselfishness.

I love my family, but I also have a tendency to tell each of them, "this is what you should do." My parents did it even more. When Tena and I had Peter and went to visit at the bungalow, my parents would say, "Let's go out to the movies tonight." If we couldn't find a babysitter, they would say, "Fine, we'll stay home and play cards." Whereas my wife's family would say, "We'll babysit, you two go out to the movie." My parents always wanted to do things together with us no matter what our needs were. They had a notion of love as possession, rather than as sacrifice.

The irony was that, because we had such a great relationship with Tena's family, we started going on vacations together with them. We did it because we could really have a vacation, because my in-laws knew how to give us room, how to take care of the kids, and how not to have arguments. Besides that, my wife had one of the kindest, funniest, most talented younger brothers you can imagine—Joey, who became my tennis partner and best friend and also went on to become a very successful surgeon, podiatrist, and part-time drummer in a popular New Jersey band called the Garden State Five.

So it only seemed natural when we bought a condominium together in 1974. It happened during the era of the great gas shortages. In those days you could only get gas on alternate days, odd or even, and sometimes only if you had a good friend at the gas station. One warm Sunday morning in March when all three kids were young and we were sitting around my in-laws' backyard in Jersey City reading the *New York Times,* I saw a notice advertising a new condo for sale on the Jersey Shore: two bedrooms, convertible living room, on the beach, with an indoor pool. What really sold me, though, was the coupon at the bottom of the ad. It said that if we showed up, the local Hess station would give us a free tank of gas, at the condo seller's expense!

Well, that did it. It was nearly unthinkable in those days to take a long ride anywhere, since you were never sure you'd be able to refill your tank. So, as much for the sake of the expedition as anything else I announced, "Let's pack up. We're all taking a ride to the beach."

"What are you talking about?" my wife protested. "It's sixty degrees and the middle of March. You'll run out of gas and strand me, the kids, and my parents!"

"Please, just listen to me," I declared. "We're going to take a ride!" So we all got into my Pontiac Bonneville and I hoped and prayed that the story about the gas coupon was true. We arrived at the shore, and the condos themselves were more than I could ever have dreamed. They cost only $37,500, with a guaranteed $88 maintenance fee for the next three years. Best of all, the builder was offering to hold a thirty-year mortgage at a terrific rate.

"What, they want five thousand down?" my father-in-law protested. "I paid three thousand for my house in Jersey City when I bought it in 1941!"

I quickly made him realize that the $5,000 was a bargain. By the end of the weekend not only had we bought a condo together, but my brother-in-law bought one as well. What's more, afterward we went to the Hess station and collected on that free tank of gas.

6

Koch vs. Cuomo

It was 1973 when I first won the Democratic primary and general election for New York City Council member from Astoria. By the time of the next municipal election year cycle, 1977, the leadership of both state parties had moved the date of all primaries from June to September (a way of making it more difficult for challengers to defeat incumbents). In any event, I had no serious challenge, and no one had filed to run against me by the official deadline in July. As a result, I ran unopposed in the September 8, 1977, primary for council member from Astoria. That Democratic primary remains important, however, for another primary result that shaped much of politics in New York for over a decade: the emergence of Ed Koch and Mario Cuomo as the top Democratic vote-getters in New York City.

The mayoral primary of 1977 was the most widely contested race in a long time. Poor Mayor Abe Beame had had the misfortune of presiding over the near-bankruptcy of the city, and seemed a vulnerable target. Nearly every major city politician threw his or her hat into the ring: besides Beame, Koch, and Cuomo, there was Herman Badillo, my opponent in the 1969 Triboro congressional race; former Manhattan Borough President Percy Sutton; and flamboyant Upper West Side congresswoman Bella Abzug, who had made a name for herself during the Watergate hearings. The results of the primary: Ed Koch narrowly led Mario Cuomo with 20 percent of the vote; Cuomo had 19 percent, and Beame, Abzug, Sutton, and Badillo each took sizable but smaller slices of the vote. The split vote forced a runoff primary between the two top candidates. It was to take place ten days later.

I had known Mario Cuomo since the early '60s. We were both Italian-American lawyers from Queens with grassroots connections and higher ambitions, and the two of us used to have breakfast or lunch together. My father thought the world of Mario, and as I came to know him I grew to like him more and more. Early in my career, I relied on Mario's good political advice. When I felt I had to dispute the election results in my 1969 congressional race against Herman Badillo, it was Mario I called for help, and it was Mario who recommended to me his law partner Fabian Palomino, whom he described as "the best and smartest elections lawyer in the state."

Mario had also won my respect and admiration for his terrific job of mediation in the Forest Hills Housing project conflict of the early 1970s. The Lindsay administration had wanted to build a low-income housing development in the middle of a high-income area in Forest Hills, Queens. No question that there was a need for such housing, but I always believed that this necessity had to be balanced with the needs and character of the neighborhood. Many Queens residents moved there to get away from ghetto-like conditions, and had a natural aversion to living in apartment houses—after all, they had finally "made it" into their own homes. They knew about city neighborhoods where, as soon as a "project" came in, the area changed ethnically or racially and deteriorated economically, and former residents, rightly or wrongly, felt chased out. Anything that even sounded like a "project" was a red flag. Besides, many of the residents of Forest Hills were Jews who had run away not only from congested conditions, but from death itself, and they didn't want to be "chased away" again.

I'm a grassroots person, as is Mario, so when somebody wants to come in and build a group of 24-story apartment houses in the area, I say, "Wait a minute." The Lindsay administration, operating from a city-wide perspective, knew that it was necessary to bring minority groups into middle and upper middle class communities, but they had a hard time separating prejudice and bigotry from legitimate fears. A smart lawyer like Mario Cuomo was able to come along and say, "This is no place for a project. Let's talk instead about ownership, about condos and coops." For people like Mario and me, it was a question of addressing the fears in such a way as to bring in minority people without driving out the middle class. That is really the only possible basis for a healthy city. And that's what Mario managed to put through. With Mario as mediator, supported by groups like my own Astoria Civic Association, a great compromise took place. The Board of Estimate approved a smaller "scatter-site" development of three 12-story buildings, organized as a low-income cooperative, unique in the country.

In 1974, right after I became a councilman, Mario and I had coffee across the street from City Hall. He was deciding whether or not to run for lieutenant governor for the first time. He told me, "Peter, you should run for it instead. You're better known than I am, and you come from a strong political club. I haven't been as active politically as you."

A man who can do what Mario did in the Forest Hills controversy was a born leader and I told him so: "Mario, I think you're more qualified than I am. Don't worry about not having an organization; you'll have mine, and a lot of help." Unfortunately, Mario lost that race for lieutenant governor to Mary Anne Krupsak. I remained confident that Mario's day would come, and in 1977 I served as co-manager of his Queens campaign for mayor. As for Ed Koch, in 1977 he was to me a largely unknown quantity, as he was to most Queens Democrats. All we basically knew about him was that he had been a very liberal Congress member from Manhattan, that he had beaten the "machine" Democrat Carmine De Sapio for leadership, and that he ran good commercials. In recent years he had taken more conservative stances, associating himself with some of the Forest Hills protesters against the new housing development, and was in favor of the death penalty.

Unlike Queens native son Cuomo, Koch, with his roots in Greenwich Village Independent Democratic politics, needed to establish his credentials beyond Manhattan. While Mario, ever idealistic, refused to cut political deals, Koch, unsurprisingly, sought the backing of district and county leaders in the Bronx, Brooklyn, and Queens. An early result of Ed Koch's alliance building was an endorsement from my former opponent, Bronx congressman Herman Badillo. In Queens, our county leader Donald Manes officially endorsed the hometown candidate Mario Cuomo, but made no effort to press his candidate upon individual district leaders and elected officials, who divided largely along ethnic lines. Most Jewish leaders (except Assemblyman Saul Weprin) worked for Koch, and most Italian leaders for Cuomo.

In my own area of Astoria and Long Island City, district leaders Ralph DeMarco and Gloria D'Amico sensed in Mario, as I did, a very bright young star on the rise—and not just because we all were Italian. To us who loved Mario he was not only the son of an immigrant who became a legendary lawyer, he was also a different breed of Italian-American candidate. The ones we were used to were more like the mustachioed, slick-haired Mario Procaccino, who when he ran for mayor came up with such memorable phrases as "He grows on you, like cancer." Procaccino was a nice man, but he did not represent the image that Americans of Italian descent wanted to project. Mario Cuomo, on the other hand, was a brilliant lawyer who could rally voters of all colors and creeds. In debates with Harvard men he made them look feeble.

Not all Italian-American leaders felt as we did. Some were more calculating. The important Brooklyn political leader Meade Esposito, for example, saw his alliance with Ed Koch as a way of ensuring his continuing influence over judgeships and other appointments to city office. For his part Koch effectively courted Esposito while at the same time asking him to keep a low profile.

My father had known and liked Esposito: although he could be crude, he was so affable and disarming that he was hard to dislike (and too powerful to mess with, anyway). Shortly after I was elected, Brooklyn council member Howie Golden insisted I come out to Brooklyn to meet Esposito, because Meade had told him he thought I was "a flake." There he was, holding court at his usual table at a restaurant on Court Street in downtown Brooklyn. Sure enough, he began by saying, "I hear you're not like your father Charlie. He was a good guy, but you're a flake who wants to get rid of the Board of Estimate and turn the city upside down."

The conversation could not help but remind me of a meeting years earlier with the Manhattan political boss Carmine De Sapio, whose first words to me were: "Are you Charlie's boy?" I had never met anyone who didn't like my dad. Politicians, princes, popes, or ex-convicts, they always knew my dad and liked me because of him, even if many of them voted against me politically. Esposito and I had a pleasant lunch, we laughed, and became friendly. Once again my dad had paved the way for me.

My father's background and my own roots in the Astoria clubhouse identified me as a regular or "machine" Democrat. The truth is, however, I could never help siding with the reformers on basic principles, and in the City Council I formed natural alliances with other reformers like Manhattan's Bobby Wagner and Ruth Messinger, or the group from Brooklyn that included Herb Berman and Abe Gerges. In some ways I believe I have been the biggest reformer in the last quarter-century of New York City history, though I probably won't be known as that because I still have the image of the conservative Italian guy from Queens.

In the Democratic runoff election on September 19, 1977, Koch defeated Cuomo 55 to 45 percent. However, Cuomo had already received the smaller Liberal Party nomination, and before Primary Day he had pledged to run in the general election on the Liberal line no matter what happened in the primary. Now he followed through on that pledge to run, even without the official Democratic Party blessing. Mario's strong challenge made it imperative that in the general election Ed Koch rally to his side as many of the prominent Democrats who had backed Cuomo as possible. Every one of them—from Governor Carey to Attorney General Robert Abrams to Congressman Mario Biaggi to our Queens county leader Donald

Manes—fell into line. The only two he couldn't get were my fellow councilman Thomas Manton and I.

In my diary on primary election night I wrote: "Cuomo was too good for them . . . I'm still personally committed to Mario and loyal to the Democratic Party. I believe what is best for the city is what is best for the party—and Mario is best for the city." The decision to support Mario on the Liberal line was hard for me, because I was always an organization guy and this was the first time I ever broke from the Democratic Party. In most cases I believed that it was best to clean up the party from within. I had never met Ed Koch, but I had a personal relationship with Mario. And besides, even if it was a long shot to think Mario could pull it off without most official Democratic backing, it was still a realistic run, especially since the Republican candidate, Manhattan's Roy Goodman, had no prospect of winning, and John Lindsay had already proven that you could win running on the Liberal line alone.

The endorsements of Koch by Democratic Party leaders proved surprisingly ineffective with the general voter, and as our campaign brought attention to Koch's political deal making, Cuomo enhanced his standing with minority groups and liberals. Not enough, however, given Koch's historic ties to these groups in Manhattan. In the more conservative, heavy-voting neighborhoods of Queens and Brooklyn, Ed and Mario split the vote, largely but not solely along ethnic lines. Koch was already sounding conservative, so he got a lot of Italian votes when he joked that he was "a liberal who got mugged." Cuomo was an unabashed liberal, although very much filled with middle-class values and a champion of the common man.

Unfortunately, the campaign turned nasty when a misguided Cuomo backer, an attorney from Queens, organized the circulation of hate literature that read, "Vote for Cuomo, Not the Homo." An unauthorized draft of a never-run Associated Press story containing smears about Koch's alleged sexual orientation was also making the rounds. Mario and I condemned these outrages. At first we believed they were a plant intended to motivate the liberal gay vote against us. In the end, the smears definitely did more to hurt Mario than anything else. Everyone at campaign headquarters was furious. The person responsible later confessed and apologized and exonerated Mario, me, and others in our Queens campaign offices.

In the general election on November 9, Ed Koch won the race for mayor against Mario Cuomo by a margin of 50 to 42 percent. As disappointing as Mario's loss was, I found some consolation in my own margin of victory over my nominal opponents, winning 87 percent of the vote. Throughout the campaign, and in my public career, my priorities remained the same: public safety, moderation, providing a community voice, combating homelessness. My campaign spent not a cent on advertising, and I ran only on the Democratic line.

The campaign dust had hardly settled when the troubles began between me and the new mayor-elect and his staff. In early December I heard that Koch and his right-hand man John LoCicero "wanted to know" which committees I was sitting on. Why were they looking at me so intently, I wondered. Did they perhaps want to maneuver me off the important committees I was currently serving on and onto lesser ones? It certainly appeared that way. A day later a bill I had sponsored that would have granted "advise and consent" powers of the City Council over the mayor's commissioner-level appointees went down to ignominious defeat in the council's own Charter and Governmental Operations Committee, 5–4 (the four negatives were actually abstentions).

My bill had been inspired partly by the Charter Revision Commission of the mid-1970s—the one chaired by Republican state senator and unsuccessful mayoral candidate Roy Goodman. This commission had established community boards all over the city and granted the council veto power over nine boards and their commissioners. In its hearings and general recommendations it called for increased legislative oversight over the executive. It had done this in lieu of specifically granting broad advise-and-consent powers or adopting my own call for the outright abolition of the Board of Estimate. As Goodman had pointed out in his unsuccessful run for mayor, the Beame administration had stymied many of that charter commission's recommendations. My Advise and Consent Bill was an attempt to thwart the executive tactics mayors used to manipulate the council. I saw it as a "logical, legal extension" of the powers the Charter Revision Commission had given the council.

Needless to say, Mayor-elect Koch had lobbied long and hard against my bill. Having lost that vote, a week later I felt obligated to vote against a $10,000 pay raise for myself and my fellow council members—who seemed to find it easier to reward themselves monetarily than to give themselves the power to effectively oversee the people's interest in government. This vote was particularly painful for me not only because it came on my birthday, but because it seemed to validate the media criticism of the council as a collection of "The Forty Thieves." In the end, the pay raise passed 33–7, although I returned my raise to the city treasury.

The year 1977 marked the end of an era for me. I had always been respectful of the political traditions of my elders, and two important ones were passing from the scene. My second political "father," Ralph DeMarco, had died unexpectedly in March. And now Abraham Beame, a man who had served the city for some forty years, had been rejected by the voters. I found it tough to adjust to Abe Beame's loss. Even though we had never become close, he proved himself to me a few weeks before he left office when he remembered a few words I whispered in his ear at Ralph DeMarco's funeral and pushed through an appointment for a brilliant young assistant DA, Neil O'Brien, to become a judge of the criminal court, an appointment that held no political advantage for Beame. Neil went on to become one of the most respected jurists on the appellate division before his recent untimely death.

Besides the nostalgia engendered by Ralph DeMarco's death, I was nervous about what the political future held. After my strong push for the Advise and Consent Bill—including my insistence on a vote even though the mayor-elect specifically requested me to withdraw it—I had heard stories that Koch had vowed to "politically destroy me." When John LoCicero attempted to apply pressure, I told him, "Screw you." The lines were drawn, and I expected the worst—not only from Koch, whose retribution I had risked by going out on a limb for Mario Cuomo—but from my ex-rival, deputy mayor Herman Badillo. From experience I knew Badillo was a tough guy to take on, although we later became quite friendly.

So it came as something of a surprise when, shortly after Koch was inaugurated, I was paid a visit by John LoCicero. I had been sitting in a Government Operations Committee meeting at 250 Broadway when I was told LoCicero wanted to say hello to me, that he had walked across the street from City Hall to see me. I approached John with a smile and an outstretched hand, and was greeted with, "I just want you to know we know you were responsible for the 'Vote for Cuomo Not the Homo' signs." As if that weren't enough, he then repeated to my face the threat I had heard secondhand for over a month: "We are going to destroy you politically!"

Anyone who knows me will attest that the worst thing anyone can do to me is threaten me. I think it goes back to the bully on the bus back in my middle school years. In this case I told LoCicero to go to hell and that I intended to convey the same message to the mayor in person. Sure enough, I crossed Broadway, the "street of no return," to have my first face-to-face encounter with the indomitable Ed Koch. I was furious: partly because by this time I really knew who *had* put out the leaflets, partly because I had denied it publicly before and was ticked that LoCicero (and his boss) did not seem to understand that lying was not a part of my political character.

Ed Koch agreed to see me right away. At first he had a look on his face of "Who does this guy think he is?" The big blowup, however, did not happen. When I laid my cards on the table he seemed to know at once that I was telling the truth, even if I did not divulge who had done it. I in turn felt a sense of sincerity from him. We had an unexplainable, immediate rapport. As soon as he realized this he sat down, started to laugh, and said, "Let me get John in here."

John, now set straight, offered his hand in friendship. The moment of near confrontation had defused all the tension between us and crystallized an understanding of mutual respect. With LoCicero looking on, Ed and I talked for five or ten minutes. That conversation set the tone for a new relationship. After it, I saw Ed Koch and John LoCicero almost daily for the next twelve years. I was the Queens borough representative on the council's budget committee, so I had reason to work closely with the mayor's office. They knew I was respected, hardworking. Ed must have realized that I was one of the five or six council members who would eventually get somewhere. Our relationship remained healthy, even if we disagreed on some matters. It's easy to see the tone of this developing friendship in entries in my diary over the next few years. At the end of 1978 I wrote: "Get more from Koch than I did from Beame . . . Koch doing A-OK"; at the end of 1980: "Mayor Ed Koch is the best mayor NYC ever had, and he and I are now good friends. Talk of my becoming majority leader if post ever becomes vacant."

7

The Creator: The Basic of All Basics

While attending Power Memorial Academy in Manhattan I took a course entitled "Apologetics" which convinced me beyond a shadow of a doubt that not only did God create this earth of ours and bestow on us the rights to life, liberty, and pursuit of happiness, but that every single human being is made in the image and likeness of God. The earth, sun, moon, stars, and the intricacies of this planet of ours could no more have just come together without an intelligent maker than could the watch on your wrist.

I will also never forget Brother Ryan telling us why a belief in God was the best bet a gambler could ever make. If there is a God and you try your best to live a good life and practice the golden rule of treating others the same way you would like them to treat you, not only will you be happy on earth, but when you die you will go to heaven and live happily for all eternity. If, on the other hand, you hurt others and live a life of selfishness, not only will you be unhappy on earth but you will be held accountable and continue to suffer for all eternity. If there is no God, and there is nothing out there, you have lost nothing—your life will have been lived as happily or as miserably just the same. Obviously I placed my bet on there being a God, and I have never regretted it.

Just look at the principles that flow from a belief in the Creator. If you really believe that we are all made in the image and likeness of God, then how could you discriminate against any other human being simply because he or she is of a different color or religion or different in any way whatsoever? God certainly does not create junk, so every living creature should be treated with respect, as well as all aspects of our environment. And as a Christian who believes that God Himself came down to earth in human form and allowed Himself to be crucified to atone for our sins and then rose again, I can more easily understand why suffering and sacrifice were necessary companions along our way to our individual judgment days. That Final Day certainly will be the ultimate accountability for all of us. Those principles also make it that much easier to see how obscene it is for humans to kill in the name of God, whether it be terrorists who attacked innocents in the World Trade Center on September 11, 2001, or the latest cold-blooded murder reported in today's newspaper. Such mindless and blind hatred does not come from the mind of God, but from the warped minds of humans who live in selfish misery.

Some people think I am a religious zealot because I attend mass and take communion every morning. No. I have been doing it since I was thirteen not just because of Sister John Alicia, but because I have found it is a wonderful way for me to begin my day with God, and I really enjoy it. And while I am a Roman Catholic, I believe it is far more important to have a firm belief in God than to blindly follow any organized religion, and I refuse to condemn anyone who believes differently. So when it comes to matters of conscience such as abortion or the death penalty, I take great pains to try to respect everyone's opinion even if it is different from my own. I leave judgment up to the Creator, who knows best. As far as my own judgment goes, the worst hypocrites are those who are quickest to condemn others.

As far as the particular doctrines of the Catholic Church, the most enlightening experience for me was when I was asked to teach catechism to Catholic high school students who were attending public school and coming in voluntarily on Sundays for formal religious instruction. I was attending law school at the time and took on the task very seriously. I brushed up on such complicated doctrines as the Immaculate Conception, Assumption, Incarnation, and others that I had found confusing at their age. What a surprise to discover in the very first question after my long discussion of these various doctrines that what the students really wanted to know was: "Why do you believe in God?" I never did get off that subject. That's when I learned how important it is in life and in government to get back to the basics, to never assume that people know them.

I sincerely believe that the Declaration of Independence would never have come together without the help of human beings who had a firm belief in God and the sense of justice that flows from it, and that a firm belief in a God of love is the surest road to success in a world full of pitfalls. The God I speak of knows that all humans make mistakes and fail now and again, but just as any parent forgives and helps her or his child in any way possible, so too does this Creator expect us to get up again and try our best. My God does not set up one religion over another (or no religion) but judges people rather by how they treat their fellow humans.

Perhaps most important of all, my God asks each of us not to set ourselves up in judgment of another person's conscience. That is up to God alone. This philosophy has helped me immeasurably in dealing with fellow elected officials. My election in 1986 as head of the New York City Council was marred by betrayals and discontent. During my first months in office both the city as a whole and some of my personal friends suffered terribly from the worst corruption scandal in years. Yet it was easy for me to convince my colleagues that I bore no hard feelings, that I wanted to start fresh, because I really believed it. Credibility and truthfulness cannot be feigned.

While attending Fordham College, I went with other students on so-called religious retreats that lasted from three to five days. In 1964 my father asked me to accompany him to the Bishop Molloy Retreat House in Jamaica Estates, Queens, for a three-day retreat. I enjoyed it so much I have been going every year ever since, and now bring one hundred men with me (there are also separate retreats for women, teens, and married couples). Many know that business retreats are opportunities to spend quality thinking time with higher-ups and improve your financial position in this world. A religious retreat is quite similar, except you spend quality time with your Creator and improve your position in this world as well as the next. You can't get much higher than that. It was at these retreats that I began to understand the meaning of the idea that "God does not create junk."

In an earlier chapter I mentioned the attention I received from a Mountain Lodge community paper praising me for all the lives I had saved as a lifeguard. This attention, along with the fact that I once played semiprofessional football, still played tennis twice a week, and worked at keeping in shape in spite of my hectic double career as a lawyer and a councilman, left me with the false impression that I was physically invincible. In 1978, at age forty-three, I believed that I needed my Creator only for spiritual reasons. It wasn't until the summer of that year that I found out just how wrong I was.

Tena and I were sunning ourselves on a beach blanket with friends at the Jersey Shore when I heard the lifeguard's whistle. I looked up just in time to see my son Paul come surging joyously toward us on a big wave.

"Hey, will you look at those nice rollers," I said, jumping up. "They must be at least four feet!" I saw the displeasure on Tena's pretty face.

"Peter, don't go in again. Mass is at five o'clock. You're going to make us all late."

"It's the last day of vacation, honey," I protested. "Just one more wave!" I dashed eagerly toward the surf.

My idea of relaxation was bodysurfing with my three sons. But the ocean had been disappointingly calm all summer. That Saturday of Labor Day weekend in 1978, the weatherman had said that Hurricane Edna would be passing off the Atlantic coast, well out to sea, making higher-than-normal waves. Some hurricane! The sun was beating down out of a cloudless blue sky. Two-foot-high mini-waves had been all that Edna could give us, until now.

This is more like it, I thought as I plunged into the surf and swam with swift, sure strokes to a spot about seventy-five feet from shore, where I could catch the swells. This was our fourth summer vacation at the Jersey Shore with my in-laws, and I loved every minute of those precious weekends, times of respite from the pressures of City Hall. The fiscal nightmare that had gripped the city and had brought it to the verge of bankruptcy two years earlier was far from over, but the city I loved was making a comeback.

I plunged into the sea. The waves were now about five or six feet high, and a surprisingly strong undertow quickly swept me out to where I could ride them back in. I felt a surge of excitement at the sight of a huge swell building behind me. I was about to catch it, when I heard a familiar but distant voice shouting, "Help me, Dad! Help! Help!" Turning, I saw my son Perry, fifteen, about seventy-five feet farther out. He was struggling to hold a girl above the water.

Around me, the ocean was suddenly a churning, roiling maelstrom. The waves, which a few seconds before had been "just right" for surfing, were now giants of really menacing size, maybe ten feet high. It was tough going, but I kept up a steady, powerful stroke. I was in charge; I was sure I could handle the situation.

As I reached them, I grabbed the girl's arm and said to Perry, "Don't worry. It's all right now—I have her!" I recognized the girl as Barbara, the teenage daughter of one of our summer neighbors.

"Thank God, Mr. Vallone . . . !" she gasped in relief.

"It's a good thing you got here, Dad!" Perry shouted, frantically treading water in the great waves. "I've been yelling for ten minutes, but nobody heard me. I just couldn't hold her up any longer."

"You go in first, Perry, and get help," I said. He nodded his head in assent and moved away from us through the tossing sea.

Barbara was rigid with fear, but I managed to turn her on her back and grab her under the chin in the traditional lifesaving hold. I began to swim. A huge wave broke over us; Barbara sputtered and coughed, water in her mouth and nose. She clawed at my arm in panic. Desperate, I turned her on her side, trying to raise her face higher out of the water. Another wave hit us, plunging us under. Barbara came up choking, her arms flailing wildly. *It isn't working!* I thought to myself.

I turned and faced her. Ropes of her long hair entwined her face and neck like seaweed. Her eyes were wide with terror.

"Barbara, give me your hand," I cried. The only thing to do in such rough seas was to let her face me and literally pull her along as I swam. It was slow going, and for the first time since I had plunged into the surf, I felt every one of my forty-three years, as my strength ebbed rapidly away. To make matters worse, I couldn't see the shore; I didn't even know in what direction we were moving. Where were Perry and the lifeguards? Surely they were just beyond the next wave.

"I don't want to die! Please . . . I don't want to die!" Barbara kept sobbing over and over. The roar of the breaking surf almost drowned out our voices.

"Take it easy, Barbara," I said, trying to calm her. "Nobody's going to die." But even as I spoke the words, I began to doubt in my heart that we were going to make it.

I thought of Tena. Incredible to realize I would never hold her again—never talk to her or my boys. It looked as though I had run out of time. A great sadness filled me; there was still so much to say, that would never be said now. . . . *The insurance policies; she doesn't know where I keep the insurance policies.*

I looked at Barbara. All at once I felt a twinge of resentment for her helplessness, her clinging, insistent hands that were dragging me down. The waves crashed over us. We were going down and her hair was streaming up.

Let her go, a subtle voice whispered, *You've got a wife and sons who need you. Save yourself . . .*

I tried to ignore the voice, stroking harder. My strength was almost gone.

Nobody will blame you. You're not the lifeguard . . .

I had trusted in my own strength, and it was failing me. All the skill and polish of the successful lawyer, all the power and drive of the politician, the pride of the former lifeguard could not help me now.

She's not your responsibility. . . you're not even supposed to be here . . .

Her eyes were wide in terror, riveted on me. I looked into them. Suddenly I knew there was no way I could let her go. And as soon as I decided to go down with her, a great calm came over me.

Suddenly we were going up, up, and Barbara was shouting, "Mr Vallone . . . Mr. Vallone, look! The shore!" I turned my head and through the tossing waves saw the beach. The lifeguards were running about getting the last stragglers out of an ocean gone completely wild. I thought, *My God, they don't even know we're out here!*

I saw that we had covered only about half the distance to shore, but Barbara had taken heart at the sight of land. She asked, "Are we going to make it, Mr. Vallone?"

"You bet we are, Barbara!" I shouted. "Look, here comes a wave. Don't be afraid—I'm going to give you a push and we're going to ride it in. Swim to shore with all you have. I'll be right behind you."

From some hidden reserve we found new strength. We caught the wave and rode it. I grabbed Barbara again, just as her momentum was giving out, and with a few last desperate strokes, we struggled out of the undertow and found ourselves able to stand.

Stumbling forward, half dragging Barbara, I handed her over to a lifeguard. I stood knee-deep in the water, my chest heaving with exhaustion. I realized I had pulled a muscle in my leg. As I limped onto the sand, I looked back at the raging sea I had escaped. And froze with horror: *Perry was still struggling in the water!*

"Dad!" he cried out. In my efforts to save Barbara and myself I had forgotten about my own son; I thought he had made it safely to shore.

"Swim, Perry, swim!" I shouted over the roar of the surf. If I dived in to help him, I knew I could never make it back. But there was no choice. Our eyes locked for an agonized instant, and I said aloud, "God in Heaven, help us!"

Then suddenly it happened: Perry was borne up on the crest of a monstrous wave, like a huge hand, and was catapulted forward. An instant later he lay gasping and sputtering at my feet. I had never seen anything like it before, and I'm sure I never will again. That wave had carried Perry at least thirty feet. It was as if the Lord Himself had plucked my son from the ocean.

Arm in arm we stumbled along the beach. We passed Barbara, who was receiving emergency treatment, crying and coughing up water, surrounded by curious onlookers.

I fell on our blanket. Tena, unaware of what had happened, exclaimed, "Peter, I've never seen you so pale!"

After a few minutes, Barbara and her parents came over and tearfully embraced Perry and me. I could not hold back my own tears of gratitude to God, who had saved us all. I knew in that moment something I had never learned in all my years at City Hall: we can do nothing without God's help. I was just too weak and the fierce ocean too strong.

I didn't know it at the time, but the cartilage in my right knee was torn apart and I would need complicated surgery to repair the damage. In all the years I played football I never sustained an injury requiring me to be removed from a game, but this one event almost removed me from the game of life altogether. If I had not already been certain that we were creatures of a loving Creator, this frightening experience alone would have made a believer out of me. All the false pride I once had in my physical strength was swept away in the waves by the hand of God, or by an angel that was sent to lift the three of us to safety.

It is also interesting to note that once your name appears in any newspaper or magazine, it can come back to help or haunt you in the future. The true story you have just read appeared in nearly identical form in the July 1980 edition of *Guideposts* magazine. About twenty years later, I won the Democratic nomination for governor of the State of New York. Kevin McCabe, my close friend and former chief of staff who took a leave of absence to become my campaign manager, warned me that negative campaigning was inevitable, and that I had better own up to any unpleasant or untruthful events at the outset of the campaign, because if I didn't, my opposition would certainly find a way of uncovering them.

I had completely forgotten the swimming incident that occurred twenty years earlier. Besides, it was entirely true. The young woman's name was not really Barbara (it was Marcy) and it was changed in the story at my request so as not to embarrass her. At least one of my opponents somehow found this now happily married woman in Florida. Some members of his staff went to visit her with a copy of *Guideposts* magazine. They expected her to say that I had made up the whole thing. Instead, she told them it was true. After they left with a polite acknowledgment that they were "just verifying the story," she looked up my son Perry in the New Jersey directory and called to find out if I was all right. He assured her I was. It was only when Perry called me that my campaign and I found out to what lengths and expense the opposition would go to discredit its principal opponent. Dad's golden rule of always telling the truth had helped me again. If this published story had been made up, my career in government might have ended then and there.

8

One Man, One Vote?

During the first of Ed Koch's terms as mayor, I had to decide whether to stay focused on the city or to try a run for statewide or national office. Locally I consolidated my position by becoming chair of the Standards and Ethics Committee of the New York City Council, a position that seems insignificant outside the council, but significant within it, since you cannot hold the position unless your fellow council members have confidence in you to use it wisely. In 1979 I had an opportunity to make a run for U.S. Congress when the Triboro district disappeared again to make way for a more traditional all-Queens congressional district. The congressman who had long represented voters in the area, James Delaney, had been living mostly in Florida for some years, and when he finally decided to give up the pretense of continuing to represent Queens, I became a heavy favorite as the strongest contender for the seat.

It's true I had a strong reputation and, as a City Council member, a useful platform for a congressional run. Yet I was enjoying my new visibility at City Hall. Speaker Cuite was getting on, and sooner or later I knew a good position might open up closer to home. Most of all I remained ambiguous about going to Washington. I wanted to stay close to my wife and three sons. As a councilman I represented some 170,000 voters; as a congressman I would have represented 500,000. It did not seem a big enough difference to make moving to Washington worth it. In the end I declined to run and a largely unknown assistant district attorney named Geraldine Ferraro, who benefited from her association with her cousin Nick Ferraro, ran in my place and won the seat.

At the end of 1979 I was named chairman of the Carter-Mondale campaign in Queens and soon came to realize that, while Washington held little appeal for me, Albany was another matter. Although Governor Carey had been reelected by a comfortable margin in 1978, his popularity had taken a beating in recent years as gossip columnists headlined his remarriage and eccentric social behavior, leaving an impression that he was distracted from state politics. I myself had no chance of attempting a run for governor without prior experience at the state level—but any statewide official who decided to challenge Carey might leave an open position I could run for. I was getting a fair amount of publicity—far more than any other council member—for my work with the Administrative Code, and my name came up repeatedly, especially as a possible candidate for attorney general.

The first indications that statewide office might be a real possibility had come through my experience several years earlier stumping as a surrogate for our Queens borough president Donald Manes. In early 1974 Donald got bit by the notion that he ought to run for governor. He had no trouble raising money, and spent some $400,000 on an abortive primary race. Unfortunately his personality on television came across as gruff and a little unmannered—a kind of Buddy Hackett from Queens Boulevard—and he had trouble connecting with voters outside the city. So he decided to ask two of his favorite young politicians, me and Alan Hevesi, to go around the state on speaking engagements representing him. He knew the biggest vote in the state was the Italian one. Even if I was a comparative unknown, having lost my congressional race and just won my council race a year earlier, my father had had a big reputation, and Donald thought the name might even mean something in Buffalo and Rochester. "Look," he said to me, "You're a well-spoken Italian, and certainly a better public speaker than me. I want you to speak for me around the state."

I first knew Donald Manes from various Queens courthouses where he, like I, had been a trial lawyer. During the 1960s we regularly bumped into each other either in the central criminal court or in the civil courthouses that in those days were spread all over Queens as far away as Rockaway. Then, when I first ran for office in 1969, Donald was another City Council member from Queens, and he and I naturally had reason to interact as we both moved in political circles. I liked Donald. At the time I found him gregarious, funny, and ambitious. He was always telling jokes, always laughing. The first Queens borough presidents had been Irish, followed by a series of Italian ones. Manes was only the second Jewish borough president.

I wasn't one of Donald Manes's buddies like Matty Troy or Howie Golden, with whom he went out drinking, or to the races; I went home to my wife. Still, one-on-one, Donald was very appealing: knowledgeable, smart, and no-nonsense. I agreed to make an appearance at a forum in Westchester in his stead, and maybe at one other place. It did not work, since obviously the voters wanted to see the real candidate, not a surrogate. I called him up and told him, "Donald, it won't work, you've got to go."

"No, Peter, I have the money, but I'm not as good as you are at public speaking."

"Donald, it won't do you any good to have me or anyone else speak for you. The people want to hear and see you. Otherwise you haven't got a shot in hell of winning, and anyone who advises you differently is just going to take your campaign money and squander it. I won't have any part of it." He was determined to do it his way; he kept sending more surrogates. Even Matty Troy, who was then still Queens Democratic county chairman, rejected Donald's attempt to win state office. The campaign went nowhere. Before his downfall, Matty Troy had helped engineer Donald Manes's rise to Queens borough president. That did not prevent Donald from helping to ease Matty out of office shortly after Matty pooh-poohed his bid for governor.

A few years later Matty Troy pleaded guilty to unlawfully using a client's escrow funds. His troubles seemed truly inadvertent, not purposeful. He was simply not a criminal type, and most of his friends thought he could probably have beaten the charges if he had found himself a good criminal lawyer. Instead he was disbarred and served a year or two. He had already lost his county leader position, and with the legal charge he lost his Finance chair and eventually his council seat. This, of course, ended his political reign, though he was later readmitted to the bar.

Matty Troy's legal problem was the reason the city revised its charter to preclude City Council members from becoming political county leaders. As council Finance chair as well as Queens Democratic leader, Troy was seen as an example of too much power in one person. Somehow the Charter Revision Commission failed to see the logic in applying the same exclusion to city executives, such as borough presidents. To some it seemed only logical that Manes take over Troy's county leader position, even if this meant another concentration of power in one person. Manes, by deposing his former mentor, did not ingratiate himself with Troy. (Nonetheless, Matty and Donald were reconciled after Matty served his jail term and was no longer a political force.)

Troy and Manes came from the powerful area of Queens that includes Bayside, Forest Hills, and Queens Village. They were products of the Democratic clubs there, which are particularly powerful because it's a heavy voting area with a large Jewish, Italian, and Irish population. By nature Manes was no more a criminal type than Matty, but he was a plotter, and he knew pretty well how to manipulate people. Matty, who had never been able to keep his mouth shut, would blurt out everything; Manes was much too smart for that.

My brief taste of campaigning in place of Donald Manes outside New York City whetted my appetite for a larger platform. During the 1970s I also had come to realize that the fate of the city depended enormously on what happened in Albany. At the end of 1980 I wrote in my diary about "making long-term political plans, possibly statewide," and in 1981 the same diary read: "Looks like I'm becoming an instant candidate for NYS Atty. Gen'l." Everything seemed to point in the direction of my winning my 1981 council race by a large margin and being perfectly positioned for a statewide run in 1982.

So you can imagine my disappointment on September 9, 1981, two days before the scheduled primary elections, when I heard that a three-judge federal panel had barred the election from taking place in Brooklyn, Manhattan, and the Bronx—making it all but impossible to hold the vote in Queens and Staten Island as well. The reason for the decision was a suit brought by African-Americans, Hispanics, and others who objected that newly drawn City Council district lines in those three boroughs discriminated against them. The primary election for all offices was postponed for two weeks, and ultimately postponed for all City Council races for at least a year. This completely fouled up my plans to float a test balloon for a statewide race. As a sitting council member I could have run for state office and still kept the seat if I lost. I could not, however, run for two different offices at the same time.

So, instead of becoming an "instant candidate" for state office, my diary on Election Day, 1981, read: "No council elections (Depressing!) Koch wins in landslide." Ed Koch had been nominated not only by the Democrats, but by the Republican and Conservative parties as well. I had been the only city legislator planning to run totally unopposed, even though I accepted only the Democratic Party nomination. The result of the court's ruling—that the U.S. Justice Department would have to clear any new district lines—meant that I and all the other council members were in political limbo, prevented from running for reelection, yet unsure whether our terms, scheduled to run out on January 1, 1982, would be extended or not. The only consolation was that the political confusion gained me more TV coverage than ever before, from *Good Morning NY* to Gabe Pressman's weekly show.

In many ways the breakdown in the voting system for the City Council was not surprising, though it caught the powers-that-be largely off guard. By 1981 I had largely completed the revised codification I had been working on for seven years, shining light into the arcane rules of the old Administrative Code and bringing it into the late twentieth century. I was only part of an ongoing citizens' reform movement, however. We believed a true democracy means granting the local community and its representatives a fair share of real power and bringing city governance—in particular the Board of Estimate's backroom deals—into the light of day. Because this broad-based movement had its roots in the civil rights and community control campaigns of the 1960s, the media saw it largely as a challenge from minority black and Hispanic groups. True, those groups deserved to gain influence more in line with their growing share of the population. But the move for citizen power was also an institutional one that involved community groups of all ethnicities and races, from Forest Hills and Astoria to Harlem and the South Bronx.

The Goodman Charter Revision Commission proposals voted into effect in late 1975 had established community boards throughout the city, but many of its other efforts to increase legislative oversight on mayoral prerogatives had been blocked by executive resistance. My effort in 1977 to implement some of those ideas was one of the reasons that Mayor-elect Koch and his staff had threatened to "destroy" me politically (until we met in person). Ironically, it was an earlier, 1961 Charter Revision's creation of "minor party" at-large council elections that posed the single most complicating—and ultimately critical—factor in the early 1980s effort to sort out what a truly "representative" City Council should look like.

The purpose of those at-large elections had been "to provide representation to minority parties and to avoid a monolithic one-party City Council." The system tried to accomplish this by stipulating that each borough elect two council members in borough-wide elections, one of which had to come from a "minor party." In practice this meant that in Brooklyn, in the '80s, the at-large council members were a Democrat and a Conservative, while in Manhattan they were a Democrat and a Liberal, and in Queens they were a Democrat and a Republican. The second seat always went to the candidate with the second-highest number of votes, running on whichever party line was considered "minor" in that particular borough. Twenty years' experience showed that the at-large system had not accomplished its goals. Over twenty years it had produced, out of fifty elected members, only one minority member, a Hispanic councilman. As for "minority parties," the system may have indeed artificially propped up the Liberals and Conservatives, but most of the at-large members who had run using those labels could just as soon have run as Democrats or Republicans.

It's not surprising that this byzantine council election system began to break down by 1981. For years, the U.S. Justice Department had been dissatisfied with the way council district lines were drawn in heavily minority areas of the Bronx, Brooklyn, and Manhattan—usually in a way that made it harder to elect minority council members. The federal court decision that delayed our primaries for a full year came in response to that challenge. As the city and its council struggled to redraft the district lines to the Feds' satisfaction, a simultaneous, parallel challenge to the at-large members of the council threw yet another wrench into the system—this time with even wider implications for the very form of New York City government.

This secondary challenge started innocently enough one evening during a social engagement when a young lawyer who had recently moved to New York, Kim Sperduto, met a Brooklyn Heights neighbor interested in politics. The neighbor mentioned his thought that having the same number of at-large members for boroughs of vastly differing populations must be illegal. Kim, who had worked at the White House in Washington, D.C., agreed. He then broached to his law firm the idea of bringing a pro bono suit challenging the system. On November 17, 1981, federal judge Edward R. Neaher agreed with the suit begun by a meeting of two Brooklyn neighbors. He declared New York City's at-large seats unconstitutional because they "didn't accord due recognition to the population differences among the boroughs." The Justice Department had already asked the City Council to redistrict itself. Now it was being asked virtually to redefine itself.

These two challenges—forced redistricting and the possible abolition of all at-large council members—were serious obstacles to the council's effective functioning. They also posed a serious threat to the political careers of many council members. Tom Cuite, in consultation with the mayor's office, decided to appeal the "at-large" decision but not the Justice Department decree on redistricting. The argument used against the court's "at-large" ruling—of special circumstances due to New York City's unusual status as a conglomeration of boroughs—foreshadowed claims that would be raised repeatedly by the city's executive branch later in the decade in defending the Board of Estimate.

However, the appeal was dropped in March of 1982 when Mayor Koch appointed a new Charter Revision Commission to be headed by Michael Sovern, president of Columbia University. The task of this commission was to create a new legal basis for City Council elections and to restore "the legitimacy of government" in the city. Shortly afterward Judge Neaher, who had made the ruling in the "at-large" case, held that no "at-large" elections could be held until at least 1983, and then only if the charter commission changed them drastically enough to meet the constitutional principle of one-man, one-vote. We other council members, meanwhile, were "held over" in our peculiar political purgatory, waiting to see if the council, the city, and the Justice Department would agree on new district lines in time for us to face election in the fall of 1982.

Other politicians were not so constrained, and while we council members stewed, the prospect of a vacant governor's seat in Albany attracted the attention of now Lieutenant Governor Mario Cuomo and Mayor Ed Koch. Mario was first. He threw his hat into the ring even before mid-January, when Governor Carey announced his planned retirement. Koch, however, waited for a draft movement, which was not long in coming, especially from Rupert Murdoch's *New York Post.* Given Koch's recent gargantuan victory in the city, the mere prospect of his running scared off all challengers except Cuomo. Mario was much too stubborn to give in to the man he had nearly beaten five years earlier.

The rematch of Cuomo and Koch posed a particularly uncomfortable dilemma for me. The Cuomos and the Vallones had been friends for over a generation, and back in 1977 Ed Koch had been for me a political unknown. Now, however, I was the Queens representative in the council, chair of the Ethics Committee, and one of the acknowledged leaders of the council. Even more, I had developed a warm personal daily working routine with Ed Koch, whom I would have to continue to work with if he failed in his quest to become governor. For more than a month I wrestled with whether and how to make my decision between the two men, and wondered whether one or the other might not withdraw from the race. In my heart, though, I knew both men too well to believe either would withdraw.

There was no way I could decide between the two men, and when I attempted to make an argument to myself on one side or another, all I did was go around in circles. So in the end I went to the mayor and said, "Ed, I'm sorry I can't endorse you for governor. Mario and I have been friends for years and you recall I was even his Queens co-chair when he ran against you. I also think you would make a great governor and would be best for our city, but under the circumstances I will remain neutral." Ed seemed to understand completely, and gave me his blessing.

I then went to Mario and explained. "Mario, you're the only person I have ever stepped back for because I believe you're more qualified.

Remember years ago in the coffee shop across from City Hall, where we argued who should run first statewide? I won the argument and you ran and eventually went on to win. I did it because I think you are the brightest and most qualified person in government today. You would have made a great mayor and are certainly more than qualified to be governor. But Ed Koch and I now are also good friends and I work closely with him every day in City Hall. Under those circumstances, I simply have to remain neutral."

Mario was gracious, but he was clearly not happy. "Peter," he said, "I'm obviously disappointed, but you obviously have to do what you think is best for you."

The weeks since Ed Koch had decided to challenge Mario for the nomination could not have been easy for Mario. Donald Manes, who had endorsed Cuomo back in January when Mario first announced, wiggled out of the Cuomo camp over the next few months. In early May he appeared alongside the other three Democratic county leaders—Stanley Friedman from the Bronx, Howard Golden from Brooklyn, and Denny Farrell from Manhattan—at a joint press conference to endorse Koch. Mario's comment: "The last time four political leaders got together to endorse someone who won was in the Iroquois Confederacy." Meanwhile, I maintained publicly the same neutrality I felt in my heart. I liked both candidates, and I said only positive things about both.

Back at City Hall that spring, the council staff was working around the clock to come up with an equitable solution to the council redistricting crisis. The key leaders were Tom Cuite's legal counsel, Tony Caracciolo; Gary Altman, counsel to the Speaker's office, who would become an institutional fixture at the council over the years, and Mario's old law partner Fabian Palomino, hired as a consultant because he was the best elections lawyer in the country. These three huddled and knocked heads with the Justice Department representatives, moving district lines this way and that on incredibly detailed maps, until they figured out a redistricting plan that Justice agreed would pass muster. Then hearings had to be held. One of the more pointed ironies of the whole redistricting predicament involved the chairman of the Rules Committee, Ted Silverman, a tough guy from Brooklyn. He was forced to preside over the hearing that established the lines that drew him out of his own district, and into one in which he could not win. A year later he had moved upstate and was driving a bread delivery truck.

In due course the lines were redrawn and approved by the Feds. Primary voters went to the polls on September 23, 1982. After all the intense wrangling and the year-long forced postponement, the 1982 primary races for City Council brought only a small increase in minority candidates and few major surprises—except for one important near-upset. In the Brooklyn district that included Park Slope, Red Hook, and Sunset Park, Thomas Cuite, council member for nearly twenty-five years and council leader for over a dozen, barely won the Democratic primary over a popular young district leader, Stephen DiBrienza.

The Koch-Cuomo rivalry had played a role in Cuite's near-disastrous campaign. Cuite's Democratic club had given its endorsement for governor to Mario (an old army buddy of Cuite's counsel Tony Caracciolo). All the literature with Cuite and Cuomo's names on it had been printed up. A few days before the election Cuite and his club switched their endorsement to Koch, and Koch spent important hours near the end of his gubernatorial campaign in Cuite's Brooklyn district stumping for himself and Cuite. Because of the switch, Cuite's campaign workers found themselves at the end of the campaign passing out pro-Cuomo literature while their campaign loudspeakers roamed the streets urging the election of Koch.

Cuite's last minute switch to Koch reflected a growing realization in the last days of the Koch campaign that what had once seemed a cakewalk or coronation was anything but. Shortly after he announced, some surveys had put Koch 35 points ahead of Cuomo. After all, despite Mario's statewide name recognition, his only electoral win had been as part of the 1978 ticket with Governor Carey. Then it turned out that Koch had made some offhanded comments to *Playboy* magazine shortly before he declared for governor. He had belittled life in the country as "wasting time in a pick-up truck," and called "this rural-America thing . . . a joke." These remarks doomed his chances with upstate New York voters. As a result, Ed had to press all the harder for his voters to come out in the city. But here, too, his pugnaciousness toward minority voters and unions worked against him. When Primary Day came, Mario won big upstate, came close in the city, and bested the mayor 53 to 47 percent overall.

Ed Koch graciously conceded and immediately lent his endorsement to Mario's campaign for governor against Lewis Lehrman, the millionaire businessman whose family had built up the Rite-Aid pharmacy chain. Likewise, I looked forward to playing a public role in Mario's general election campaign, which promised to be a difficult one. Despite the nearly mythic quality the press had built up about the Koch-Cuomo rivalry, it had been a hard-fought but decent campaign, unlike the bitter mayoral primary of 1977. Many voters, like me, genuinely liked both candidates. It seemed to me that a unified Democratic city leadership could help provide Mario the margin he needed to edge out a Republican in the suburbs and upstate. As part of that unity effort I went to Ed Koch after his gubernatorial defeat and told him he had "always been a winner to me." And I approached Mario's campaign through the intermediary of a confidant of both his and mine, Mike Partridge, to offer my services in whatever way they thought they could use me.

I felt I had to use an intermediary because I had heard through the gossip mill that some people on Cuomo's campaign staff had accused me of "vicious rumors" and that Mario's son Andrew claimed that I had not really maintained my neutrality during the recent campaign, but had been "playing it cute" and privately supporting Ed Koch.

Mike Partridge and I made a date to go down together to the Cuomo campaign headquarters in Manhattan. Mike went into the office first. Soon after, I heard yelling from inside. Mike came out. "They won't see you," he said. "Andrew says you're only here to spy on them."

Needless to say, my blood pressure went right through the ceiling and I walked away. I had been truly neutral; I had said good things about both candidates. As far as I can recall, I voted for Mario over Ed in the primary, because our friendship was older—though I must admit that I was so conflicted, and after this episode so disappointed, that today I cannot be sure which lever I did pull in the voting booth.

Back in September and October of 1982, the race for governor was too important for me not to do whatever I could to support Mario in his campaign against Lewis Lehrman. But needless to say, I did not figure prominently in his close but ultimately successful campaign to become governor of New York. In my own general election campaign, I faced only token opposition from a Republican candidate who carried a gun and dressed as a priest and lived right down the street from my office. I did not spend a dime on the campaign and won reelection by an 8-to-1 margin. At the end of the year I wrote in my diary: "1982 certainly was an up-and-down year. I won election to the council bigger than ever, and Cuomo beat all odds and edged Koch for governor. Because I stayed neutral, he hasn't even talked to me, the only elected official of any importance who stood up for him four years ago." So much for my relationship to the new governor of New York!

As for my political prospects within the New York City Council, I wrote that I was "due in 1983 for the key Government Operations

Committee." Given my landslide reelection, my record in the council, and popularity among fellow members, I expected to be given the coveted, salaried chair of this important committee. Not so quick: behind the scenes, political powers were anxious not to elevate me prematurely, especially given the weakened position of council leader Cuite, who after the preceding fall's near-loss looked more and more like a lame duck. Everybody noticed it; few expected him to go through another run for office in the elections that would be coming up now in only three, not four years.

I also had to reckon with the changing face of borough politics, especially in Brooklyn. There, longtime Democratic county leader Meade Esposito, whose political machine had long kept a fractious borough largely united, decided to step down from his official post. He anointed former council member and now borough president Howie Golden as his successor, but not everyone was happy with the idea of Golden consolidating so much political power in his own hands. Black Brooklyn leaders, Canarsie political chief Anthony Genovesi, and even Mayor Koch all played a role in the power struggle. The infighting left a bitter aftertaste. Council members from Brooklyn split between Golden and Genovesi. This rift complicated the daily political life of the council and would prove crucial in the upcoming battle for successor to Tom Cuite.

By early 1984 Howie had won as the Brooklyn Democratic county leader, and I was given the chair of Government Operations. It could not have come at a more opportune time. The judicial and charter revision process that had thrown a wrench into, then forced an overhaul in the election system for City Council members, had drawn to a close a few months earlier. The Charter Revision Commission decided that minority group representation in the council was more important than minor party representation, and abolished the practice of electing at-large council members. This reduced the legislative branch of the city government to thirty-five local districts of approximately 200,000 constituents each.

Governmental reform was not over with, however. The one-man, one-vote principle that ultimately led to that decision was now being tested on the one truly questionable arm of the city government, the Board of Estimate. A suit brought by the New York Civil Liberties Union on behalf of a group of Brooklynites was now winding its way through the federal courts. It maintained that because their borough president had the same vote as Staten Island's in the board's critical legislative decisions—despite a population six times greater—they were being deprived of their constitutional right of equal representation. The judge who had thrown out the council's at-large voting system at first refused to apply the one-man, one-vote principle to the Board of Estimate as well, contending that the Board's functions were more administrative than legislative. Not so, ruled a federal appeals court on May 16, 1983, reversing the lower court judge and instructing him to find a way to make the board conform to that principle.

It's not surprising that shortly after the federal court ruling, I declared in one of a new series of radio broadcasts that "the outcome" of this decision "could dramatically shift the balance of power in favor of the people of this great city." I went on to point out that the Charter of 1936 had "first created the City Council . . . to be the sole legislative body of the city," but that later charter revisions had "thrust the Board of Estimate squarely into the legislative process . . . mandating" that it and the mayor "share the budgetary power with the legislature of the city. This is an absurd result, and serves only to weaken the City Council, which should and *must* be an equal branch of government!"

I proceeded to call for a new charter commission "to reform city government, not only to have a true and independent City Council, but also to abolish the Board of Estimate as presently constituted. . . . The federal courts have given us an opportunity to rise above politics and reshape and repair our city, an opportunity we cannot afford to let pass us by."

By this time I had realized that the established power structure within New York City would never reform itself out of existence. I still had hopes that another Charter Revision Commission or the state legislature might do the trick, but I suspected this could only happen in conjunction with court rulings. There were still great powers ranged against any change in the Board of Estimate, not to mention my quest to turn the City Council into a coequal branch of government. In Brooklyn itself, for example, Howie Golden, now both county leader and borough president, was dead set against the reforms that would have meant much greater power for his own borough's people.

Howie was as powerful in his own borough as Donald Manes was in Queens. Donald saw clearly that I was a likely successor to Thomas Cuite. Traditionally, Queens and Brooklyn had shared the dominant roles on the City Council, Brooklyn getting the leadership position, and Queens getting the finance chair. Donald figured that next time around a switch might be possible, with my taking the leadership and Brooklyn settling for finance chair—after all, Brooklynite Herb Berman was well qualified for the job.

Donald made it clear just how inconvenient he found my stand against the Board of Estimate. Every time the subject came up, he would tell me, "Look, Peter, you gotta get off the Board of Estimate kick. How am I supposed to get Howard Golden to support you?"

"But it's unconstitutional," I would repeat over and over to Donald, knowing perfectly well that Donald was just as happy as Howie with the power and privileges he gained from being one of the Board's exclusive eight members.

9

January 8, 1986

In my freshman year at Power Memorial our history teacher Brother Kostka said that if we wanted to make a difference and become part of history, we had to keep a daily diary. He held in his hand a small annual diary that cost no more than ten cents at the time and said that it was only necessary to write a few of the most important happenings of the day and we would never regret it. He was so right, and I now have more than a half a century of my life recorded, for better or for worse. On May 24, 1985, it reads, "Tom Cuite not running again!" Rumors about Cuite's failing health, combined with his very close victory last time out, had made his announcement nearly a foregone conclusion. That formal statement was important mainly so that contenders could now openly solicit other members' votes. A scramble for the next leader of the City Council—the Vice Chairman—began that day. The actual day of decision would come some seven months later, on January 8, 1986, at the scheduled charter meeting of the council that was to be elected in November.

I was confident I could gather the necessary votes for my own election because I knew each of the members and they knew my record: I had never missed a meeting, and I took public service very seriously. They knew I stood for reforming and strengthening the council and abolishing the Board of Estimate. All during the spring season of 1985 I was getting favorable publicity for my seven years of work revising the city's Administrative Code, which was finally formally adopted in April. At the end of March I accompanied Tom Cuite to Washington on a train ride we dubbed "The Fairness Express"—the opening segment of a successful lobbying effort to pull in more federal dollars for New York City. In Washington we were aided by my friend, Queens congressman Tom Manton. It's not surprising that secret straw polls showed that if the vote for council leader were to be based on experience and qualifications alone, the other members would have elected me unanimously.

That was without factoring in the vagaries of borough politics, however. The magic number for victory was 18, a majority of the then thirty-five-member council. Under the old county leader system each of the large outer borough delegations—Brooklyn, Queens, the Bronx—tended to vote as a bloc. Of these three, Brooklyn and Queens were the only two that between them had enough council votes to command a majority (the reason they held the two most powerful positions). Manhattan's delegates were too independent-minded to bend to their county leader's will. As a result, they were almost always short-changed in chairmanships of the important council committees.

In recent experience the expression of this Brooklyn-Queens dominance meant that Brooklyn's Tom Cuite was council Vice Chair and Queens's Ed Sadowsky was chair of the Finance Committee. I personally liked Sadowsky, but I was definitely in the minority. To me, he was the only member of the council more qualified than I was to lead the council. After all, Ed had been the real power behind all the budget negotiations during Cuite's long tenure as Vice Chair. Because or in spite of that, Ed had trouble generating support for a run at Vice Chair even among his own Queens council members, let alone from members of other borough delegations. More than a month before Cuite officially stepped down as a candidate for reelection and when he knew he could not get the votes to replace Tom, Ed announced bitterly that he was tired of "taking care of potholes," called the council ineffective, and said he would retire from it altogether.

After me, the next highest vote-getter in the council was undoubtedly Brooklyn's reformist council member, Herb Berman. To us with a Queens perspective who also wanted to safeguard the council's effectiveness, it seemed only logical that I become council Vice Chair and Herb Finance chair. The fatal flaw in this arrangement was that it would have exacerbated the bitter political split between Brooklyn's two political factions: Herb Berman was a Genovesi Democrat, making him unacceptable to Howie Golden as highest-ranking Brooklyn member in the council.

As the maneuvering developed during the summer and fall of 1985, it slowly became clear to Queens leader Donald Manes and me that because of its fractionalized politics, any alliance with Brooklyn was liable to become undone as soon as it was agreed upon. By that reasoning it seemed that it might be possible to find one or two votes there even while looking for alliance elsewhere. But which borough to turn to for alliance? I already had all nine Queens votes. Staten Island had only two votes (luckily I could count on both). Manhattan's members had never voted as a bloc, but I was confident I could win over at least one or two of them. That left only the largely unified Bronx council delegation as the most likely partners. The Bronx was the smallest borough except for Staten Island, with only six council members. I knew the Bronx members well, and was confident I could get their votes on the merits.

What I did not know that summer and fall was that while Brooklyn's political elite was being consumed by infighting, part of my own borough's political network was also about to come apart at the seams. The small-town Queens Boulevard culture that produced people like Donald Manes, Matty Troy, and was so well portrayed by Jimmy Breslin in *The Gang That Couldn't Shoot Straight* was under investigation by federal prosecutor Rudolph Giuliani.

Like my father, like my mentor Ralph DeMarco, my social life revolved around my family. Guys like Donald Manes and Matty Troy, like my brother Buddy, had a different idea of what constituted a good time. They would go out drinking, have a good time together, go to the track and play the horses, and otherwise horse around. I did not care and I did not want to know what they did with their personal lives, but sometimes personal and political lives crossed. And unfortunately, with Donald Manes, at some point large amounts of money entered the equation.

Anyone who knew Donald inevitably liked him. He was full of life and had an engaging sense of humor. He had risen quickly in Queens and citywide circles. From a start in the 1960s as the hardworking chair of the council's Housing Committee he rose quickly to become both borough president and Democratic leader of Queens county. Somewhere along the line he went wrong. Because of his position on the notoriously powerful Board of Estimate, he was able to raise hundreds of thousands of dollars in campaign funds, even when he had only token opposition.

Back in 1974, when he ran for governor, I had told Donald he could not win with surrogates and money alone. Sure enough, he spent all his money and never got past the Democratic primary. Of course, he quickly replaced the money. It's my belief that in this mad rush to run for higher office, a "donor" slipped him an envelope of cash saying something like, "Here Don, use this for your campaign, and don't worry about reporting it. I have something coming up before the Board and I know you'll be fair."

What a terrible waste of a good man, and a good life. I am convinced that money and power can only corrupt us when we lose sight of underlying larger truths. During this period when it looked as if my own political career might finally lift me into a position of great power, God gave me several reminders about what is truly important in life and death. Both my mother and my father-in-law had been going downhill for several years. He died in September of 1984 and my mother only four months later. Meanwhile my brother-in-law, tennis partner, and best friend Joey was stricken by leukemia. These developments significantly tempered the sense of ambition that had driven me for several years. At the end of 1984 I wrote in my diary: "Got my chair of Government Operations, also established as front-runner for majority leader of the council. Not so important to me anymore, though I still love government. Not so much, though, as Tena Marie." It was always important to keep things in perspective.

Meanwhile my personal relationship with Ed Koch grew warmer as prospects of a leadership position grew stronger. In June of 1985 the mayor came to a memorable dinner at my home in Astoria with the closest members of my extended family: my brothers-in-law Tony and Joey and their wives Lisa and Sylvia, Uncle George and Aunt Grace, myself, Tena, and our three sons. Ed fell in love with the Vallone-Buttigheri clan. He was particularly taken with Uncle George and his tales of the rich and famous who came to his Fifth Avenue salon, not far from the UN, and paid $1,000 a session for hair styling. And when George told him the story of his first encounter with President Mobuto of Zaire and how Mobutu paid him $10,000 for a haircut and flew him on the Concorde to and from Africa, Mayor Koch nearly rolled off the couch with laughter.

So all in all, things looked pretty good for my chances to be elected majority leader—until one day in late October when Brooklyn's Howard Golden launched his bombshell against me. On the morning of that day, October 28, I had breakfast with Donald Manes and the other eight Queens council members. I had heard rumors that Howie was hatching a plan with Manhattan leader Denny Farrell to take the leadership post away from me. Donald, however, maintained that he had Howie "under control," and the other Queens members all repeated their support for me.

Later that morning in City Hall I attended a signing ceremony in Mayor Koch's office for one of the bills I had sponsored. Looking out the door I noticed Howie in the hallway getting ready to leave. Without waiting for the ceremony to end, I ran after him and cornered him: "Howie, what the hell's this business about you and Denny?"

Approaching Golden was a breach in the traditional protocol of city politics: county leaders were expected to deal only with other county leaders. So what? I thought I knew Howie well. He always had a chip on his shoulder, was always in the middle of a fight, but unlike the indirect Manes, he was brutally honest; at least you also always knew where you stood with him. Once again, Howie was crystal clear: "You're out of this!" he declared to me bitterly.

"What?" I responded, stupefied.

He told me that he and Denny were supporting Sam Horwitz for Vice Chair, and that between the two of them they had the eighteen votes.

"But Howie, we're friends. You know I'm the most qualified." I could not believe that all my colleagues in Brooklyn and Manhattan would go with Sam Horwitz over me. I had had conversations with all of them, and I knew that in their hearts they preferred me. Sam Horwitz was a nice guy and everyone liked him, but it was impossible to picture him as a strong independent leader who could stand up to the mayor—or to the two county leaders who were apparently planning to prematurely announce his victory.

"Howie, you know me, " I tried to argue with him, "and you know my record. How could you support Sam over me?" Howie nodded impatiently, unmoved. "Besides, Manes says you and he agreed on me as the best to lead the council."

The mention of Manes unleashed a stream of expletives that took me totally by surprise. "Manes is a f------ liar!" he exclaimed. "Look, I have nothing against you," he went on. He said I had always been honest and had a great record in the council, that he had nothing bad to say about me. "Except for one very important thing. And that's the one thing wrong with you. You are not from Brooklyn. It's war!" Howie rarely if ever smiled. But this time his anger was nearly palpable as he emphatically repeated "It's war!" Brooklyn would settle for nothing less than Vice Chair.

It looked like the party fix was in, and I was out. Shocked yet relieved to know the facts behind the rumors I'd been hearing, I thanked Howie for telling me the truth. In my diary I wrote: "At least you know now." That same day he and Denny Farrell, the Manhattan county leader, held a press conference in City Hall and confidently announced that they had the eighteen votes in the thirty-five-member council to defeat me for Vice Chair, to elect Sam Horwitz instead, and to make sure that Manhattan at last received its fair share of chairmanships.

The Golden "Blitzkrieg"—that's what it felt like—had taken me off guard, but it alerted me that something fundamental had gone wrong that needed attention. One of the first things I did was get ahold of Manes. "What the hell's going on," I shouted at him. "You told me you talked to Howie!"

"Yeah, don't worry about it," Manes said, utterly unemotional. It was as if the entire subject had nothing to do with him. And then he repeated, "I've got everything under control."

In retrospect, I probably should have realized by mid-October that things were simply too good to be true. I had had no opponent in the September 10 primary, and would be running equally unopposed in the November election. By the end of September most of the council members had seemed to be coalescing around me as their natural leader. But on the citywide level something smelled fishy. On October 15, I had written in my diary that Manes and Friedman were "too slow" in closing around me. My good friend Nick LaPorte, Staten Island Democratic county leader, and a council member until he left to become deputy borough president, had been the very first to back me publicly for Vice Chairman. On November 1 he told me that it was obvious to him that Manes and Friedman had made a deal in my favor—but that for some reason they wanted to keep it quiet. He found their silence "disquieting."

In any event, the county leaders should not have been the ones picking the majority leader. The legislators should have decided for themselves. Given my stance in favor of abolishing the Board of Estimate (and with it a large share of the power of Donald Manes and Howard Golden), I had thought it only politic to pay at least some respect to their traditional prerogatives as county leaders. Now that Howie Golden had come clean, I knew that if I were to realize my dream to lead the council, I would have to do it myself. Of course, that did not mean I would purposely step on the toes of the county leaders who might be helpful to me—whether it was LaPorte, Manes, or the Bronx's Stanley Friedman. As for Howie, I will always be grateful to him for telling me the truth, and for making it clear through his anger that Brooklyn would not be fertile prospecting territory for me. I have told him so myself many times since.

The irony is that years later, people still believe that I was elected because Donald Manes and Stanley Friedman shook hands. As if I had nothing to do with it. True, selection of the Vice Chair used to happen at a meeting of the five county leaders. Even worse, it used to come down to a huddle between Brooklyn and Queens, since between them they had the votes and tended to vote as a bloc. Still today, if Brooklyn and Queens get together, they can do whatever they want.

In the situation surrounding my election, however, I was nobody's tool—least of all in regard to the Queens council delegation. It's true that Donald and I liked each other. "Don't worry," Donald would tell me when he started talking about how he was laying the groundwork for my election, "I got you the support of all of Queens." If anything, the reverse was true. Because I already had the grass roots as well as council support of all of Queens, I got the support of Donald Manes. It certainly wasn't because I called for ditching the Board of Estimate and handing its legislative powers over to the council. On that issue Donald thought I was committing political suicide.

I, however, had cast my lot with the council. I believed that only a strengthened council could adequately represent the sole legitimate source of power in my beloved city: the people themselves. Other council members sensed this, even when they felt obliged to kowtow to the dictates of their party leaders. Because of my hard work on codification and other legislation, I was respected by them. Because of my willingness to listen to everyone, I was on friendly terms with every council member—even the irascible, elderly Arthur Katzman, who did not have a car and who had been happy to accept rides in mine during my early days on the council.

I still believed that, no matter what the county leaders of Brooklyn and Manhattan said, some of their members might still support me if I appealed to their higher interests. Several of them came out and told me so. Bob Dryfoos, from Manhattan's Silk Stocking District, had said he would vote for me based on my record, and I believed him, despite what Denny Farrell had implied. Also, right around the time of Howie Golden and Denny Farrell's press conference, I heard from two Brooklyn council members who told me, "Don't worry, no matter what you see, where you see us standing or what we say, you've got our votes." There were other supportive members as well. The Reverend Wendell Foster, a member of the critical Bronx delegation who refused to follow his county leader Stanley Friedman, was quite friendly with me. And the tiny Staten Island delegation was almost definitively in my corner. I had worked closely with Jay O'Donovan and Nick LaPorte's Democratic replacement, Frank Fossella. His Republican opponent, Susan Molinari (who went on to beat Fossella and become the only Republican council member) also promised to vote for me. Given that kind of backing it was not surprising that John LoCicero offered me congratulations on having the leadership position sewn up. "I wish I could be so certain," I told him. In the days before the general election of November 5, while the media still talked about me as the front-runner, they also now hedged, mentioning the possible candidacies not only of Sam Horwitz, but of Herb Berman, also from Brooklyn, and Mike DeMarco, from the Bronx.

On Election Day 1985, I was re-elected to my fourth term as council member with 100 percent of the vote. No one had ventured to oppose me.

But then, there had been no serious opposition to Koch, Golden, Manes, or many of the other council members, either in the primary or the general election. Despite my unanimous reelection to the council, I was not cheerful. I remained angry at Howie Golden, and at Donald Manes for letting me down. My resentment at Donald was tempered by pity for what I presumed was a serious physical malady. For some time Donald had been acting strangely. Where once he had been gregarious, cunning, a bright light shining through the zigs and zags of city politics, now he often seemed preoccupied and strangely detached. People around Donald had known for some time about the mysterious polyp in his throat and his constant hoarseness. Everyone presumed that the reason Donald went into these odd moods was because the polyp was cancerous. Thinking he must have cancer of the throat, I forgave him everything.

But that did not mean I could rely on my county leader. Contrary to popular opinion at the time, Donald Manes had not even secured any votes in the Bronx, let alone in Brooklyn. He had much more urgent matters on his mind. Unbeknownst to anyone, he was in deep psychological distress during the late fall of 1985, as federal prosecutors in Chicago and New York came closer and closer to implicating him in a bribery corruption scandal involving his associate Geoffrey Lindenauer and the New York Parking Violations Bureau.

In his lucid moments, when he wasn't torn up by this terrible thing that was happening to him, Donald would tell me that I was hurting myself politically with my provocative position on the Board of Estimate. In his less lucid moments, he would fantasize that he still controlled the power to make things happen, even as he knew that power was about to slip through his fingers forever. He would tell me that Howie was only bluffing; that of course Brooklyn would agree to give up the leadership position and settle for Finance chair only.

Sometimes, even today, I wonder whether Golden, who was much more of an intimate of Donald than I ever was, did not already sense just how deep Manes's political troubles were becoming. Golden, Manes, and Matty Troy were known for going to the track and out on the town together. Golden would have had nothing to do with anything criminal. And had he somehow learned of the payoff schemes that Donald had become involved with, he would have been furious at Donald's stupidity. Why, I ask myself even today, was Howie so angry at me—and at Manes—during our encounter in the corridors of City Hall? Something must have been seething underneath that exploded with my innocent mention of the Queens leader's name.

In my call to Manes shortly after Howie Golden lowered the boom on me, I had asked where my campaign stood with Stanley Friedman and the Bronx delegation. "I got him for you, too," Donald told me. Remembering Golden's intensity and my own pledge of self-reliance, I decided to call Friedman and ask him myself. "No, you don't necessarily have my votes," he told me, politely but firmly. "You will have to come see me yourself. I want to ask you some questions before I commit myself or any members of the Bronx delegation to you."

So we made a date to meet on November 14. I was very nervous about this upcoming meeting. I remember going home and saying, "That's it, I'm sunk." I figured that Friedman was going to want to plug his men into one patronage job or another, and make other unacceptable demands. I knew Stanley from the few months we had overlapped at the City Council after my election in 1974, when he had served as chief of staff for Tom Cuite. Since then I had met him a few times, but I had had no other dealings with him. There were some troublesome rumors going around, however. Such as that Stanley was about to make a lot of questionable money off a business deal for a handheld, computerized parking violations machine that he was selling to the city. This became a matter of great concern to me because I had no idea what questions he would ask, but I knew my answer would be "no" if he sought commitments that would in any way tie my hands.

I also realized that my entire political future might hang on this single meeting with Friedman. If I alienated him, it would be all over. I had gone to Fordham's Bronx campus with friends who were also friends of his, and I asked them to call Stanley and vouch for me to him. Not only that I was a "a good guy," but a man of my word. There were many things I would not agree to, but the commitments that I did make, I kept.

My friends told me in turn that Stanley might look like a crafty, "old-time" leader, that indeed he was a shrewd operator, but that he "never breaks his word."

It helped to know that Friedman had some objective reasons for siding with me, as a representative of Queens, even if I did not make any outright commitments to him. Even if the Queens population and share of council members was slightly smaller than Brooklyn's, it had been the most powerful borough politically for some time. Mayors and Democratic presidential candidates always went to Queens first, knowing how important it was to pull out a united Democratic base there. The days of Bronx political glory had faded since the Irish and Patrick Cunningham had lost control of the borough, and poverty and urban crime took a deep toll on the Bronx economy. With Howie Golden ruling out a Brooklyn-Queens alliance, it was in Friedman's interest to cement one between the Bronx and Queens and restore some of the borough's lost political clout.

If Donald Manes had been his old self, I never would have had to have a meeting with Stanley Friedman. So it was somehow appropriate that on the night of November 14 I met Donald in a restaurant in Manhattan before my rendezvous with Friedman. He had dinner and I had coffee. He was in a morose mood, depressed, and seemed to have a complete lack of knowledge of how things stood in the upcoming vote for my election as Vice Chair. How could he not know about Howie Golden? How could he not know that Golden and Farrell were making a marriage to screw me? I told him that so far I thought I could depend only on the nine votes from Queens, two from Staten Island, one from Manhattan (Dryfoos), and one from the Bronx (Foster). That was a total of 13. I needed five more. In other words, the entire remaining Bronx delegation. Donald sat there and nodded, nearly mute.

From the restaurant we walked to Friedman's suite of law offices, which he shared with political lawyer Roy Cohn. Friedman's legal office was fairly large, with glass doors opening onto a courtyard or terrace. I came walking in with Donald, went straight over to Stanley, and shook his hand. To my great relief, he put me at ease immediately. "Peter," he greeted me, "I have five votes for you from the Bronx, not counting Foster. You have these votes no matter how you answer a few questions I want to ask you." With that first greeting, Friedman had let me know that he was not going ask me to trade chairs for votes. I breathed a heavy sigh of relief.

Donald went and sat on a couch out of our hearing range. Against my expectations, he did not take part in the conversation. It did not really matter. I did notice that he was reading a Chicago newspaper. What was he doing reading a Chicago paper? Poor guy, now I was sure he had lost it altogether. (Later it turned out that Chicago was the place where the story that would expose him was breaking.)

"So, do the five votes get you there?" Stanley was asking.

He did not know that I had Foster, and Dryfoos. "Yes," I assured him, "I have the eighteen votes I need." As I spoke I noticed that there was a man sitting outside in the courtyard or terrace. I recognized him. It was Mike DeMarco.

DeMarco was bright, headstrong, ambitious, and had served on the City Council longer than I. He also wanted the same job I did. I knew that he had been making a case to Friedman and others that in any Bronx-Queens alliance, he should have the majority leader position, leaving me with Finance chair.

While I was absorbing the fact of DeMarco's presence, Friedman was asking me whether I would seriously consider a member of the Bronx delegation for Finance chair. I had already let it be known that Mike DeMarco was my favorite for the position. Was that why DeMarco had shown up at Friedman's office—to argue with Friedman for his own leadership? Whatever, I knew I could handle him. Mike was fearlessly independent, bright and tough, and a person I believed would fit the bill during tough economic times.

So in answer to Stanley I said, "I have a lot of respect for Mike DeMarco. He's outspoken and in touch. I also know that he's been lobbying intensely for the same position I intend to win. So the one condition, before I ask him to be Finance chair, is that he knows that I'm the leader. We have to have a face-to-face discussion, alone, and come to a personal understanding. There can be only one Vice Chair. He has to accept that."

"Don't worry," Stanley reassured me. "I'm sure Mike is smart enough to know that. . . . And I have a few other questions," Stanley went on. "I have a lot of retired judges. They are well qualified, they have time on their hands, and they could use the extra income. Can you hire them on a part-time basis for your legal division?"

"My dad was a judge," I told Stanley. "And I know what deference lawyers have for judges. But there's no way I would want retired, part-time judges telling my full-time staff what to do. I need full-time lawyers, not judges. I will seek to hire the best lawyer I can to head the legal division and let him or her hire the best full-time staff."

"Well, then, can I send you references?"

"Of course I'll accept references from you. And I'll hire the most qualified people. Party affiliation is neither an advantage nor a barrier, but it sure helps if people I respect vouch for them."

The conversation went like that. I remained open to his suggestions, but made no commitment other than to appoint Mike DeMarco. This choice was on merit, seniority, and geography. It was not a quid pro quo for Friedman's support. (Anyone who doubts this need only look at my other committee appointments, made on the same criteria, and not because of how council members voted.) Later on, it's true, I would regret selecting DeMarco, but that story I'll save for later.

I suspect that Friedman pulled his punches with me because of what my friends had told him: that if he said the wrong thing to me, I would have walked out. He already knew I was ready to give Mike DeMarco the Finance chair. That in itself was probably enough to satisfy him.

During the last part of my conversation with Friedman, Donald Manes had been mumbling to himself while reading the Chicago newspaper. When I stood up to leave, we both got up, and the two of us headed back to his car. He was going to drop me off in Astoria on his way back to Forest Hills. Needless to say, I was impressed with his setup: personal driver, roomy car, with car phones in the back. The conversation, however, really disturbed me. "You have no idea how lucky you are," Donald told me. "You're close to God, you have a wonderful wife and family, you're a successful lawyer."

He sounded seriously depressed. "Donald," I said, "you have a wonderful wife and family, too. What's the problem?"

"Oh, it's okay, everything's fine."

"Is it your throat?"

"No, everything's fine."

"I'm going on a retreat soon, Donald, let me bring you with me. The monks there are very good, they know rabbis, they know doctors."

"No, everything's fine."

I was 99 percent sure that he was dying of cancer. I felt terribly sorry for him.

Less than a week later, the entire delegation from Manhattan came to talk to me. They asked, in effect, what chairmanships I could promise them if they agreed to support me. I told them I was not going to promise them anything specific, that I would try to be fair to all the boroughs, but also to pick the best people for each committee. In other words, I would "do the right thing." One of the members of that delegation was Bobby Dryfoos. Bobby was an intelligent and active council member, and he had told me repeatedly that he would vote for me. During the fall, he and I had worked closely on legislation that centralized and computerized purchasing and performance records of those doing business with the city. New York had a history of contractors who after failing to complete a job with one city agency would immediately get work with another. The new law changed the bidding procedure for contracts so that the winner would be not merely the lowest bid, but the lowest responsible bid, and the bidder's previous work performance would now be available on a VENDEX computer system.

It was around this same time I learned that leukemia had struck my dear brother-in-law Joey: the doctors gave him a 60 percent chance of survival, but only if he underwent a bone marrow transplant. The only potential donor was his sister, my wife, Tena Marie. She was determined to do everything she could to save her brother, and much of the last part of December we spent in consultations with doctors at Sloan-Kettering where Joey had been admitted.

While I worried about Joey, the Brooklyn and Manhattan county leaders filled in the contours of their coup. Rumors flowed this way and that: one of them had it that Governor Cuomo was working behind the scenes to deny me the leadership position. I did not doubt that Andrew Cuomo might still harbor resentments on his father's behalf, but I refused to believe that Mario would stoop to that. On December 30 I finally heard details of Golden and Farrell's plot: not only would Brooklyn's Sam Horwitz get Vice Chair, but Herb Berman, also from Brooklyn, would get the Finance chair; Manhattan would get nearly every other significant chairmanship.

It all fell into place: Howie Golden was passing out council positions as a way to reunite Brooklyn's split delegation. Since Berman was a Genovesi loyalist, Golden had not been willing to allow his appointment as Brooklyn's lone leadership position. But if Golden got his own man Horwitz into the Vice Chair *and* Berman into Finance, he could not only placate the Genovesi faction, but get credit for bridging the bitter split. Only problem was, by hogging the top two positions, Brooklyn had to be very generous to Manhattan in all the other ones—which is why Howie promised Denny Farrell everything else. Such a scheme would effectively eliminate from the council any real political influence for all of Queens, the Bronx, and Staten Island.

It was an outrageous plan, and that night I lost an entire night's sleep. In my diary I called it "definitely immoral & possibly illegal," and complained that, "if it succeeds, it will sell the soul of the council to the highest bidder." Luckily, I was not alone in identifying the skullduggery behind this attempted coup. The story in the December 31, 1985, *New York Post,* headlined "The Night of the Long Knives," had one politician asking, "How are they going to run the government without Staten Island, Queens, and the Bronx?" and quoted predictions that the mayor would step in to break up the deal. Nevertheless, the mathematical fact was that Brooklyn had eleven and Manhattan seven votes, and if Golden and Farrell could keep both of their entire delegations united, they had the 18 votes to do what they wanted.

The local press grabbed me as I was walking up the steps of City Hall the last day of 1985. "Howie Golden says you're finished, you're out," the reporters yelled at me. "What do you have to say about that?"

"No matter what they say," I responded, "my eighteen votes are there."

"Golden and Farrell say the same thing."

"All I can say is, if such a thing really were to happen, it would be both illegal and immoral."

"Does that mean you're going to sue?"

"I don't have to sue, I have the eighteen votes."

When *Newsday* interviewed me on New Year's Day, I appealed in print to my secret supporters: "There must be at least one council member from Brooklyn and Manhattan who won't sell out the soul of the council." Meanwhile I had to be wary of my open supporters. Without asking me, Donald Manes met with Mayor Koch shortly after the New Year and asked him to try to influence one or more of Brooklyn or Manhattan's members in my favor. This kind of arm twisting could only backfire—not to mention that it would have made me and the council more beholden to the mayor at the very time I was trying to make it more independent of him. Also, I sensed that a backlash was already building up against the Brooklyn-Manhattan deal. I complained openly about mayoral interference, and *Newsday* obliged with a January 3 headline that read: "Vallone to Koch: Butt Out!"

Manes was nothing but trouble for me in these final days. Roger Starr of the *New York Times* editorial board, who was composing an editorial that strongly endorsed me on January 4, called Donald to get some background for "a forceful case for Vallone." According to Starr, Manes apparently "didn't give a damn. . . . It was as if I was dragging him back from a distant place . . . as if he were somewhere else." Indeed, when I saw Donald at his inauguration ceremony at Queens Borough Hall on the day before the fateful vote, he looked ill; he kept putting his whole hand into his mouth—not his fingernails, but his entire fist. I later learned that sometime during this ceremony Manes asked Geoffrey Lindenauer, the bagman who would soon bring Manes's house of cards tumbling down around him, whether he was "going to run away." Lindenauer, attempting to reassure his old friend with a lie (that would have helped neither of them), told Donald he was going to do just that.

Howie Golden's opportunistic deal with Manhattan was not playing particularly well on the editorial pages of the city's newspapers. If it went through, the council might well be paralyzed by division—and the possibility of a lawsuit from Queens. To the *Daily News,* I outlined an alternative vision, promising, if elected, to treat every borough fairly in the distribution of committee chairmanships. I knew that public opinion, even in Brooklyn and Manhattan, would not tolerate Howie's "selling" of committee chairmanships. Sure enough the *New York Times,* in an editorial apparently written by Roger Starr, criticized the proposed deal as "distasteful bargaining" that was an assault on "merit as well as taste," and went on to call me not only "the best-qualified candidate" but the "most promising and plausible," one "who in twelve years of council service has demonstrated patience, good sense, and the ability to accommodate opposing views."

I also found support from Manhattan in the form of my good friend and former council president Paul O'Dwyer, who called me "a man of integrity and great ability" and declared that "the city would benefit" if I became majority leader. O'Dwyer was a distinguished Irish politician who always stood up for the little guy. As former Manhattan borough president, he was also a power in liberal Democratic circles. He had helped quash a silly *Village Voice* "exposé" about Ralph DeMarco, and marched with me through the picturesque district of Hallett's Cove in Astoria to help save its historic Victorian-era houses.

As January 8, 1986, dawned, no one was taking bets on the outcome of the impending election. Since my warning to keep from stirring the pot, the mayor had retreated into a role as neutral mediator, saying that he preferred Vallone but describing Sam Horwitz as "affable and decent." He called the election "too close to call. . . . Both sides swear to me they have a solid eighteen votes, and both sides are counting the same people. Someone has sold himself or herself twice." It's not surprising that later Ed Koch dubbed January 8 as "the most exciting day in the history of the council."

For me it was the most nerve-wracking day in my life. Would Wendell Foster keep his word? Would Bob Dryfoos keep his? At mass that morning I prayed that God's will be done, not mine . . . but could He please make an exception this one time in my life?

Over my objection, my son Peter Jr. took the day off from Fordham Law School. As things turned out, his presence was a blessing. He kept me calm and was there when I needed him the most. He exemplified then those qualities of leadership that he now manifests as chairman of the council's Public Safety Committee.

Perception is very important, so as I entered the council chambers I smiled and looked confident. I took my seat and the meeting was called to order by council president Andrew Stein. I noticed that members of the Brooklyn and Manhattan delegations were smiling and congratulating Horwitz on his imminent victory. How will I even stay in the council if I lose this? I asked myself. How could I bear watching Howie Golden order Sam Horwitz around?

One persistent rumor was that Queens council member Joseph Lisa had secretly pledged himself to Horwitz because of his friendship with the Brooklyn assembly leadership with whom he had served in Albany as an assemblyman for many years. I had known Joe for years, and his dad and mine had been close friends years before. Besides, at a recent caucus of the Queens council delegation when this rumor came up Joe had pounded his fist on the table and declared, "I'm voting for Peter Vallone even if all the rest of you S.O.B.s don't!"

Unfortunately, Joe was brilliant but absentminded. In Albany Joe had been called "the phantom" because of his reputation for being late or absent at key meetings and votes. Today, as the historic charter-mandated meeting began promptly at noon, only one member was not seated in his chair: Lisa. Joe Strasburg, soon to be my chief of staff, approached me to say that council member Lisa was nowhere to be found. My heart sank. Was this the end for me? Was this why my opposition was so confident? I caught Peter Jr.'s eye and he came over quickly. "Peter, find Joe Lisa or it's all over!"

I immediately reassumed my look of supreme confidence. I had no choice: if I looked worried, my supporters would run out on me. "Are you sure you have the votes?" they'd asked me up to the last minute. "No question about it," I had replied serenely. In my mind at this minute, however, an entirely different story was streaming: about Joe Lisa being promised a lucrative Albany post or a key council chairmanship; that Esposito, still a powerhouse, had made a deal with him. Oh my God, they've got Joe, I thought; he doesn't have to vote against me, all he has to do is disappear. Dryfoos was a very shrewd political person. I knew the reason he was backing me was not only because he believed I was most qualified, but because by casting the crucial vote in my favor, his own status was magnified. If he saw that Lisa was gone, there would be no point in voting for a lost cause and my chances to be elected would fly out the window.

Just then, as the attendance roll call came to an end, Joe Lisa came marching in. "Present!" he yelled out to the waiting chamber and, as he passed by me, whispered in my ear: "Peter Jr. found me in the basement making telephone calls. I'm sorry. Why were you worried? I just forgot the time, but I'm here for you."

After the preliminaries, the roll call for Vice Chair/majority leader began, in alphabetical order. Unsurprisingly, the two council members from Brooklyn who had once told me that when push came to shove they would vote for me "no matter what you see . . . or what we say," voted for Horwitz. Luckily I had never really counted on them. They had disappeared from my view shortly after their early vow to support me. Still, it was not an auspicious beginning to the roll call.

Bob Dryfoos tapped me on the back and said he would "pass" to make sure I had the other seventeen votes. I knew that the pressure on Bob was intense. The Manhattan delegation had already made all of its members hold hands and swear that they were going to vote for Horwitz. Voting for me would mean at least some degree of ostracism from his own borough's members. But Dryfoos's "passing" now might endanger Foster's vote a minute or two later. I turned and said, "Bob, you can't pass. The time is now or never. Just do the right thing!"

When Bob Dryfoos's name was called, you could cut the tension in the room with a knife. A great silence enveloped the standing-room-only ornate council chamber. This would be the most important vote he would ever cast, and he knew it. Bob was an extremely intelligent lawyer with an excellent reputation in Manhattan. Would he blow it all by voting for a Queens member? He later admitted to having prepared two speeches, one for Horwitz and one for Vallone. In this instance he used what I am sure was the more eloquent one, declaring that he was voting for me based upon my "qualifications and merit"—the same words used in the *New York Times* editorial supporting me. As soon as he named me, a huge commotion broke out, and council president Stein had to gavel the chambers to order.

With Dryfoos's defection from the Manhattan group, most everyone was sure that I had won. Not me. As far as I was concerned, the Reverend Wendell Foster's support was still questionable. In the past he had often changed his vote in the midst of explaining it. The temptation of voting differently from what his borough leadership desired must have been strong; still, my commitment from Wendell preceded that from Friedman about the rest of the Bronx delegation, and it was hard to believe that he would come out and vote against me. That's when my heart began its slow ascent from my stomach. For if Wendell abstained, I had one ace in the hole that few people knew about. The council president could vote in the event of a tie, and Andrew Stein had already privately pledged himself to me in the event of an absence or an abstention.

Predictably, Wendell went into a long diatribe about the needs of his district and the lack of his county leader's or party's support. Finally, he said, he had found one leader he could trust—his good friend Nick LaPorte, the county leader of Staten Island. (Thank God it wasn't the leader of either Manhattan or Brooklyn!) Furthermore, he went on, he believed that Peter Vallone was a God-fearing man who, he hoped, would keep his word to help his impoverished district. And then, finally, he voted for me.

The final tally was 18 to 17—not counting the years I lost from my life in the meanwhile. The drama had been intense. Years later I learned from Ken Fisher, the council member from Brooklyn who acted as parliamentarian for the Horwitz forces, that when he and my acting parliamentarian Stanley Schlein met that morning with Andy Stein to discuss which council members would do the nominating for Vallone and Horwitz and in what order, Ken had decided that Bob Dryfoos would present the first nominating speech—for Horwitz. Stan, who of course knew that Dryfoos was supposed to be voting for me, apparently managed to keep his composure. As soon as he was alone, Ken called Bob to inform him about this new "honor."

"I can't do that to Pete," Bob Dryfoos had told Ken. "Look, I want to remain friends with him. It's enough that I'll break his heart when I vote for Sam." Dryfoos's refusal sent Howie Golden into a tailspin of rage, which was only calmed by reassurances from Manhattan's Ruth Messinger and the delegation leader Stanley Michels, who promised that there was no way that Bob would ever "break his word."

After all the tension of this cliffhanger election, I received a one-minute standing ovation when I stood to deliver the remarks I had prepared for this outcome. There must have been hundreds of people jamming every available place on the floor and in the balcony: anybody with any real political power in New York City had been in City Hall that day. In my diary I wrote, "Someday I will have to write a book about today"—my way of thanking Brother Kostka for getting me to keep a diary in the first place. With an overwhelming sense of relief and elation, I said to the assembly:

> First of all, I want to thank my colleagues who had the courage of their convictions to vote to continue the integrity and independence of this body. Second, and perhaps more important, I want to assure those of you who did not vote for me that there will be neither recriminations nor retribution. As I have said on many occasions, I expect to be the Vice Chairman and majority leader of *all* five boroughs, or I will not agree to serve at all.
>
> I regard the Charter Office of Vice Chairman as primary, and the party position of majority leader as the tool necessary in a legislative body to ensure that a majority vote will be there for the tough decisions so that government will function for all of the people, and not just some of them.
>
> As your Vice Chairman, I pledge:
>
> 1) That the council will become a truly independent and equal partner in the government of the greatest city in the world;
>
> 2) No member of the council will be excluded from the process because of political or philosophical differences of opinion;
>
> 3) No member of this legislature will ever be politically censured for voting his or her conscience on any matter that comes before us;
>
> 4) The central staff of the council will be strengthened to ensure that we can perform our charter-mandated legislative, oversight and budgetary duties, and;
>
> 5) Every committee of this council will have the investigative tools at hand to ensure a thorough and proper hearing on vital issues.
>
> We are, after all is said and done, public servants, and our first obligation is to all the people of the City of New York, and not just to our districts or boroughs.

After paying tribute to Tom Cuite, I ended with "my hope and fervent prayer that together we will *make* rather than merely witness history."

It was certainly providential that I eked out a win on January 8. If defeated I expected either to resign immediately or leave after serving out my term. To this day Bob Dryfoos has had to endure the anger of disappointed party members in Manhattan and Brooklyn. Some even began wearing "Benedict Bob" buttons. From me, he had a deep appreciation for doing the right thing. I rewarded him by making him part of my inner circle and appointing him chair of state legislation. Unfortunately, a few years later he arguably skirted the election laws when he used funds from a political committee to buy himself clothes. While not illegal, his actions were questionable, and I had no choice but to strip him of his chairmanship. He decided not to run again and eventually became a City Hall political consultant and lobbyist. To this day he remains a good friend.

Joe Lisa went on to distinguish himself in the council as the first elected official to call attention to the new disease called AIDS and the need for education, help, and treatment.

Sam Horwitz was always a gentleman who never made waves, but he later got into trouble for making Off Track (OTB) bets on city time using city phones. Sam unsuccessfully pleaded with the *New York Post* not to run the story exposing his gambling (he had sworn to his wife that he had stopped gambling and he knew her punishment would be far more severe than anything the media or the council could do to him). After all was said and done he repaid the several thousand dollars in phone bills owed to the city and apparently stopped gambling once and for all. He retained the respect of his constituents and colleagues enough to continue in his post until he moved to Florida in 1993 at the end of his term.

After the vote and my speech, we improvised a victory celebration in my offices in City Hall. At some point someone on my staff handed me a note from Donald Manes that read: "Dear Peter, Congratulations, you deserve it, YOU are going to make a great Vice Chairman, Love, Donald." I was a little surprised that my county leader had left without seeing me, so I called him at the borough president office, but he wasn't there. I had had enough contact with him recently to know not to expect him to be celebrating with me. But I remained worried about him.

PART III

Overturning the System

10

The First 100 Days

> Newly elected City Council Majority Leader Peter Vallone told *The Post* last night his top priority would be the creation of a special unit to probe waste and inefficiency in city agencies.
>
> The Queens councilman's proposal is a sharp break with his predecessors, who herded mayoral initiatives through the council.
>
> "While we're spending hundreds of millions of dollars, the City Council as a legislative body ought to go out to check figures and see what's being done," Vallone said.
>
> He added that education, the homeless, and housing would be the first targets of the investigative unit.
>
> —*New York Post,* January 10, 1986

The principles upon which this country of ours are based are carried out by balancing the powers vested in three great branches of government. In the City of New York today the executive branch consists of the mayor, the legislative arm is the council, and the judicial branch is capped by the Court of Appeals. The people who granted these extraordinary powers in the first place wanted, and still want, their peers who are selected to represent them to "do the right thing" by and for them.

When I was first elected as the council leader in 1986, I pledged to reform government by changing the city charter to abolish the Board of Estimate, to adopt a balanced budget which shared the benefits and burdens equally and on time, to make our city safe once again, improve our quality of life, to work with the mayor to remake our Board of Education and make our public schools the best in the nation as they were when I attended PS 122, and to hold an open hand out to the homeless instead of a closed fist. This was an ambitious agenda, and it soon became apparent to me that it was the chief executive mayor who set the policy of the city, and the council could only change it through legislation that sometimes had to pass judicial review.

In 1986 the office of the mayor had over six hundred lawyers in the corporation counsel's office alone, as well as thousands of other mayoral staff in the Office of Management and Budget, City Planning Commission, and in scores of other agencies at his beck and call. By contrast the total central staff of the council, including lawyers, numbered 78, smaller than each of the borough presidents. In addition to passing laws the council could, through its power of subpoena, exercise oversight of every executive agency from the police department to the massive Board of Education itself. Sooner or later, I knew, it would also have the awesome responsibility, on its own, of reviewing and adopting the fourth-largest multibillion-dollar budget in the country (the only larger ones are for the United States itself, the State of California, and the entire State of New York). I intended to take whatever powers the council already had, implicit as well as explicit, and utilize them. Fortunately for the council and the city, Ed Koch was the mayor at the time I became majority leader and started the transformation of the council into a real legislature. Both as a former member of the council and of the U.S. Congress he understood the necessity of both professionalizing and increasing the legislative staff and the importance of working together for the good of the city.

Ed Koch was also a genius at handling the press, as when he asked, "How am I doing?" According to Ed the answer he got seven out of ten times was "great" or "terrific." He was never afraid to use that positive rate of response in retort to his critics: "Imagine a baseball player getting a hit seven out of ten times. That would be a pretty good batting average, wouldn't you agree?" I'm not sure if Ed knew the difference between a baseball, football, or golf ball, but he sure knew how to handle a crowd. Sportsman or not, he also presided over the Big Apple when the "Amazing Mets" came from behind and won the World Series on October 27, 1986, and on January 25, 1987, when the New York Giants won the Super Bowl. It was during this same period of "coming from behind" that the City Council finally gained some respect. But not before many good people in government became tarnished by the wrongful actions of a few.

Several times on my first day as majority leader Donald Manes stuck his head in my office. I nearly missed talking to him since I was on the phone almost continuously—even John Lindsay called to congratulate me—but the last time I jumped up in time to invite him in for cup of coffee and a moment's relaxation. I remember he was sweating a lot, and his armpits and shirt collar were wet.

"I just wanted to see you sitting behind that desk," he told me.

"Is everything all right?" I asked him, still thinking that he was dying of throat cancer.

"Yes," Donald assured me, as he rushed out of my doorway.

But Donald had problems worse than throat cancer. The next morning members of my staff told me of news flashes on radio and TV about a mysterious crime or accident involving my county leader. As the *New York Times* reported:

> Donald R. Manes, the Borough President of Queens, was found by the police in his car near Shea Stadium early yesterday morning, bleeding heavily from a slashed wrist and an injured leg.
>
> It was unclear whether Mr. Manes, an affable and well-known figure in New York politics for more than 20 years, had been the victim of a crime or had inflicted the wounds on himself.
>
> He underwent almost three hours of surgery on his left wrist, and his doctors said he could not be questioned immediately.
>
> The delay in questioning him only added to the confusion and the growing speculation about the 51-year-old politician—about how he was hurt and by whom, and why he was driving a car that was weaving along Grand Central Parkway in Queens early yesterday morning, just six hours after he was the host of a reception at the Queens Borough Hall for the new Israeli Consul General.
>
> "The only person who knows what happened is Donald Manes," District Attorney John J. Santucci of Queens told reporters.

I was shocked and distressed by this news. With no explanation of what had happened and why, speculation and rumor overtook the city's political classes. My staff and I tended to credit the idea that Donald had been somehow involved with a call girl who had a knife—I was still convinced he was dying of cancer and was trying to get the most out of life while he still could. I did not believe he would attempt suicide. As I told reporters, Donald Manes "had too many friends and too much to live for."

Like many of Donald's friends and associates who went to the hospital to wish him the best, I was denied permission to see him. News and police reports over the next few days did nothing to dispel the confusion surrounding what had happened. Donald remained in isolation in the hospital while stories about him made the front page of every newspaper. His family and his doctors successfully protected him from press, police, and other politicians. That only heightened the mystery about whether he was a victim of himself or others.

On Monday, January 13, newspapers reported that Donald's wounds appeared self-inflicted. Over the next couple of days he was quoted as claiming he had been abducted by two men he could not identify, hit on the neck and back and made to feel "metal on his neck the whole time," while forced to drive his car around Queens for several hours. This far-fetched story sounded to me like a cover for something more embarrassing. The *New York Times* called the affair "bizarre" and warned that the failure of those who were counseling Manes to offer more convincing explanations invited "the public to suspect the worst . . . loss of mental balance . . . political corruption."

Corruption or criminal behavior still seemed to me the least likely cause for what was happening to Donald, even a few days later when Geoffrey Lindenauer, a Traffic Bureau chief and one of his political associates, was charged with extortion by federal authorities. For more than a decade, rumors had floated about Stanley Friedman or Meade Esposito, but not Donald. Even the *Daily News* reporter who was covering the federal investigation of Lindenauer did not initially suspect Manes of any involvement. To me and to many others, Donald had clearly suffered some sort of nervous breakdown. Beyond that, it seemed pointless to speculate. That, of course, didn't stop every cabdriver on the streets of New York from developing his own theory about what had happened, even if it involved UFOs. On the evening of January 16 I stopped by at Antun's in Queens Village for the long-planned celebration of Donald's fifty-second birthday. Shortly before it began, the chief of detectives of the New York City Police Department called a press conference at which he rejected as impossible Manes's claim to have been abducted. The party went on anyway, without Donald.

A few days later, Stanley Friedman was implicated in news stories about the Parking Violations Bureau. In the wake of the arrest of Lindenauer, Mayor Koch had ordered a review of the bureau's recent contracts. One such review involved the lucrative contract, recently approved by the Board of Estimate, for hand-held computer devices meant to keep track of parking violations. During the review it was noticed that the principal shareholder of the company that received the contract, Citisource, was none other than county leader and former deputy mayor Friedman, a fact Citisource had failed to disclose. (They had listed him simply as a "special counsel.")

On that Monday, Martin Luther King Day, I found myself speculating on the strange twists of fate. The two county leaders who had supported me in my recent dramatic election had suddenly landed in severely compromising situations. I could not help but remember how my wife's grandmother, who worried that my fellow politicians were going to eat me alive, had always warned me: "You're too honest; they won't trust you. In politics you have to be a little crooked." Honest or not, I could not turn away the hand of friendship from Donny Manes in this time of great trouble. I asked for God's guidance in these troubled times, and over the holiday I reached Marlene Manes and asked how Donny was doing. I told her to tell him that "God loves him and I love him."

All during this turbulent political maelstrom I was trying to come up with a fair distribution of committee chairmanships and a workable way of restructuring the City Council. On the same day of my election I had nominated Morty Povman as chair of the Rules Committee (because that committee selects the other committee chairs) and Mike DeMarco chair of Finance (because Koch was submitting his budget within a week and I needed to have a chairman in place in order to receive the budget). Otherwise I spent all my working hours at City Hall interviewing council members and weighing my choices. I knew that if I rewarded the people who had voted for me—especially after winning by only one vote—I would only perpetuate a divided council and ruin my own dreams of strength in unity.

The hardest decision for me involved one of my oldest council associates and partners in reform, Abe Gerges. A few days earlier I had learned that during the pre-election maneuvering for my position, Gerges had been the mastermind behind Howie Golden's effort to block me as majority leader. I was left with no choice other than stripping Gerges of the chairmanship of the Economic Development Committee—a decision that only hardened after Howie Golden spent a half hour on the phone with me trying to save Abe's position. Abe was smart, domineering, and a strong leader;

to reward him with a leadership position, at the moment I needed to consolidate my own leadership and refashion the council into an effective lawmaking body, could have proved fatal. There were only twenty chairs to be distributed among the thirty-five members, so fifteen would be disappointed in any event.

The council vote on the new committee assignments took place the morning of my ceremonial swearing-in. I could tell from Abe Gerges's expression just how painful it was for him to lose a chairmanship. To tell the truth, it choked me up to publicly embarrass him, and only the arrival of my family and brother-in-law Joey for the ceremony shook me out of that mood.

The swearing-in was one of the proudest moments of my life. Tena and the boys stole the show around City Hall and my brother-in-law had the time of his life sitting in my office chair pretending to be council leader. Six hundred people showed up for the event, including Assembly Speaker Stanley Fink, Geraldine Ferraro, Mayor Koch, and my old classmate Joe McLaughlin, one of the brightest federal court judges ever to serve. After I introduced him with words describing him as "a class act," Joe sent the audience into howls of laughter with the clarification that "Peter and I were not in the same class, even if we may have been in the same classroom—I graduated *magna cum laude,* he graduated *magna cum difficultate.*"

In my own brief acceptance speech, I hailed the fact that charter changes and recent court decisions had moved the legislative branch of New York City government to the forefront of "where the action is," and pledged "to work hand in hand with the executive branch to ensure that all of the people in this town benefit from this new legislative awakening."

The triumph of my inauguration day was brief. The day before, Donald Manes had confessed that his story about being abducted had been a total fantasy. He had indeed tried to kill himself—but he said nothing further about why. At least twenty media people stormed my office in search of comments. Continuing the strange conversation that was taking place through the media between Donald and his political friends, I addressed myself to Donny directly, reminding him that "people will forgive you if you tell the truth."

The morning after my inauguration, the *Daily News* published on its front page a column by Jimmy Breslin providing specific evidence of Manes's complicity in the Parking Violations Bureau bribery scheme. The source was attorney Michael Dowd, a former officer of a collection agency known as Computrace. The headline, in giant bold letters: "MANES ACCUSED OF EXTORTION."

This damning print indictment was followed by a live news conference the following day from the same Michael Dowd and by comments from federal prosecutor Rudy Giuliani confirming that Dowd was indeed cooperating with the Feds' investigation. Michael Dowd was no stranger to me. A former law associate of the man who would become the new Queens county leader, Tom Manton, and like him Irish, Dowd had also been an important official in Mario Cuomo's 1977 campaign for mayor, the one plagued by smears and homosexual hate literature. The night after Dowd's news conference, Channel 2 News wanted to meet me in Astoria Park, ostensibly for an interview about the new council, but actually to get my reaction to the latest revelations. It was 10 degrees and snowing, I had nothing on heavier than a sports jacket, I was shivering, and all they could talk about was Manes. Breslin's article and Dowd's allegation were indeed shocking, and no less than Mayor Koch had declared that Dowd's allegations had "great credibility." Like Ed Koch, I felt it necessary to recommend to Donald, "or anybody else" likely to be caught up in Rudolph Giuliani's probe, "to suspend himself [from office] and hope for a speedy resolution." Manes decided to do just that, suspending himself from both his post as county leader and as borough president for the foreseeable future.

The two or three weeks that followed Breslin and Dowd's revelations about Donald Manes were depressing times for all Queens politicians. It was difficult to get important work done: all the media wanted to know about was Manes, Manes, Manes. Manes himself, who knew better than anyone what he had thrown away, teetered on a knife's edge. Things were not helped by the media feeding frenzy that always happens in scandal situations.

Jimmy Breslin and I had been on cool terms since the late 1970s, when he printed a story about an old classmate of mine, Vito, belittling the former chauffeur to the then borough president of Queens by calling him the borough president's "bagman." Not only was Vito dying of cancer at the time, but Breslin and I had been two of the sponsors of a fund-raising party held to raise money for his medical expenses. And yet there was Breslin, the day after the party, making it sound as if Vito had been engaged in some kind of criminal activity. All that Vito had done was facilitate the payment of reduced fees for traffic summonses, and there was nothing illegal or immoral about that.

Now, two weeks after he published the story that broke Donald Manes, Breslin called up my friend Marty McLaughlin, a PR advisor to me and several other city politicians, and told him that he had a source who had seen Marty give Bob Dryfoos a brown bag with $50,000 in it—supposedly as payment for his vote in my favor during the recent election for Vice Chair of the City Council. Marty was as familiar with Breslin's supposed "source" as I was—a mentally unbalanced former aide to Bob Dryfoos who had become disgruntled after Bobby Dryfoos fired him some months earlier. After my election, this man had attempted to peddle his brown-bag story to the Manhattan DA as well as Rudy Giuliani, and everyone but Breslin had immediately recognized that the guy was bonkers. Marty threatened to kill Breslin if he printed the story and called me up to warn me. While I was still on the line with Marty, Breslin himself called on another phone and declared point-blank: "I have an informant that tells me you gave fifty thousand dollars to Marty McLaughlin."

This was the first time I had heard Jimmy's voice since the Vito episode many years before. Whether it was the ludicrousness of the accusation or the coincidence of having these two angry men on the phone with me at the same time, I burst into laughter.

"This is not f------ funny," Breslin scolded me.

"Not funny?" I replied. "You think that's all I'm worth? Get serious, I won't consider a penny less than two hundred thousand!"

Finally Breslin joined in the laughter, and then Marty, who had heard the whole conversation over the other phone, was laughing, too. Needless to say, the non-story was never printed.

It's just as well, because that same day Donald Manes formally resigned his position as borough president and as county leader, landing the responsibility for selecting the next Queens borough president squarely in my lap. As it happened, I had a dinner date that evening with Mayor Koch and Governor Tom Kean of New Jersey. All the television stations followed me to Gracie Mansion. I greeted Donald's resignation with a sense of relief, declaring that he ought to "finally get a chance to defend himself. And that we, the people of Queens, should finally be able to get to the truth of what was going on here. . . . Anyone who knows Donald Manes," I stated, "feels very sad about it. If there is any wrongdoing or corruption involved, then Donald Manes will have to pay the price. But let's get to the proof and see what the facts are, and let the chips fall where they may."

Before the charter change of 1989, it was up to the council, acting on the recommendation of the county caucus in question, to fill in a vacancy in the office of borough president. That did not stop Governor Cuomo from almost immediately announcing his intention to play a role in the selection, and Mayor Koch from calling me up to tell me when and how to go about the City Council's business. As I told everyone who asked, I was not about to cede the City Council's authority to Governor Cuomo, Ed Koch, or the Pope. Nothing was more important at this point than to prove that I was nobody's pawn. This unsought responsibility for orchestrating the selection of Donald Manes's successor fell upon me just as Lent began, a holiday for which I always gave up pipe smoking. Without that particular crutch, I knew it would be extra hard for me to be "calm and kind," as I urged myself in my diary.

Media speculation about the next borough president centered first around Queens assemblyman Alan Hevesi and former Queens council member and Finance chair Ed Sadowsky. Hevesi, who had a decent shot at becoming the next Speaker of the assembly in Albany, quickly withdrew his name from consideration. Ed Sadowsky agreed with me that he stood little chance of being elected by his former fellow council members, and that if he wished to run he should wait for a general primary. From the very beginning I was convinced that Donald Manes's deputy borough president, Claire Shulman, would be the best choice to replace Donald. Shulman was a bright light of honesty, integrity, and competence. Unlike Donald, she was all business and minimal schmooze. She knew every pothole in Queens County. Naturally, she wanted to maintain the Board of Estimate as it was, but I would have been daydreaming to expect anything else from any candidate for borough president.

Unfortunately for both Claire and me, we were viewed by many in the Manhattan-based media elite as products of a disreputable Queens organization. In an editorial calling our public hearings about the replacement "a sham" and in effect labeling our borough delegation an "oligarchy," the *New York Times* praised Ed Sadowsky over Shulman, saying she had "given no sign of being eager for a cleansing of the Queens clubhouse or reexamination of the way borough presidents function on the Board of Estimate." The *Times* was mild by comparison to the *Post, Daily News,* or *Newsday,* all of which blasted me because Claire had been Manes's deputy during his fall from grace and "knew or should have known what was going on." Claire was an easy mark for the press, and indeed for other candidates who were interested in the position. Two of these, Queens council members Sheldon Leffler and my own favorite perpetual grumbler, Arthur Katzman, questioned Claire sharply during our public hearings, saying that "people would not believe that she did not know the people who were meeting with Mr. Manes and did not know they were talking about corrupt schemes."

"Whether you or anyone thinks that I should have known, I didn't," Claire responded.

A day or two after this hearing, *Newsday* ran a story characterizing Claire as Donald Manes's "conservator," implying that he could not have done anything she hadn't known about—and that if she did not know, she was incompetent.

It was clear to me that this story was nothing but a fabrication, and I immediately defended her. The incident depressed me, however. In my diary, I wrote that I was convinced that crazies would kill Claire's chance and "crucify me in the process." As a saving grace on this troubled day, I heard that *The Tablet,* the newspaper of the Brooklyn-Queens diocese, the largest in the nation, had just proposed me as a candidate for mayor.

Somehow that vote of confidence was enough encouragement to light my way out of the dilemma. Two days later I called in Ed Sadowsky and encouraged him to submit his credentials to actively seek the borough presidency now, instead of waiting for the September primary. Although I myself had always liked Ed, I did not think he had the personal or political qualities to handle the job. He had never gotten along well with the council members who would now have to elect him, and he had further hurt his own chances with them by ridiculing the body as a whole just before he left office a couple of months earlier. Nonetheless, it was critically important to keep the process open and give Ed a chance to change the hearts of his former colleagues.

How we decided the borough presidency in this moment of scandal and crisis had crucial implications for the business of the council over the upcoming four years. To ignore the public's depth of disgust with the recent corruption would have been fatal. Potentially even more insidious would have been eliminating the only qualified person out of guilt by association. At the same time I desperately wanted to reach a consensus on this first vital piece of business for Queens and the city. In my heart I knew that Ed Sadowsky would almost certainly never be a consensus candidate for our Queens delegation. Neither would the candidate council members, Sheldon Leffler and Arthur Katzman. However, one further serious candidate emerged from the twenty-one who had appeared at our hearings: Dennis Butler, an Irish-Catholic Queens assemblyman of perfect integrity. Butler was very Catholic, very proper, and pro-life; his nickname was "the monsignor of Albany." His moral integrity and no-nonsense approach would have sent many of the right signals about how seriously we were taking the current crisis.

Near the end of February we adjourned our borough presidency hearings for two weeks to allow time for the city's Department of Investigation (DOI) to conduct thorough background checks into four possible choices: 1) Ed Sadowsky; 2) Claire Shulman; 3) Sheldon Leffler; 4) Dennis Butler. This kind of thorough vetting of possible conflicts of interest had become all the more important after the tumultuous season we had just been through; we were also well aware that Rudy Giuliani's federal investigation was far from over, and that further surprises on the near horizon might alter the city's political landscape—as indeed they did.

The atmosphere along the corridors in City Hall and Queens Borough Hall was hard to bear in these days. Many city employees had become demoralized and paranoid. Multiple investigations were going on, not only into the Parking Violations Bureau but into every aspect of Queens government and the city's Transportation Department, headed by Anthony Ameruso, an associate of former Brooklyn county leader Meade Esposito. Some opportunists used the atmosphere to try to settle old scores. Unsurprisingly, attacks were launched on Bob Dryfoos and others.

On March 6, Doug Johnson of *Eyewitness News* asked me during a televised conference whatever had happened to make nice, respectable, middle-class Queens seem to come entirely apart? It had been, I told him, "the roughest two months of my life," a shocking jolt of disillusionment "to anyone who knows the people named."

"Maybe Queens got a little too smug," I admitted, including in that criticism the Democrats who enjoyed a complete monopoly on political power. The Republicans, I complained, were too state-oriented. They should not have written off the City of New York, but built up their party here, just as the Democrats needed to do a better job of building up their party on the state and national levels. If Queens were a state, I pointed out, we would be the nineteenth largest in the nation. There was an enormous potential to improve things county-wide and citywide, and among the first things to take control of was the amount of money being spent on political campaigns, which poisoned the system against the little guy. The current scandals at least made many things, like campaign finance reform, politically possible for the first time.

Queens council members reassembled on March 11 to consider the four remaining candidates for borough president after all of them had received clean bills of health from the DOI. Leffler and Sadowsky quickly dropped from serious consideration. Butler, however, had attracted new interest among most council members as an alternative to Shulman (except for the usual dissenter Arthur Katzman, who declared that there was no way he would vote for "an Irishman for borough president"). Still favoring Shulman myself, but afraid that we would be pilloried for bucking the entire media establishment, I had a last-minute conversation with my good friend Gloria D'Amico, powerful Democratic district leader in Astoria and a confidante. Gloria, who was almost as opinionated as Katzman but usually in favor of Italians, surprised me by encouraging my original intentions. "Peter," she said, "you've got to vote for Claire. She's the most qualified. Dennis is a wonderful guy, but he knows nothing about being borough president."

On the day of the vote I brought in all council members. We took a straw poll, and it was evenly divided between Butler and Shulman. I then told them that I thought the right thing to do was to go with Claire. They all agreed, and we unanimously elected Claire Shulman borough president. Amazingly, we received not one criticism from the press for our choice. Somehow I had rolled with the punches and succeeded because I had done what I knew all along was right. The next few years proved that Claire was bright, honest, and above reproach. As the first woman borough president of Queens she compiled an unblemished record of achievement and may well go down in history as the best of all the presidents who preceded or followed her. I say this despite the fact that fifteen years later she failed to support me in my primary bid for mayor.

Two days before we picked Claire Shulman as borough president, Donald Manes's one-time bribe collector, Geoffrey Lindenauer, appeared in federal court and confessed to extortion. After two months, he had finally reached a plea bargain with federal prosecutors. In sworn statements he said he had worked on behalf of himself and others, without publicly identifying the "others." Some of the contractors who had paid bribes to Lindenauer, however, had already identified Manes. Lindenauer also admitted to making false statements to help Citisource, Stanley Friedman's company.

According to his attorney, Donald Manes was aware of Lindenauer's court testimony. He must also have been aware of our electing Claire Shulman to replace him as borough president. Shortly after 9 P.M. on the day after our vote, Donald's daughter noticed her father in the kitchen of their home, "fumbling erratically in a kitchen drawer." Sensing something amiss, she rushed to get her mother. Too late. By the time Marlene Manes came on the scene, Donald had stabbed himself fatally with a knife. When emergency personnel arrived a few minutes later, he was already dead.

Back in 1971, Donny had told me: "Did you ever see anyone get so much publicity as me? I'm going to make you the second-most important politician in the State of New York." He had been nothing more than a council member at the time, and we were both trial lawyers. Fifteen years later, Donald had inflicted on himself a judgment far more severe than any a judge or jury would have rendered. The only consolation was my hope that the ultimate judge who now had him would be merciful and grant him eternal rest and peace.

The saga of the rise and fall of Donald Manes is an excellent example of why it is so important to take the lure of money—truly "the root of all evil" when it comes to governmental wrongdoing—out of politics. Power and money, as attractive as they may seem, are fleeting and temporary. One life in the image and likeness of God is worth far more. I believe Donald Manes understood this as well as I. He liked me and supported me because he saw something in me that he sensed in himself but found impossible to reach. Our conversation in his car the night of my interview with Stanley Friedman convinced me of that.

Donald was right: I was lucky to have such a loving wife and family. Coincidental with the unfolding of Donald's tragedy came proof of my family's strength. In early December my brother-in-law Joe Buttigheri underwent preparatory surgery to have his spleen removed. If the operation went well and he gained sufficient strength, the plan was to give him a bone marrow transplant from Tena Marie a couple of months later. The expectation was that only her bone marrow stood a good chance of being accepted by Joey's immune system.

In my diary over the critical weeks in February and March I kept track of Joey's ups and downs and Tena's tremendous courage in donating her own marrow—a lot of it, because, as the doctor told her, "your brother's so big." Tena was nervous and nauseous from the procedure and developed a fever, but vowed to "always take care of" her brother. From the beginning until the end of March, as I and others donated blood and prayed that the transfusions would make J.B.'s platelet count rise, we were all on pins and needles. It did rise the first week—only to plunge again to zero for the next week before finally rising to an acceptable level. Finally, on March 29, my family and I took off for our New Jersey beach condominium for the first time since the previous summer. It was my first taste of relaxation in three months, and on a cold and windy beach I savored a can of beer and a cigar for two meditative hours, staring at the ocean.

It was inevitable, and welcome, that the worst city scandals in decades would lead to a reexamination of the governmental system that had permitted them to evolve undetected for so long. I was delighted when, in early February, Governor Cuomo asked for a thorough reexamination of the role of the Board of Estimate, and declared that the investigations into corruption provided the city a chance to change the way "politics was practiced in New York City." In mid-February I reminded listeners of this in my weekly radio address:

> Nowhere in the Federalist papers, or in the United States Constitution, or in any derivative state or municipal constitution, does there exist a branch of government called the Board of Estimate. . . . In New York City, however, while the charter says the City Council is "to be the sole legislative body of the city," subsequent charter revisions [mandated] that "the Board of Estimate and the council . . . shall adopt a single budget." . . . The same holds true for land use and capital projects.
>
> This is as patently absurd as expecting the Congress of the United States to have to obtain the permission of all the state governors before our federal budget could be adopted, or the New York State legislature having to obtain similar permission from each and every county executive before our state budget could be adopted.
>
> Moreover, if the Board of Estimate does *not* agree, the City Council can *not* adopt a new budget. There is no provision for legislative power to override this group of *executives*. . . .

> It is time, therefore, to move on a bill which I first submitted in 1974 . . . to create a true and independent legislative branch of government in the City of New York. It will also require action by the New York State legislature and, perhaps, a referendum by all of the registered voters in our five boroughs—but move we must. Budgetary and land-use powers must vest in the legislative body, as they now do on the federal and state levels and in virtually every other jurisdiction.
>
> We are also still waiting for a federal appeals court to follow through on its May 16, 1983, decision requiring the Board of Estimate to conform to the United States Constitution's principle of one man, one vote. While that is an important element in this discussion, it is not as vital as the fundamental constitutional question I have repeatedly raised concerning the *existence* of the board.

Finally, *finally,* my criticisms were finding a real echo, not only among the usual band of reformers, but the governor and the mayor (who previously had dismissed all proposals for change). Although Howie Golden continued to like the Board just the way it was, many people began to realize that it was, as Professor Richard Wade of CUNY put it, a "theater of corruption." The fact that the corrupt contracts at the center of all the recent investigations had all won Board approval, often outside of any meaningful public hearing or review, made that all too apparent.

That did not mean there would be political will within the city to do away with the Board, as I was suggesting. In Albany, though, I expected to get a hearing, and indeed received it. On March 10, 1986, I made a combined courtesy and official visit to the state capital to press my plans to reconstitute and/or abolish the Board of Estimate of the City of New York. I conferred with both Republican and Democratic leaders of the senate and assembly, made an address to the Democratic conference, and met with Governor Cuomo. Both my ideas and I were treated positively—nearly "regally," as I said in my diary. It looked as if passage of the necessary legislation was only a matter of time.

For me it was essential that the current opportunity be used not just to punish individuals, but to reform the system. I worried about the general perception that everybody in government was corrupt, when in truth, for every person who was indicted or convicted, hundreds were doing a very good job. Unless the system were brought back into balance, however, with the City Council an equal partner and exercising appropriate oversight over the executive in forums open to the public, the same kind of graft could recur.

For me those early days as council leader were the best of times and the worst of times. Every day, it seemed, I hit a new high and fell to a new low. It was exciting getting the council into a position where we could make a difference, but the scandals were also demoralizing and debilitating. My chief of staff Joe Strasburg would tell me I was too much of a nice guy and I had to draw the line and assert my power. After the *Village Voice* called me "the Rosemary's Baby of Manes and Friedman," I had to work particularly hard not to lose my temper. I called up Jack Newfield and Wayne Barrett to complain. I am still proud that years later Jack Newfield said that "I've called Vallone every name under the sun, and he never got angry with me. In fact, he still answers my telephone calls."

On April 18, my hundredth day as Vice Chairman and majority leader of the City Council, I began my annual weekend retreat at the Bishop Molloy house in Jamaica Estates, Queens, for some needed soul healing. Before I left, I was lucky enough to record two radio broadcasts in which I summarized my first hundred days in office. Some highlights of the council's achievements I mentioned:

- Establishing a new Office of Oversight and Investigations, which gave the City Council the resources, for the first time in its history, to investigate how allocated money was being spent and to rein in waste and inefficiency. Appointing the head of this new office had led to my first confrontation with Finance chair Mike DeMarco. The day after I announced the appointment, Mike asked why I had not consulted with him beforehand. My temper went out the door and Mike found himself the object of an intense dressing-down as I reminded him that the condition of his appointment had been his acceptance of my leadership.

- Bolstering the council's Finance Unit and Legal Bureau, each of which until then had consisted of no more than fourteen staffers—including secretaries.

- Reforming city government through new legislation aimed at campaign practices, disclosure laws, and so on, as well as holding comprehensive ethics hearings.

The second prerecorded broadcast was a lengthy conversation with Gabe Pressman, the thoughtful city affairs commentator from Channel 4 News. That interview touched on a wide range of subjects:

PRESSMAN: You've said repeatedly that you've wanted to take the Board of Estimate out of the budget-making process in city government. Do you think you're going to succeed in that endeavor?

VALLONE: I think for the first time, we have a real chance. I've been saying it . . . since the day I was elected. . . . Stripping the Board of Estimate of its budget power is the minimum. I've been to Albany already, and just this week I sent up legislation to the leaders. . . .

PRESSMAN: Have Assembly Speaker Fink and Majority Leader Anderson agreed?

VALLONE: They've agreed to the principle.

PRESSMAN: What about the mayor, is he letting you get away with this?

VALLONE: The mayor, deep down, is also a legislator . . . he was once. I know that he agrees that if you really want to have a balance of power, this is the correct thing to do. Whether he'll actually support it is something only the future will hold.

PRESSMAN: He'd be committing political suicide in a way, because he'd be giving up some of this powers.

VALLONE: But I think this mayor will try to do the right thing. . . .

PRESSMAN: Ultimately do you want the Board of Estimate abolished?

VALLONE: There's no question in my mind that it has to be restructured. I think you could strengthen the borough presidents as county executives.

PRESSMAN: Do you think that taking away the board's budgetary power would be conducive to avoiding corruption in the future?

VALLONE: I think it's much less likely that corruption would exist if what's going on is in the eyes of the general public. The City Council does things in public. With the Board of Estimate, the opportunity for things to go on behind the scenes is more likely.

PRESSMAN : You became majority leader after a deal between two party leaders. Does the fact that Friedman has been indicted and that Manes was mentioned in indictments affect your own credibility?

VALLONE: I hope not. I like to think that the twelve years I put in have something to do with my election. It became a turf fight as to where the power of the council was going to go. I tried to have a coalition of all five boroughs. As it turned out I had three of the five. What happened with Donald and what's happening with Stanley now had nothing to do with that election. They were trying to do what any county leader would do, to make sure that there was a fair share of committee chairmanships, I'm trying to allocate them - fairly to all five.

PRESSMAN: Do you feel that the city's government business has been seriously affected?

VALLONE: I think yes, unfortunately, it has, because of the horror of the scandals. I found as I was trying to put together a team on the council, it became very difficult for people to understand that all I care about is honesty and ability. If you don't make mistakes, I don't think you're doing your job. . . . People became almost like statues. I see it's now being healed. If you can't get on with some confidence in doing your job, knowing that a mistake is not the same as corruption, then you don't belong in government in the first place.

PRESSMAN: What about in the executive branch? Have they circled the wagons?

VALLONE: I happen to think that Mayor Koch is one of the finest ambassadors the city has ever had. I see him now getting back to what he always meant to have, hands-on control of his people. I think he's going to be a better man for it.

PRESSMAN: Let's talk about power, We have a strong mayor system of government. The council has been accused of being a rubber stamp. Obviously you feel that should change?

VALLONE: It sure should.

PRESSMAN: If you're going to take more power, the mayor's going to have less power.

VALLONE: The whole country is supposed to be based on a system of balances. If there's a problem we don't go to war, we go to court. . . .

PRESSMAN: The real tragedy, you said once, is that Donald Manes sentenced himself to death in a court that had no jurisdiction over him, a court of public opinion. What are your thoughts now?

VALLONE: My thoughts are really of sadness for Donald and his family. No matter what Donald might be guilty of, no court would have sentenced him to death. I only hope and pray that his family will have some peace down the road.

PRESSMAN: Do you think the mayor did wrong when he sat in the chair you're sitting in and said Manes "engaged in being a crook"?

VALLONE: I think that reflected the mayor's humanity. I think it was an overreaction on his part. Understandable because of the personal relationship he had.

PRESSMAN: Did it hurt Donald Manes?

VALLONE: Well, I don't see how it could have helped, but in the mental condition Donald was in, I'm not sure anything really hurt him or helped him at that point.

11

Challenging the System

After I supervised and completed the arduous task of organizing the council members into the various committees and chairs according to my stated criteria of ability, seniority, and geography, the next most important matter was to select a chief of staff. Joe Strasburg had served as Tom Cuite's chief of staff. While his role there was as a gatekeeper to maintain the status quo, I knew he was as anxious as I to give the council wings. Therefore I chose him to be my chief of staff as well and to begin the process of putting together what many have called the best governmental staff in the entire country. Joe was not only bright, intelligent, and familiar with the ins and outs of City Hall, but he and I shared a basic conception of how to do business. We both had an ability to absorb the facts in any crisis and come up with a bottom line and marching orders. We also both had photographic memories; the problem was, mine lasted for about a week, while Joe's seemed to last forever.

My friendship with Ed Koch had grown stronger in my years on the City Council. When I finally became leader in 1986, that friendship was the bond that led to the passage of the first gay rights bill. Of all the bills that had ever come before the City Council this one, aimed at prohibiting discrimination based on sexual orientation, had engendered the most debate, the most friction, the most agonizing consideration. Because of these emotions, the legislation had been bottled up in committee for years. Cardinal O'Connor and the Bishop of Brooklyn vocally opposed it, and there were threats that even if it passed, the Catholic Church would try to tie it up through litigation.

I had no problem with the anti-discrimination aspects, but I thought the form of the law was wrong, that the issue could be handled under our other anti-prejudice laws. I did not favor adding homosexuality as a category to civil rights law along with race and religion. Also, the emotional arguments engendered by the bill—the fear that passing it would give a "stamp of approval" to a way of life of which so many disapproved—took away from the real issue of tolerance. As I explained to the mayor, discrimination is anathema to me. It contradicts my belief that every single human being is made in the image and likeness of God. At the same time he agreed with my concern that the law should not be used to proselytize for homosexuality.

Vice Chair Cuite had always prevented the bill from coming to the floor. Ed's calm reasoning in its favor, however, persuaded me to let it out of committee. I thought there were people with good conscience on both sides of the issue and that they would provide the pros and cons. Although I voted against the bill, I instructed the committee "to vote their consciences and . . . vote without fear of reprisal or promise of reward." The bill came to the floor in the middle of the Parking Violations Bureau scandal and others that were coming to light, and it passed, and the world did not end. I later came to understand and agree that the law was necessary for its value as a tool to prevent bias and violence against differences in sexual orientation—not as a lifestyle endorsement.

The whole episode confirmed my belief that, while we have the God-given right to disagree, no one has the right to condemn anyone else because of his or her beliefs. The law must allow for that discourse. My vote was no, but my heart said yes. The light of knowledge is far better than the darkness of ignorance.

By the end of April not only was my brother-in-law Joey on the way to recovery but the worst of the paranoia and panic from the Manes and Friedman scandal was over. It even seemed to me that a certain rhythm had developed in my relationship with the mayor. On the one hand he paid me the compliment of stealing the reform bills I'd developed with the council and presenting the package as his own. On the other he insisted on asserting his power to frustrate me by trying to turn the recently closed Flushing airport into a car pound. I was furious with him: "This is my district, and you want to create a slum!" I told him angrily in a long, three-hour meeting. Despite these games, we agreed on plenty, and the day after our row we had a press conference where we jointly introduced a bill declaring that New York City would do no business with South Africa until their apartheid policy was dismantled.

Ironically, it was during the first few years of my council leadership, when Ed and I had some of our strongest disagreements, that we also solidified our friendship. We were in complete agreement about the need for campaign finance reform and for strengthening transparency in government by increasing the number of city employees who had to reveal their sources of income. In fact, it had been Koch who first taught me how important it was to make full disclosure.

Like any other person in or out of politics, I value my own and my family's privacy. Why should being well-known to the public have to endanger them? Considering the firebombing of my office a decade earlier, I had good reason for concern. After my election as Vice Chair in 1986, I refused to make public my tax returns because they contained my home address and other identification information. Some reporters who usually did not see me afternoons at City Hall assumed that I was refusing their release because I was making oodles of money in my law office. My refusal to release my tax returns added fuel to their mistaken assumptions. In fact, because of my 8 A.M. arrival at City Hall, I was often finished with meetings and work downtown by 1 P.M., and would go afterward to my Astoria office to tend to district as well as citywide concerns.

Ed Koch advised me to simply delete my home address, Social Security number, and other identification information and make public my tax returns. Otherwise the stories about how I was using my position to enhance my law practice would never stop. I did as he said, and indeed the stories stopped.

Ed and I disagreed, however, on the need for a basic change in the structure of city government. He had found he could be effective with the Board of Estimate. He liked dealing with a few people he knew well. He sometimes called the council members "Indians" and said he would rather do business with seven Board of Estimate members than fifty Indians. He had no problem dealing with me, he said, as long as he didn't have to talk to the others.

Given this attitude, I knew Ed would be no ally in my fight to do away with the Board and empower the council in its stead. I also knew that Albany, not City Hall, would be the key to accomplishing my goals through legislation. Luckily some legislators there, such as Senate Minority Leader Manfred Ohrenstein, recognized that, as important as ethics codes and campaign finance reform were for stopping scandals before they started, "the process of letting government contracts is probably 90 percent of the problem." Even Governor Cuomo had expressed interest in "reexamining the Board," but hedged his bets by saying he would await recommendations from a joint city-state Commission on Government.

Then, on May 14, 1986, Assembly Speaker Stanley Fink announced that he would resign at the end of the year (tragically, he would die a year later). With his resignation impending, my chances of getting rid of the Board through legislation decreased dramatically. Stanley was a good lawyer to whom government was more important than politics; he was willing to risk political capital for the sake of principle. His possible successors were unlikely to want to risk their political capital early for an issue like abolishing the Board of Estimate. As if to confirm this analysis, Mario Cuomo let it be known the day after Fink's announcement that the bill I had introduced in Albany to abolish the Board of Estimate would not pass.

There were only three ways to rid the world of the Board of Estimate: through an amendment to the city charter approved by the city's voters; through an act of both houses of the state legislature; or through the federal courts. I was doing what I could to assist all three avenues. The court had already ruled against the Board years earlier, but the wheels of justice ground exceedingly slowly and the city's entrenched powers knew how to create nearly infinite legal delays. The charter amendment route would require a commission established by Mayor Koch. Such a commission might well "agree" with my position in theory but be unsympathetic in putting it into practice. So by far the quickest way was to get the state to abolish the Board. In issuing his statement that my bill was doomed, the governor was only being honest. That didn't make me any happier about it. I didn't want it said publicly, especially since Mario had not spoken a word to me about the bill.

The scandals in the city took their toll on the 1986 budget process. To close a budget gap between needed expenses and revenues, Mayor Koch had been relying on taxes that needed to be approved by the state legislature. The legislature did not want to increase taxes in an election year. The council and I were determined not to increase property taxes on the city's beleaguered homeowners. The mayor was weakened and distracted, and had not done his homework in Albany or in the city's neighborhoods. In early June he finally appeared to wake up after I appeared on television accusing the mayor's staff of balancing his proposed budget "with blue smoke and mirrors." Ten days later in Albany I hosted some one hundred legislators at a breakfast meeting. By the time the Board of Estimate, the council, and the mayor sat down to hammer out the details of the budget on June 27, we had approval from Albany for tax and fee increases to cover some three-fourths of the shortfall.

Although the press tried to make hay from the inevitably changing nature of power relationships at City Hall, the last-minute negotiations actually went quite smoothly, as is attested by a letter I received shortly after in which Ed expressed his "appreciation of [my] leadership." A certain tug of war is a sign of healthy tension between an executive and legislative branch. Until my arrival the City Council, if not exactly dormant, had certainly been quiescent. The summer of 1986 saw the first signs of a healthy competition. For example, when I promised to transform the City Council and thus "do for New York in a civil and productive way what Elliot Ness did for Chicago in a criminal and prosecutorial way," the *New York Post* quoted Mayor Koch as shrugging me off with the comment, "Who's Al Capone?" then went on to suggest a regular boxing match:

> Vallone also hinted that he was prepared to take on Koch.
>
> Vallone questioned the legality of some of Koch's executive orders. . . . "I want to make sure the mayor knows and the corporation counsel knows at what point I believe they can issue executive orders and at what point they can't," Vallone said.
>
> Koch said he would not give up his prerogative to issue executive orders.
>
> He also said he was disinclined to discuss the orders in advance with Vallone.
>
> "That's not the way it's done. I might and I might not," Koch said.

This kind of coverage allowed me to finally get media attention for the proposals that most of the city establishment had ridiculed since I first introduced them more than a decade earlier: arguments, for example, that the budget should be worked out between the mayor's office and the council alone, without the Board of Estimate. In what proved to be an act of prescience but might just as easily have turned into empty grandstanding, I staked my future as majority leader on the necessity of getting the Board out of the budget business, publicly "guaranteeing" that the Board would be stripped of its budget power before my four-year-term was out.

Unsurprisingly, my fellow council members were delighted by this aggressive posture on behalf of the council, even those who had voted against my election. I mustered a unanimous vote from them for a resolution calling for the Board of Estimate to be stripped of its right to approve the budget; appointed a representative to lobby for the council's interests in Albany; brought in public relations advisors to represent the council's viewpoint during the budget negotiations; passed legislation over the protest of major landlords making them disclose enough of their incomes and expenses to allow the city to more realistically assess the value of the buildings for tax purposes. Most important, I actively wooed the members who had done everything to prevent me from becoming majority leader, rewarding competence over political affiliation. Ruth Messinger soon became an ally. I even went out of my way on behalf of Abe Gerges. After stripping him of his committee chairmanship for organizing the attempt to stop my election bid, I ended up creating for him, against the wishes of my chief of staff, a subcommittee on the homeless which would turn in spectacular work over the next few years.

Needless to say, the borough presidents were not happy with me. Claire Shulman was disappointed, and Howie Golden went from his usual anger to a raging fury. True, budget negotiations might have been smoother if I had played along with them, but that would have been irresponsible, especially after all we'd been through the past six months. I finally had a united legislative body who didn't care whether or not their own county leaders were also members of the Board of Estimate. They saw what we were doing as a legislative prerogative; they knew by now that it was the right thing to do.

That did not necessarily make it a politically promising thing to do, as I was reminded that summer when I became the only major public official to openly criticize the Board of Estimate in my address to the joint state-city Commission on Integrity in Government. The group was headed by Michael Sovern, president of Columbia University. Mario Cuomo had appointed him with much ceremony and said he would wait on the commission's conclusions before committing himself to any structural reforms in city government. I knew that the problem we were experiencing was not merely one of a few corrupt politicians, but of a basic corruption in the system of government as represented by the Board of Estimate:

"It is time to restore to this greatest of all cities a truly balanced government with a truly independent legislature," I declared, pointing out that my efforts along these lines, far from being an "overreaction to the current municipal scandals" as many of my critics charged, had begun in 1974 when as a freshman city council member I tried to introduce a resolution to do away with the Board of Estimate. "There is no hysteria or overreaction in this campaign. It is, rather, a reasoned program which has been joined by the Citizens Union, New York Public Interest Research Group, and other nonpartisan and good government organizations."

I pointed out that three years earlier a federal court had ruled the Board unconstitutional as it was then functioning. "Let the Board perform its executive functions," I exhorted. "Let the judges preside in our courts without interference from the other branches of government. And let the legislators legislate, accepting full responsibility for the laws that govern our 7.5 million citizens. . . . The Board of Estimate participates in the spending of billions of dollars each year but has no responsibility for coming up with ten cents in revenue for those expenditures. You couldn't run a household or a corporation where the people spending the money are unanswerable to those who raise the money. Why should New York City government . . . be different?"

Testifying before the Sovern Commission felt like an exercise in futility. The more I said, the more I earned the hostility of the five biggest power brokers in the city, many of whom were also the Democratic county leaders. The powers that be were trying to limit reform efforts. In my diary I wrote: "Someone has to speak out . . . but why you?"

What a difference one year can make! Twelve months after Mayor Koch was reelected to his third term in office with the largest majority in modern history, the *New York Times* ran a major story claiming "The Next Mayoral Election Is Already in the Air" and that four politicians had already staked out their positions as Ed Koch's opponents, one being Peter Vallone. It did no harm to those who were jockeying to keep my name in the running when the *Daily News* published a major story on me a week later entitled "Not Just Another Queens Politician," suggesting I might be "the cure" for the city's corrupt politics.

While it was true that there was "a continual confrontation between the mayor's staff and the council staff," as I admitted at the time to the *Times,* I also knew that it was the job of the mayor's staff to undermine us, and ours to challenge them. Two hundred prominent people in the city might know I was going to be mayor, but what about the two million who voted? Although I was pretty confident that I could become mayor if I put my heart in it, I was becoming more interested in being governor, since I realized that it was Albany that pulled most of the city's strings.

More important than these speculations in the press was shepherding the council through its first steps to real power. Later that November I was handed a big shot in the arm when the same federal district court that had issued a preliminary decision calling the voting structure of the Board of Estimate unconstitutional reaffirmed the ruling, demanding that the city come up with more than voting "remedies," but begin to consider true "alternatives." The next day Mayor Koch announced that although the city would appeal the court ruling, he would also soon appoint a charter commission panel to reexamine the makeup and possibly the very existence of the Board of Estimate.

Although the mayor claimed the city had every intention of battling the district court's decision all the way to the Supreme Court, I knew from my own talks with him that he was dubious about winning the city's appeal. The scope and powers he granted the new commission spoke for that. They were far broader than the ones the Sovern Commission had been given or assumed. (Unsurprisingly, the five reports issued soon after by that commission, worthy as they were, did not tackle the main issue of structural corruption. The commission members had been presented with sharply differing views about the Board of Estimate and had not been able to reach a consensus on what to do about it.)

I was elated by the court's ruling. At last it was clear that the city would have to subject itself to the scrutiny of some higher authority. Unlike the Sovern Commission, the federal courts were beyond the power of the city's bigwigs. As if to punctuate the role of the Feds and the disappointing results of self-reform, Stanley Friedman and several of his associates were convicted in federal criminal court in New Haven, Connecticut, little less than a year after the scandals broke. In winning a high-profile case played out on the evening television screens for several months, Rudy Giuliani had not only won a major prosecution, but a prominent spot in the city's political future.

These developments in November had an immediate effect on my own credibility and standing. Now that the establishment saw that what I had been saying stood a chance of actually happening, my power and influence started increasing. So did the respect granted my fellow council members, which in turn improved my standing with each of them. The year-end summary in my diary speaks for itself: "You've scrutinized, organized, and supervised to the point where the council is on the way to becoming a real partner in government. All that remains is getting the Board of Estimate where it belongs, that is, out of the legislative process!"

That winter and spring I concentrated on making my case for a structural overhaul of city government. It was important to me that those in power not be successful in deflecting the impetus behind reform onto the wrong target. In a December radio talk entitled "Princes and Paupers," I criticized the misdirected efforts of some "good government" groups to abolish legislators from having any outside employment. I pointed out that lawmakers, unlike judges and administrators, needed to live and work among the people they represented in order to "bring to the halls of government that sense of reality that is essential to true representative government." In truth, the only legislators who could afford "sole-income" positions would be those who were either so wealthy they did not have to work for a living, or people who were so dependent on having such a job they would do anything—honest or not—to avoid losing it.

But I reserved my strongest efforts for my testimony in late April and early May before the mayor's charter commission headed by Richard Ravitch, former head of the Metropolitan Transportation Authority. I had been delighted to learn of Ravitch's appointment, since my special counsel Ralph Miles spoke so highly of him, and I used my platform to go to the heart of the issue.

The courts had concerned themselves, I pointed out, with the fundamental imbalance in proportional voting, the violation of one-person, one-vote. They had not addressed the fundamental corruption that lay at the root of the Board's function: the failure to separate executive and legislative powers. Even if as individuals the members of the Board were talented and dedicated public servants, the confusion of executive and legislative duties was intrinsically corrupting. For the people of this town to have had to wait for the federal court to point out the Board's illegitimacy was outrageous.

People who argued that the Board served as a legitimate watchdog on the executive and legislative ignored the imbalance of power and the lessons of history. Some even proposed that an imbalanced, unconstitutional city government was justified because the greatest city in the world was not really a city at all, but five separate entities with little in common but geography.

It was essential to me to have the Ravitch Charter Revision Commission address the fundamental issue of separation of powers because past charter commissions had failed to do so, or had even confused matters more, as in 1983 when they created a Districting Commission appointed by the mayor, although the courts had repeatedly ruled that redistricting was and must remain a solely legislative responsibility. I was hopeful that the Ravitch Commission, even if appointed by the mayor, would have the courage and wisdom to finally restore the City Council as an equal branch of government. Back in the early 1980s, when the City Council was held in contempt by many and the focus had been on the discriminatory effects of electing council members-at-large, it had seemed logical to that charter commission to create a Districting Commission independent of the council. Of course, Mayor Koch had taken full advantage of this bias to gain near total control of redistricting. For years I had been whistling in the dark about this problem. This time, however, while I was testifying, I noticed that I was talking to serious people who cared about our great city—and that they were actually listening to me. In fact, my testimony helped convince the Ravitch Commission to throw out the mayor-appointed districting commission in favor of one in which the council appointed a bare majority. The results of this formula brought to City Hall a council much more representative of the city's diversity than its predecessors.

Although pleading the case for increasing the council's share of power, I was careful to stress as well the importance of the grass roots represented by the fifty-nine community boards. I considered the boards essential to the involvement of local citizens in city government. Established in the 1970s through legislation sponsored by Republican legislator Roy Goodman, the boards created a monthly forum for dialogue between city agencies and local citizens regarding everything from potholes to gangs in the streets. Members were appointed by the borough presidents (half on the recommendation of the local council member), and although strictly advisory groups, they sometimes overreached and ran into conflict with officials. Mayor Koch started out strongly supporting the community boards, but grew less tolerant of them over the years. Some legislators at the city, state, or even national level resented them as a breeding ground for future rivals. I saw that there was a movement afoot to convince the Ravitch Charter Commission to abolish or significantly weaken them, and urged against any such move, pointing out that these boards represented a great experiment in decentralized municipal government and that since I became majority leader, twenty legislative measures had been introduced to strengthen their role. I supported the boards because I believed that dialogue and neighborhood involvement, even if it involved healthy tension, was important for good government. If this meant that for once I was actually on the side of the borough presidents, so be it.

By the spring of 1987 an unorganized coalition involving minority groups, the federal courts, some prominent reformers (like Robert Wagner Jr. and Ed Sadowsky), the City Council, and I had finally succeeded in getting the establishment to question the future of the Board of Estimate. A little more than a year earlier I had been voted into office with the support of several members of the Board who had always considered my quest a quixotic idiosyncrasy. Yet a few days before the Ravitch Commission opened its hearings, Sam Roberts of the *New York Times* wrote that the Board faced four possibilities: 1) to adopt a system of weighted voting; 2) to be reconstituted as a body whose members represented districts the size of Staten Island; 3) to become an advisory board; or 4) to be abolished.

As much as I was in favor of abolishment, I knew the disappearance of the Board would pose its own challenges, especially for us who supported transferring most of its powers to the council. Our job was now to show that we were capable of handling vastly increased responsibilities. The most controversial of these, besides the power of the budget, involved zoning and land use. Many thoughtful people were afraid that the "not-in-my-backyard" tendencies of local communities might turn such decisions into drawn-out nightmares and infinite delay. They also feared that placing land use decisions before the council might *increase* rather than decrease corruption, on the theory that it would be easier to "buy" a council member than a borough president. The *New York Times,* for example, wanted to give the Board's budget function to the council, its contracting function to a new mayoral panel, and leave land use to what it called a "thinned-down" Board of Estimate. When chairman Ravitch grilled me about this issue I recounted a conversation I'd had recently with the majority leader of Chicago's City Council when he made a courtesy call at City Hall. I had been complaining to the Chicago councilman that in New York we did not have the power of the budget. The Chicagoan had responded: "Well, at least you have zoning and land use." When I told him we didn't have that either, he had said: "How could you possibly operate as a legislative body in the City of New York without those fundamental legislative powers?"

The "Forty Thieves" reputation of the City Council made it hard for some well-meaning reformers to believe we were capable of policing ourselves. I suppose it's part of the human fascination with power and authority. Many people seem to believe that the bigger you are, the less likely you are to be corrupt. Myself, I'm a great believer that power and money are the great motivators of corruption. During a second round of testimony before the Ravitch Commission, I was still trying to convince a doubting panel that the "people's representatives" were worthy of being entrusted with their own governance. The skeptics questioned whether City Council members were really up to the job. Who were they, after all, to take on so much responsibility? The skeptics seemed to echo the refrain of the executive branch: "Leave it to us, we know what's good for you. Don't trust these little people because they just come from a little district. They are just interested in little concerns." But wasn't it the very need to pay attention to the "little concerns of little men" that lay behind the principle of democratic representative government, whether in the U.S. Congress or a state or county legislature? Did skeptics really mean to say that the representatives of the people could not be trusted? In the end, I reminded them, "We are just as good or bad as the people. What you see is what you get."

Testifying before a commission, however, would never convince the doubting and the complacent. To do that I would have to create a track record that proved the council could act as a serious and effective legislative body. One thing I needed for that was an adequate staff. Another was to put the mayor and the press on notice that we could no longer be taken for granted. In early June, just before the budget negotiations for that year began in earnest, Ed Koch provided me with a perfect opportunity. Rather than sending us information about its candidates for various city boards in timely fashion in advance and offering them to our committees for interview, the mayor's staff had sent us an entire slate of candidates at the last minute. They had not yet even been cleared by the City Department of Investigation, yet we were expected to listen politely to their statements and approve them right away.

Rather than listening politely and relying on the candidates' and the mayor's assurances, I arranged for the Rules Committee, of which I was a voting member, to disapprove outright nine of the nominations and postpone action on two others—without even hearing testimony from the candidates, who were waiting outside the chamber. "I cannot be so stupid as to tell the mayor that he can't appoint his own people, but he can't be so stupid as to think I am going to rubber-stamp everything he does," I explained. This dramatic gesture took the mayor by complete surprise and lifted the spirits of all our Rules Committee members (except the volatile Mike DeMarco, who abstained). As the *New York Times* pointed out the next day, "It was the first time in the memory of council members and the mayor's staff that an entire slate was rejected at one time."

We had no interest in obstructing the mayor's agenda. We simply wanted to establish a procedure that gave us the chance to seriously review the mayor's candidates. It meant that the nominee would be vetted not just by the City Department of Investigation, but by our own Office of Oversight, and would meet in an open hearing with the appropriate borough delegation. That way the delegation would know who they were voting for.

At first the mayor complained, saying he didn't want to make his people "submit . . . to all that." I promised we would turn down a candidate only if we found out he or she was hostile to local interests—wasn't it better to know that at the outset? In the end my gambit worked, and we got the kind of review I wanted. Until this time we had been taken for granted. Now the executive knew what treating us as "equal partners in government" meant in practical terms.

With the advise-and-consent process clarified, we turned to the most difficult budget negotiations in years. It was June 8. The deadline, June 5, had already passed. The mayor had offered us $50 to $75 million in discretionary spending, but we at the council had not heard a "peep" from the Board of Estimate, so we went ahead and came up with our own list of $160 million in necessary "add-ons" to the bare-bones budget. For several days the Board of Estimate refused to do anything. My Finance chair, Mike DeMarco, was cool as a cookie one minute and yelling like a maniac the next. Stupidly, he leaked to the press the super-secret list of programs we planned to fund.

The Board, however, proved unable to agree, and despite talking all night and all morning we could not come up with a counterproposal to the mayor's budget. Freddy Ferrer and Claire Shulman were the only ones even willing to negotiate. The mayor's Budget Office, seeing our disarray, took from the budget the mayor's own $50 million of discretionary funds offered to the council! Finally, by keeping the talks going around the clock for another night, we arrived at an agreement with the Board for a package of $157 million. That evening I immediately opened negotiations with the mayor, and when I got home at midnight I felt completely disoriented.

In the confusion of these intense 24-hour talks I lost track of time, and the next morning I failed to remember to show up for the graduation speech I was supposed to be giving at Christ the King High School, a big local Queens school. Unable to forgive myself, I found the insult compounded when most of the Board of Estimate failed to show up that same day for scheduled talks with the mayor to hammer out the final budget. I drove down to the Jersey Shore for a few hours just to clear my head before resuming all-night negotiations. Finally, at 4 A.M. on June 14, after the mayor met us halfway and promised to add more if and when the revenue stream improved, we reached a final compromise.

In these budget talks the Board of Estimate had proved itself both incompetent and inane. Rather than negotiate in good faith, they boycotted the talks. No wonder Thomas Cuite had always caved in to the Board! In the end, statesmanship had prevailed, but how much longer could we afford to play such games?

Only a few days after the budget ordeal was over, I received a reminder that not everyone was automatically happy when things went well for me politically. On June 23 I took an early train to Albany to host my annual breakfast for state legislators and to address the State Committee on the City. I had had my difficulties getting used to Stanley Fink's successor, the abrasive Mel Miller, but in the course of the spring we had come to an accommodation, and this day we not only had a productive talk but he invited me to be his guest on the floor of the state assembly. I also had a good meeting with the senate leader, Republican Warren Anderson. In fact, the only meeting that did not go well was one that never happened: my scheduled talk with my onetime good friend and associate Mario Cuomo. He was not available when I arrived for my scheduled appointment at his office, and while we were waiting his aide Fabian Palomino ushered us into his office for an unfailingly gracious but brief interview. Finally, the governor's secretary announced that the governor was too busy to see me—or even come out for one second to shake hands and say hello. I did not feel it worth speculating on Mario's motives, but my staff—especially Ralph Miles, whom I had first sent over to work on Mario's campaign for lieutenant governor more than a decade before—was ready to break the doors down and pull Mario out. Whatever lay behind this snub, nothing was going to interfere with my "impossible quest" of getting rid of the Board and reforming city government.

12

Ed Koch, Spirit of the City

Ed Koch will go down in history as the man who single-handedly lifted the city's spirits during a period in which many people were giving up on the future of the Big Apple. I don't think anyone in office ever had a better sense of humor. The photo that appeared on the cover of *Time* magazine of him with his hands upraised with the city in the background, as if he were personally lifting this great metropolis, expresses visually just how he came to personalize New York.

So it was not surprising that the entire city seemed to stop in trepidation on August 6, 1987, when Ed Koch suffered what the papers called a "teeny, tiny stroke." In fact, it was nothing more than a spasm in an artery that caused a momentary slurring of his speech. Like all city officials I was very worried until I visited him in the hospital and found him to be his usual irrepressible self. Although in some people this kind of "attack" may lead to a stroke, in Ed's case it did nothing of the sort. Less than a week afterward he held a photo opportunity on the porch of Gracie Mansion that quickly turned into a full-blown question-and-answer session with the press. However, the incident fueled speculation about who might take over if the mayor were incapacitated (the city charter was less than clear on the issue). Only days after Koch's "stroke," my predecessor Thomas Cuite died of heart failure: another reminder of how transient we all are.

Mayor Koch was in full stride for the Bicentennial Constitutional Parade I set up in Astoria at the end of September. He, Andy Stein, my wife, Tena, and her group of student flutists, and I and three thousand others marched through the streets and rallied in front of the school I attended as a child to celebrate the signing of the proposed U.S. Constitution two hundred years earlier. This was a cause dear to my heart, not only because I'm a Constitution nut, but because I wanted people to appreciate and understand the magnificence of the Declaration of Independence and the Constitution. As I noted in my speech and later radio address about the occasion, the "system works because it was designed to prevent any one branch from ever growing so powerful as to dominate the others. . . . What a wonderful occasion for a birthday celebration!"

A week or two later, as if to confirm that reminder of the importance of balanced government, the U.S. federal appeals court rejected the city's appeal of the earlier court ruling that the Board of Estimate as currently constituted violated the one-man, one-vote principle, and set a target date of six months and a deadline of one year for the changes to be put in place. A spokesman for the Ravitch Charter Commission declared that the new ruling removed the status quo as an option, and Dick Ravitch began to talk actively about abolishment, previously seen as an "extreme" solution. The charter commission and the Supreme Court had put the Board issue back on the table.

Officials on the Board, however, continued to belittle my principal concern—namely that in acting on the budget the Board usurped a strictly legislative function. By now B of E members with strong ties to the city's minorities, like David Dinkins and Fernando Ferrer, realized they looked ridiculous arguing against the one-man, one-vote principle. Instead they began to argue for retaining the Board, but with a system of weighted voting. Freddy Ferrer had recently been appointed Bronx borough president after borough president Stanley Simon was forced to resign as part of the corruption scandals. Now he and Dinkins maintained that because Ferrer's recent appointment had increased minority representation on the Board, this was no time to start diminishing its powers. As I pointed out in another radio address, however, "any so-called restructuring of the Board of Estimate by assigning weighted votes would be nothing more than a thinly veiled attempt to preserve this political dinosaur." In fact, minority leaders in the council favored abolishment and an increase in the council's powers. They knew, as I pointed out, that the City Council could not be a balancing power "unless it has the power to check and balance the Executive Branch. . . . Reform of government is never easy," I admitted. But the time had come to abolish the Board of Estimate.

"Don't rock the boat" was no longer working, but members of the Board were having trouble coming up with any coherent governmental principles on which to base their argument for retaining their preponderance of power. Council president Andrew Stein floated a proposal that used weighted voting but also further increased the power of citywide officials like himself. Only Staten Island's borough president Lamberti supported it. B of E members were unable to unite behind any proposal.

Both proponents and opponents of increasing the City Council's power often talked about making the council districts slightly smaller and enlarging the number of them as a way of increasing minority representation. When these proposals were first made I was concerned that, minorities or not, council members from smaller districts might be weaker (and more prone to being manipulated by the mayor), a situation that could lead to a fractionalized council. Still, I remained open to the suggestion. As I moved around the boroughs of New York talking to constituents about the future restructuring of New York City government, it became clear how few understood the importance of balanced government. I was not surprised to hear from some that, although they voted in city elections, they did not even know who their City Council member was, what a council member does, or how the City Council functioned.

The only way to overcome this ignorance was to bring city government closer to the people whose lives it affected, and it was clear to me that the community boards and City Council were the vital links in this process. When Mayor Koch felt he had to close a neighborhood firehouse, he always tried to do it without notice. I told him he was wrong to do it that way. Just because the number of fires in a particular neighborhood has declined doesn't mean the firehouse is no longer needed. We were able to write such advance notification into law. (Thus, when Mayor Mike Bloomberg tried to close several firehouses a few years ago, without notice, the law required him to reopen them and give notice. After he did so, he again closed the firehouses, but not before huge community protest rallies.) In Astoria in 2001 we had three major fires, one of which led to fatalities, though we hadn't had a major fire in the ten years before that. In both situations there was a delay because the closest firehouse had been closed.

At around this same time the council and Mayor Koch joined forces to pass landmark anti-smoking legislation for the first time in a major world city. By the 1980s there was clear evidence about the dangers of smoking and smoke-filled environments. Some people close to me had died as a result. I was determined to get a tough but fair citywide bill passed: one that would protect non-smokers but give smokers a place where they could go to smoke. We had extensive hearings in our Health Committee and endured one of the strongest industry-sponsored lobbying campaigns in history. At the time the issue was quite contentious. A good percentage of the population smoked and the tobacco industry tried to mobilize them against us. Every council member was deluged with phone calls. In December 1997, however, after many amendments, the council passed the Clean Indoor Air Act, 32 to 1. In my nearly fourteen years in public office it was one of the first major initiatives ever taken via the committee system, and we got immediate recognition for it. Ed Koch called it "the most important legislation ever passed by the City Council"; national health groups came to our offices; even Secretary of Health Joseph Califano came from Washington to see me.

We passed the city anti-smoking bill because the state would not act. We would have preferred the state to go first, since otherwise they might overrule us. A statewide ban would have prevented the situation which then occurred, where smoking was prohibited only in restaurants on the Queens side of the Queens/Nassau County border. The theory in those days was that restaurants that banned smoking would lose business. As things turned out, the ban on smoking *helped* city restaurants, which started to gain clientele because of their smoke-free environment.

Another reform that really should have been a state initiative also fell to the City Council in 1987–88: campaign finance reform. When Albany killed proposed statewide legislation in the fall of 1987, council member Arthur Katzman introduced a citywide finance reform bill, as Ed Koch and I had earlier warned Albany we would do. The legislation proposed providing public campaign financing for all candidates who agreed to abide by its limits, and set the cap for spending in primaries for council members at $100,000 and at $120,000 in general elections. For citywide offices the limit was set at more than a million. The amount of the limits immediately became contentious, since we were forced to set them uniformly for all boroughs, even though historically races in Manhattan soaked up much more money than races in the "outer boroughs." However, we did not want Manhattan to artificially inflate the cost of the program, which would, after all, ultimately fall on the public. In the end we compromised on a city council spending limit of $60,000.

Getting my council members to vote in favor of this bill was a real challenge. Wealthy candidates and contributors and entrenched interest groups lobbied against it, of course. But my biggest problem was convincing elected officials to give away the natural advantage of incumbency. Why arrange to pay for someone else to run against them? they asked. State legislators had refused to do it, why should we? Ed Koch advised me: "See if your colleagues have the guts to do what's right and not popular." I had to hand it to the guy: here he was supporting a bill that offered a publicly financed platform for those who were planning to run against him a year later.

The strongest source of opposition came from an otherwise strong political ally, City Council president Andrew Stein. The position of council president in those days was an oddity. In one way it was similar to that of the vice president of the United States, in that he was to preside over the council, and vote in those rare instances when the legislature was tied. (In fact, he had been my insurance policy back in the tight 1986 vote for council leadership: if Dryfoos had not voted for me in the end, Andy had agreed to stick his neck out and break a tie in my favor.) Andy was an ex officio, non-voting member of any council committee and could attend any meeting, so whenever the full council was in session, he was there; but his real power lay on the Board of Estimate, where he had two votes. When city government was reformed a few years later, the council role fulfilled by Andy became part of the newly created Public Advocate's job.

Andy and I were good friends. We had both had powerful fathers involved in public life, who knew each other, and his politics were similar to mine: more centrist than most of the other Manhattan politicians, whom he considered too liberal. Where we differed was in our personal circumstances: Andy's father, Jerry Finkelstein, was a wealthy man, with the resources to help his son considerably after he changed his name and decided to go into politics. As a young assembly member in Albany, Andy had gained statewide publicity for helping senior citizens as chairman of a committee that investigated nursing homes; he quickly rose to become a successful Manhattan borough president and citywide candidate, and appeared to be a formidable mayoral candidate in the making. Given modest personal wealth, it was comparatively easy for me and Koch to support the campaign finance bill. But for Andy, campaign finance felt like political suicide. Being from Manhattan, Andy was the darling of many reformers and felt he could not come out publicly against the bill. But in private he tried hard to change my mind: "You have to be crazy, Peter," he told me, "to take away the hard-earned advantage of incumbency." A day later we had an outright shouting match, with him trumpeting: "Do you really need this just because you think it's right?" I hollered right back: "Yeah!"

Because it felt like arguing with my brother, it seemed okay to yell at each other. I understood his situation. I pointed out to him that with his resources he could just opt out of the public financing. He saw that as politically unacceptable, since doing so he would lose the political backing of many of the city's editorial pages, particularly the *New York Times.*

Other of my friends also disagreed, for different reasons. My political advisor Marty McLaughlin argued that the bill would create a new bureaucracy (which I'm afraid has by now become somewhat true). Other opponents asked why, when funds were so tight, we should be taking funds from police, fire, sanitation, libraries, and education, and giving it to people who are running for office. Council Finance chair Mike DeMarco made this point succinctly if awkwardly when he complained that "we can't afford good government right now." The only possible answer to him: We cannot *not* afford it. Good city government, especially after the crisis of faith induced by the Manes and Friedman scandals, was the highest priority. Many in the media were skeptical that the City Council, which still suffered from the old "Forty Thieves" image, would ever summon enough "good government principles" to pass the bill. One citizen's group went so far as to call gaining passage of the bill "an enormous test of Peter Vallone's leadership."

Among my allies on campaign finance reform besides Mayor Koch was Dick Ravitch, chairman of the commission on charter revision, who liked the idea so much that after we passed our legislation he made public financing of campaigns part of the charter itself. Even more important to me was the attitude of average New Yorkers. I decided to use two neighborhood groups I knew well, the Astoria Civic Association and the Taminent Democratic Club, as my own focus groups, presenting them with the best arguments both for and against the proposal. The results: both groups voted nearly unanimously in favor.

On January 15, 1988, I reached the magic number of twenty committed council member votes in favor. From that point on I knew the bill would pass, as indeed it did less than a month later in full session by a wide margin, despite some rancorous debate. With its passage the City Council became the first legislature of significance to ever pass such a bill—the first major city to do so and only the fourth local government in the nation. Significantly to me, Andy Stein and his wife and two-year-old son came over for dinner only a couple days after I had secured all the votes we needed, and we had a fun social evening, his wife and I talking politics while he played Nintendo on the floor with his son and my three sons Peter Jr., Perry, and Paul.

Occasionally the *New York Times* publishes an article that perfectly captures the essence of a particular city institution. One such example is a March 24, 1988, article by Todd S. Purdum entitled "Board of Estimate: A Tale of Realpolitik," which begins like this:

> It is 3:20 A.M. and the New York City Board of Estimate is voting on a developer's plan to build a midtown office tower using air rights from a school next door. It is a plan whose passage was all but assured 16 hours and 50 minutes ago when this meeting began in City Hall.
>
> The board has considered this idea for so long, at five previous sessions over three months, that a lawyer who first came to meetings in a fur hat now wears just a light raincoat. It is only now, in the middle of the night, amid empty coffee cups in its near-empty chamber, that New York City's most powerful governing body will approve this building.
>
> Though its members praise the board as a jewel of democracy akin to a town meeting, the board will pass this plan not because of any public oratory but because of private compromises and understandings reached days before.
>
> This scene is much the same every second Thursday: part Marx Brothers, part Machiavelli.

Why the late hour, the wrangling back and forth, the deal making in the situation described here? Was there something sinister going on that needed to be hidden? No. In the particular instance being described here, there was broad agreement that the proposal in question was a good deal for neighborhood, city, and school system. In fact, the delay had come about because two of the project's financial backers once had associations with the scandal-ridden administration of the ex-president of the Philippines, Ferdinand Marcos, and had also made contributions to the campaigns of Harrison Goldin, Andrew Stein, or backed a musical based on Ed Koch's book, *Mayor.* Fearing those associations might create an impression of impropriety, Board members Goldin, Stein, and Koch had basically removed themselves from the approval process, making it almost impossible to proceed.

The need to iron out such conflicts of interest through private agreements that would be ratified at biweekly all-night marathon sessions had become standard operating procedure for land use approval in New York City. Since the Board members themselves were not about to stay up at all hours twice a month, they sent stand-ins to do their business for themselves at these nominally "public" meetings. Citizens who came to testify would bare their hearts, but no one was paying attention. The real principals were not at these meetings; their "representatives" were authorized to listen to public commentary, even authorized to vote, but only by prearrangement. Who was responsible? The hearings were only for show, the proceedings rigged, and everybody knew it. The system worked because it was a closed clique whose members could trade items and favors.

This kind of land use system was worse than nontransparent: it simply stunk. There are so many people and such little land in New York City that land here has become like oil in Houston: it stands for both money and power. The Board members did not need to be corrupt because the system was; it was inevitable that they would be receiving huge contributions from the real estate people who appeared before them.

What made this system particularly galling to someone like me was that almost everywhere else in America the final say on land use, in municipalities and cities as well as in rural and suburban areas, always rested with some legislative body. That body might let a zoning board hold hearings and even make a decision, but a citizen could always appeal to it. Major cities within New York State (Albany, Binghamton, Buffalo, Rochester) gave the power of zoning to their city councils, as did such other major American cities as Chicago, San Francisco, Philadelphia, Miami, and Dallas.

Some critics point out that we legislators also do some of our work behind closed doors. That's true enough, but we stand up ourselves and vote, and we are politically accountable in our specific neighborhoods for the votes we take. Furthermore, because we are a larger and more diverse group, it is inevitable that more information about our dealings seeps out. Any group of only eight people is by nature a closed system.

The New York City Council faced another problem, however: people had become so used to thinking of us as a rubber stamp for the mayor's office that they treated us with near contempt. People may have recognized the corruption of the system, but at least it was a check on the mayor's power. They feared that the council could never effectively challenge the mayor. Of course, the Board members milked that fear for all it was worth. In an interview with me in November 1987 television broadcaster Dick Oliver talked about the current city council as a bunch of "lightweights," and said that the Board of Estimate would react "in horror" at the idea of its dissolution in favor of the council.

It was difficult to counter a perception of "Oh no, we don't want to empower *these* bums!" I was confident that the council would rise to its new mission. To me, if you diversified the council racially, ethnically, and intellectually, you'd have a good example of what representative government is supposed to be. After all, I'd been a council member—without much power—for twelve years. I had worked with colleagues of all kinds, every color, every race, every religion, and every intellectual ability. I'd seen that by patiently explaining, by not assuming what other people know or don't know, by being patient, reasonable, and not talking down to people, just giving them the facts and telling the truth, they will "do the right thing." You have to remain flexible and be willing to listen to different ideas.

Take my experience in working on codification of the city laws with Abe Gerges and Archie Spigner. I'm a good lawyer, and I'm usually right, but I get there on instinct and can often get the details wrong. In my office they have a word for it, a "Vallonism"— an exaggeration based on fact, a dramatization that, statistically, may be wrong. When something is important, however, you have to have a good technician around to nail down the facts. Abe Gerges was that kind of man. One of my other good friends on the council, Archie Spigner, used to be a bus driver. Abe Gerges was brilliant, and he'd have the technical facts exactly right. But if Archie couldn't understand what Abe was talking about, we didn't want it. Plain language became an expectation and a necessity. And that's what I always loved about the City Council: spare me from people who think they know it all.

The representative foundation of legislative groups is the essential ingredient of our democracy. Everyone knows it's not as efficient as a dictatorship, but that's not the point. Board of Estimate supporters just didn't understand the feeling at the local level that many neighborhoods were powerless against the big real estate interests, that the money interests could pretty much dictate whatever went on, even in their own backyards. Community groups and the community boards were pushing hard for more review of land use. Ruth Messinger wanted the Ravitch Charter Commission to look into ways of increasing the oversight powers of the community boards. Others wanted to take the borough presidents out of the community board appointment process and have the members be elected by "tenants associations and neighborhood groups." A reformer like Dick Ravitch recognized that local community boards had become a primary way "for local communities to express themselves and bring weight to bear." The question, as he put it, was "How do you balance efficiency of decision making with optimal participation and democracy?"

Any way you looked at it, the power of the Clique of Eight was bound to come to an end soon.

The housing situation in New York City had grown progressively worse ever since the city came back from the brink of bankruptcy in the mid-'70s. Inexpensive housing was no longer an option for most tenants, and landlords naturally wanted to maximize their investments. When I was growing up we never saw homeless people in Astoria; instead they all lived on the Bowery. After World War II society decided that people did not belong on the street and started putting them away into mental institutions like Willowbrook, even though many of the people they picked up were not really mentally unstable, just homeless. Later the pictures from Willowbrook horrified everyone. I remember my own Astoria Civic Association sponsoring a drive in which we sent clothing there to try to make things better. After the negative publicity Governor Carey, with the best of intentions, decided to "de-institutionalize" practically all of the people being held. "We'll provide halfway homes and money for programs to take care of them," came the promise. The reality, however, was "Let the cities deal with it." Suddenly New York had to cope with thousands of people on the streets. The natural reaction of the administrators in the mayor's office was to build big shelters and make sure they weren't very comfortable, otherwise people might want to stay put.

In 1986 I created a Homeless Assistance Subcommittee which for the first time brought together members of the council, advocates for the homeless, members of the administration, and leaders of the real estate industry. Initially I presided over it, and later on we upgraded it to a full standing committee and Abe Gerges became its chair. The council had allocated the money and we wanted accountability from the city officials who spent it. We found out a lot: about "boarder babies" (newborns abandoned by their mothers, a particular concern of Andy Stein); about fire hazards at the shelters; about the fact that it took more than a year to obtain screening to keep pigeons out of the Flushing Armory, where their droppings were falling on homeless women sheltered there; about the failure to plan ahead for what everyone knew would be a dramatic increase in the homeless population. We found out the city was moving homeless people into hotels in many neighborhoods; in the daytime the homeless would sit on the sidewalk and beg and at night go into the hotel. It soon became apparent that the city's policy was exactly backwards. Destroying the quality of life in the local community was not an answer. It cost $2,000 to $3,000 per month to shelter the homeless. Would it not make sense to pay a much more reasonable rent in a permanent home?

The policy up to this time was to leave the homeless on the streets on the pretext that they had a constitutional right to be there. Many advocates for the homeless went along with this approach, apparently thinking that leaving these poor souls on the streets would somehow shock taxpayers into forcing their elected officials to do more to help them. It's true that the shelters were bleak places, but as bleak as they were, states like Florida were actually giving bus money to their homeless to come to New York City to take advantage of our higher welfare payments.

In 1987 the council wrangled with the mayor over his plans to build thirteen additional homeless shelters in various neighborhoods around the city. The plan called for large shelters of 500 to 1,000 people. Since this simply took us back to square one, we insisted instead that any shelters be smaller and be focused on the transition from homelessness to a job and a home. The executive position was that the more social services you offered, the more homeless you'd attract. That point of view was understandable, but we learned that the more you helped the homeless, the quicker they got back on their feet, and the cheaper it was for taxpayers in the long run; we proved that the better the shelters were, the less likely people were to need them. The rub was, and still is, to identify the population in question.

As a result of our preliminary meetings, in 1987 the council adopted a series of laws starting with Local Law 46, which created a five-year plan to construct sufficient accommodations and, for the first time, to project the number of permanent housing units to be built. Our idea was to force the administration to take an inventory of who was on the streets or in the shelters and to see whether we could actually find decent living facilities.

In addition, Mayor Koch, with my urging, issued an executive order that required the forced removal of the homeless from the streets into a shelter when the temperature fell below freezing. The measure passed judicial review. At one point the New York Civil Liberties Union challenged our forced removal and structured medical care policies. They did so in the name of a homeless woman who, when removed, gave her name as "Billie Boggs"—because she was infatuated with the talk show host Bill Boggs. Although "Billie" claimed she was a "'professional' street person, her family identified her as Joyce Brown. She then admitted having been homeless less than two years, having earlier held several clerical positions. Ms. Brown was known for sleeping in her own excrement and screaming vile insults at passersby. To my mind, Ms. Brown was an obvious candidate for rehabilitative services.

In the midst of the press coverage about Joyce Brown/a.k.a. Billie Boggs, I appeared on Channel 2 with news anchor Jim Jensen. Jim probed and pushed me about her case and others. "I don't care whether you're a Harvard physicist and perfectly sane or anything else. You do not have the right to occupy the sidewalks or the street," I said.

Jim kept trying to pin me down: Where will you bring the homeless? Will you have them brought to jail?

I kept saying "No" and he kept pressing. It was obvious the person would have to be taken somewhere for evaluation, and in trying to explain that Jim eventually got me to say, "People who live on the streets and refuse to be taken to a shelter or a hospital should be subject to arrest and accommodated in a cell overnight for their own protection." I had said the impermissible words: "arrest" and "cell." All that appeared on the nightly news and dailies the next day was that I wanted to put the homeless in jail! I spent the next few days clarifying that I was talking about "protective custody"—not jail.

It did not help: a crazy judge ruled that "Billie Boggs" had to be released, and though several thoughtful politicians supported my position and an appellate court temporarily stayed the release, within two months she was freed and, in another burst of publicity, the misguided civil libertarians dressed her up, got her a lovely apartment, and even arranged for her to speak at Harvard. All to no avail. The poor woman was back on the streets in weeks, and as far as I know, lost forever.

This entire episode was very frustrating for me. I had no question in my conscience that the city had an obligation to pick up and help people, rather than step over them. I believe it is just as wrong to allow a person to die slowly on the street as it is to allow them to jump off the Brooklyn Bridge. The problem was devising an appropriate legal procedure. In the end we came up with a livable compromise limiting the removals. We also agreed that before the cops could *arrest* anyone, a social service worker would approach the person and try to talk her or him into going to a shelter.

At least Ed Koch thought we were doing something right. In his annual State of the City speech in January of 1988 he spent two minutes praising me and the City Council and went so far as to say that "Peter Vallone has done more as majority leader in two years than any other City

Council has accomplished in twenty." More important, in the same speech he announced plans for a major program to preserve 225,000 units of moderate-income housing, and pledged that even though "New York City's fiscal system has turned cooler" his administration would not "leave the homeless out in the cold."

Unfortunately, some of those I was most trying to engage in a process of consensus believed that a process of contention would better serve their purpose. After I became involved with the homeless issue I had breakfast several times with one of the prominent activists in the field, Robert M. Hayes. In November of 1987 we reached agreement in principle on a comprehensive law that would encourage homeless single adults to stop living on the streets. Bob and I both hoped that legislation could be approved quickly, but as the Billie Boggs case had proved, homeless issues can quickly become a minefield of complications, with publicity souring the atmosphere. Bob seemed disappointed that I couldn't accomplish things by fiat. In truth, I had to go through committee hearings, I had to persuade, I had to get the mayor's cooperation. Also, the city couldn't afford to pay for things that were the obligation of the state and federal government.

Soon Bob started criticizing me. Then he joined several liberal activists on a misguided campaign against any landlord who withheld apartments from the rental market in an effort to convert their buildings into a co-op or condominium—a practice that came to be called "warehousing." The activists were convinced there was a direct connection between apartments being kept vacant by landlords in the process of converting their buildings and the affordable housing shortage—that if these apartments were suddenly reopened to the rental market, the shortage would disappear and the homeless problem would be miraculously solved. In the spring of 1988, legislation was proposed in the City Council to outlaw warehousing altogether. Like the moratorium on the conversion of "Single Room Occupancy" hotels a couple of years earlier, this quixotic campaign soon took on overtones of a crusade. I had serious reservations about the bill, which I thought was based on faulty reasoning and was also unlikely to survive a court challenge. Since there was already a state law on the books about apartment warehousing, I didn't believe the City Council really had jurisdiction. We couldn't change the state law on our own, and to make a symbolic stand in this instance seemed wrongheaded to me.

Besides, I believed it was a good thing to convert rental buildings to condominiums and co-ops, because home ownership to me was part of the

American dream. I knew the truth lay somewhere in between what the activists claimed were unscrupulous landlords warehousing apartments to victimize tenants and what landlords claimed were unscrupulous, well-to-do tenants thwarting conversions so they could hang on to their underpriced rental apartments.

I was soon pilloried as a stooge of the landlords for failing to go along with the anti-warehousing activists. In May of 1988 a dozen or so pick-eters with signs showed up at my house, and later at my church. At the church they tried to block me physically from going in. I was willing to scuffle with them and they were not able to prevent me. Several months earlier Bob Hayes had met me at my church, and had breakfast with me several times. He knew that I was working on the homeless issue in good conscience, but he had publicized the locations of both my home and church and even saw that it got into the newspapers.

The methods of many of the activists did not improve much over the next year, although I did find another homeless advocacy group, led by Peter Smith, which was easier to work with. A year later Mayor Koch and I stood together at a press conference where we agreed to call on the state legislature to reduce the warehousing allowance from 10 to 5 percent, in recognition of several landlords who had taken unfair advantage of the 10 percent allowance. That did nothing to diminish the demagoguery of those who insisted on no warehousing and no conversions whatsoever, and continued their ad hominem pickets at my home and office.

The homeless problem has always existed, but all three branches of government must continue to cooperate to do the right thing. As a legal assistant in my father's law office I memorized this quotation from Cicero: "The purpose of government is to do for the people what they cannot do so well for themselves." Alas, legislation about the homeless that began in 1987 and has continued to this day has too often become entangled in a tug of war between city officials and the courts.

As for the "forced removal" issue: it was gutsy of Ed Koch to go ahead and say, "Pick them up." I urged him to do it, but he was the one with the power to do it. Something was done. He and I were among the first politicians willing to swim in the boiling water of the homeless issue. Much has changed since the late 1980s. Many of those now involved realize there will never be a permanent solution, but that we can do much to make it better. My dream now is that all the people who want to help in good conscience will put aside their penchant for fighting with each other.

13

Exit Ed Koch

The first few months of 1988 were a critical turning point in our struggle to bring back balance to New York City government. The first official report of the Ravitch Charter Revision Commission at the end of 1987 had so frustrated me with its ignorance of what the City Council was and could be that I made a "no more nice guy" resolution and shot off a memorandum to each member of the commission. I followed this up with detailed arguments and proposals for enhancing the council's powers in budgetary, zoning, and advise-and-consent matters.

On January 21, in two hours of grueling testimony before the charter commission, I pleaded with the commissioners to get rid of the Board of Estimate completely and allow the council its rightful, equal partnership in government. The commissioners kept questioning the integrity, reliability, and competence of council members, throwing into my face arguments about the council's "narrow" or parochial interests, repeating the idea that the Board of Estimate was best able to balance the potential competition between local and citywide interests. It was the same old song: "Council members cannot be trusted to deal with major citywide issues." I pointed out how the archaic borough/B of E system discouraged coalitions of common or interborough interest, and that a similar argument had been suggested two hundred years ago when aristocrats asked: "Can the *people* be trusted?" As my special assistant Ralph Miles told me, "They beat you up pretty good, but you counterpunched to a draw."

I knew that many of the charter commissioners were playing devil's advocate, but the day after my appearance before them I felt as if I had a hangover from the grilling. A few days later, after I had lunch with chairman Dick Ravitch, I was back on top of the world. I not only found him to be intelligent and sympathetic, but he agreed with practically everything I had said about the Board. At last I had an intellectual and political ally. I was certain then that the commission would rule to do away with the Board; the only remaining issue was the extent to which they would give the council equal powers with the executive. As with the commission as a whole, I pleaded with Ravitch to go all the way, not just pay lip service to the idea of council empowerment.

For legal reasons the idea of abolishing the Board altogether now began to take on an aura of inevitability. Lawyers familiar with voting rights adjudication had pointed out to the Ravitch Commission that the U.S. Justice Department would probably never give their blessing to weighted voting—until now the consensus solution for solving the one-person, one-vote problem posed by the Board's current composition. Why? Because weighted voting, while providing more equal representation among all city residents, would weaken the power of minorities—which was a violation of the Voting Rights Act of Congress. When Richard Ravitch talked openly about this problem to the newspapers and the word abolish made it into the headlines, Board members were outraged. Ravitch, courageously, had spoken the unspeakable. Now the genie was truly out of the bottle. A few days later even Mayor Koch was quoted as saying he was convinced that the Board was headed for abolition.

The timing could not have been more perfect. Starting February 4 and continuing throughout the winter, the council was to hold public meetings in every councilmanic district to discuss impending changes in the structure of the city government, and to build the case for further empowerment of the City Council. Those meetings were my shining hour; I went to every borough and was received enthusiastically by large audiences—even in Staten Island, a supposed hotbed of secession. I recited the Declaration of Independence and spoke passionately about the separation of powers.

I remember one meeting in the gym basement room at the Macedonia A.M.E. Church in Flushing with councilwoman Julia Harrison, where a full crowd came to hear me give a short lesson on New York City's corrupt version of the American system. While most remembered enough from civics classes to be articulate about the three branches of government, few of them understood the way the Board of Estimate had hamstrung the City Council. I told them how wrong it was for the elected representatives of the City of New York to be held back. I felt like Paul Revere, calling the people to retake control of their government. Simultaneously I had meetings with the editorial boards of all the New York papers, plotted strategy with members of our minority caucus, and worked with our Albany liaison office to strengthen contact there.

The tide was shifting in our favor, but no one expected the most powerful officials in New York to abdicate power without a fight. For the first time in history, two of the eight members of Board, David Dinkins and

Freddy Ferrer, were minority members. A group of powerful people associated with these two men, understandably frustrated that the system was about to change right when they had begun to have influence, began to argue that abolishing the Board of Estimate would violate the "values underlying" the Voting Rights Act because it would take away functions of leaders who were members of the minority. Further, they claimed abolishment would lead to an "imperial mayoralty"—the Board and only the Board could constrain an otherwise all-powerful mayor. It was around this time that David Dinkins came up with the colorful complaint that using the principle of one person, one vote to eliminate the Board of Estimate in the hope of increasing minority representation was like "saving the patient by amputating the head." The irony of all the talk about the Board of Estimate being the only possible "constraint" on the mayor, of course, was that the mayor was its *chairman!*

Luckily, black and Hispanic members of the council's minority caucus, however much respect they had for Dave and Freddie (and it was enormous), stayed loyal to the principle rather than to the principals. They understood that in the long range having a proper balance in government was more important than having any specific people in office at one time. And they were confident that on many matters they could supply minority leadership as well as the borough presidents.

By mid-March the papers were reporting a consensus within the charter commission in favor of eliminating the Board. Naturally, tempers began to fray among Board members and their lone advocate on the commission, Bernard Richland, a distinguished former corporation counsel who in the final days of hearings protested that the commission's legal consultants were applying the wrong data, did not understand New York City, and failed to recognize that the Board was "the best it has ever been."

"What we have before us is not a referendum on the worthiness of the Board of Estimate," pointed out the commission's secretary, Nathan Leventhal. Meanwhile Dick Ravitch, in response to Board members' complaints that his charter ccommission failed to consider the legal impact of boosting the mayor's power, said he and the other commissioners had no intention of giving all the Board's power to the mayor.

While members of the Board stubbornly refused to believe that the City Council might be worthy of taking over its responsibilities, the world at large was not so skeptical. On March 15, I met in Washington with Speaker of the House Jim Wright and his deputy Tony Coelho and had lunch with the New York congressional delegation. My arguments in favor of eliminating the Board and empowering the council were welcomed by everyone but Charlie Rangel (a close political ally of Manhattan borough president Dinkins). Two days later at the St. Patrick's Day Parade on Fifth Avenue, our group of a hundred-some council members and associates, led by former City Council president Paul O'Dwyer and myself—a group that until recently had been routinely ignored by the crowd—was roundly cheered. It was invigorating, to say the least, to know that we had some popular support.

Knowing we had that kind of base made it even more infuriating when the Board of Estimate voted at one of their dead-of-night sessions to give $120,000 of the public's money to Ed Costikyan, a well-connected Manhattan lawyer and one-time Democratic county leader, to be a hired gun for their interests. It didn't help that a year or two earlier, during the height of the city scandals involving Donald Manes and Stanley Friedman, Costikyan had tried to link my chief of staff Joe Strasburg to Friedman in front of a New York Bar Admissions character committee (presumably because of Joe's connection to me). One of Costikyan's first efforts on behalf of the Board was a letter in which he wrote: "There is no apparent basis to believe that an enlarged City Council would increase either the quantity or quality of minority representation." The old "Forty Thieves" argument again, however elegantly phrased!

Needless to say, the minority members of the council and I were livid. The council minority caucus issued a press release demanding an apology; Ed Koch appeared on television with our group to issue a letter condemning Costikyan's "racial slur" and demanding an explanation. At a City Hall news conference, caucus members denounced the "gutter tactics" and criticized the board for "seeking to perpetuate itself by creating confusion in minority communities with distortions about charter revision: "The very last thing New York needs is to have its black and Hispanic leaders attacking each other. The next-to-last thing New York needs is the Board of Estimate." In response to the Board's campaign, I decided to form CPAC, or Council Political Action Committee, a fund-raising group through which we would be able to counteract the Board's campaign against us.

The tension continued to build through March and the beginning of April 1988, as the charter panel heard two proposals from its chairman that both called for the end of the Board of Estimate. Having failed to convince more than a single commissioner of their argument, the Board (except for

Ed Koch) submitted a separate memo calling for its continuation, with each member's vote being weighted differently. Recognizing that they had failed to sway the commission, the Board tried an end run around them by exercising its influence in Albany. There John Marchi, the state senator from Staten Island, and Jerrold Nadler, state assemblyman, introduced legislation to change the agreed-upon rules for the upcoming November public referendum—a straight up-or-down vote on the commission's proposals—by opening up the ballot to alternative restructuring proposals (such as the Board's). I wrote in my diary: "Albany going crazy with bill to save the Board of Estimate." In my own final attempt to persuade the charter commission to grant us full equality, I personally contacted every commissioner and submitted a memorandum arguing for the following propositions:

I. The Board of Estimate Should Have No Role in the Budget Adoption or Modification Process
II. The Council Should Have Expanded Advice and Consent Powers
III. The Power to Pass the Zoning Resolution Belongs with the City Council
IV. The Members of the City Council Should Remain "Part-time" Employees
V. The Power to Appoint the Members of the Districting Commission Should Rest with the City Council
VI. City Council Members Should Continue to Serve for Four-Year Terms
VII. The Board of Ethics Should Be Independent
VIII. The Department of Investigation Should Be Independent

Then, suddenly, on April 4, the entire process ground to a halt. On that day, contrary to general expectation, the United States Supreme Court agreed to hear the City of New York's final challenge to the lower federal court's determination that the Board was unconstitutional. In my wildest imagination I could not believe that the Supreme Court would reverse the earlier decision against the Board of Estimate. But you never really know, and I had never been content simply to sit back and take the judicial route. It wasn't necessary: both the charter commission and the state legislature had the power to restructure the city government for the benefit of its people. By now there was a groundswell of popular support for what I had been proposing for fifteen years; more important, it was clearly the right thing to do. Why did we have to cede our power to the U.S. Supreme

Court? It would take a full year for the high court to hear arguments and render a decision. Why wait?

Ed Koch thought otherwise. Instead of following through on his promise to give the Charter Revision Commission full authority, he immediately came out in favor of waiting. To make matters worse my supposed ally, Richard Ravitch, agreed with him.

"Now I know what Dondi felt like," I wrote in my diary, referring to the comic strip character who always walked around with a cloud over his head. I felt betrayed by both the mayor and the commissioner. I went to see Ed Koch and reminded him that the charter commission had already decided to get rid of the Board. Why were we running to Washington?

Ed was his usual nonchalant self: "Peter, Peter, don't worry about it, what are you going to do? Overrule the Supreme Court?"

Koch knew as well as I did that the Board was doomed, whatever its members tried to do to salvage it. Meanwhile he had to work with them and, from his point of view, giving them a little more time for reality to sink in probably wasn't so bad. In retrospect, I can see that any mayor probably would be content to let the Supreme Court do his work for him. But that didn't make me feel any better. As for Dick Ravitch, I had no idea at the time that he was planning to run for mayor. If I had, I would have known immediately why he chose not to incur the wrath of many of the same politicians whose support he would be seeking.

"It appears the city's voters will have to wait yet another year before they are given an opportunity to restore representative government in New York," I declared in my radio address a week or so later: "This latest example of political wisdom—or lack of it—is akin to rearranging the deck chairs on the *Titanic*. . . . New Yorkers may feel let down by the unnecessary decision to delay the charter revision process, but as the majority leader of the City Council I guarantee that the Board of Estimate, like the *Titanic*, is not unsinkable, no matter how many times the deck chairs are rearranged!"

The round-one decision may have been delayed on a technicality, but I was not about to let up on the pressure. I needed Ed Koch to understand that in the long run he would be better off worrying about the council than the B of E, and I used the 1988 budget negotiations to make that crystal clear. When the mayor proposed a doom-and-gloom budget requiring a property tax increase of $150 million, I worked hand-in-hand with my newly hired public relations wizard, Peg Breen, to brand the document a "Chicken Little" approach to budgeting and warned that Koch should not even consider a property tax increase—especially since a recent change in the way the state calculated those taxes was already going to levy a significant increase on property owners.

We council members were familiar with City Hall's budget tactics: to underforecast revenues (the law gave the mayor's office sole control over revenue projection) and hold back on the items we considered particularly important—like cops on the beat. That way the struggle focused on cuts that the mayor knew would be restored in the end, and in the process the council's priorities could always be shunted to the back burner. I understood the concerns of many that a spendthrift legislature was less likely to check itself than an executive or administrator, but I could not agree that one person, the mayor, should have basically unchecked power over increasing or decreasing the budget by means of revenue projection.

To counter this power, we decided to hire two Syracuse University "fiscal reality checkers." Their mission: to comb carefully through the mayor's mandatory revenue and expenditure forecasts and attempt to identify questionable projections. Sure enough, by June 10 our experts had come up with a list of $214 million in possible spending cuts. Although Koch's budget director immediately questioned our list, and made even more dire predictions about falling tax revenue, he also managed to find enough unspent money from the year before to hold close to his original revenue and expenditure figures.

The battle of headlines continued past the usual budget deadline of June 16: this was one year in which we would not be railroaded. We continued to challenge the mayor's revenue projections, pointing out that the campaign finance amounts did not really need to be included since they would not be paid out until fiscal 1990, and that the city's projections assumed much too conservative a model of the national economy. As part of our public relations campaign, most council members started to wear buttons depicting the black cover page of the mayor's budget with a red slash through it and the words "Just Say No."

"We are not simply being intransigent," I declared to the press. 'We are performing our duty to scrutinize the mayor's proposal and to reshape it into a responsible document that reflects the true needs of our citizens." The Board of Estimate, needless to say, was less than helpful. Having always had the power to spend money without any responsibility for raising it, they really didn't know the first thing about the budget, or how to cut it. They refused to make common cause with our proposals; instead they asked the mayor to resubmit one more to their liking. When the mayor refused, they were stuck. As I wrote in my diary on June 19: "The mayor and the Board blinked first." Koch, increasingly exasperated, blamed the city comptroller—Harrison "Jay" Goldin, his archrival on the Board and potential mayoral opponent—for the budget logjam. The city's papers, however, correctly identified the heart of the matter as a power issue between the mayor's office and the council, a struggle in which the Board of Estimate was becoming increasingly irrelevant.

Finally, about a week after the original deadline, Finance Committee Counsel Gary Altman, acting at the suggestion of my advisor Ralph Miles, spent two days and nights scouring the charter administrative code, and laws of recent years, and came up with a $60 million brainstorm. The idea? To suspend cancellation of an energy tax on utilities instead of increasing real estate tax increases. Mayor Koch, calling the concept "ingenious," accepted our counterproposal, and even the Board of Estimate agreed. If only the state legislature had agreed to an increase in excise taxes on cigarettes and alcohol, we would have succeeded in balancing the budget entirely without a real estate tax (because the state did not, we *did* have to boost it slightly). Most important, for the first time, the council had become *the* player in the budget negotiations.

In the 1980s New York City was suffering from a severe drug addiction problem, traceable largely to the widespread availability of "crack" cocaine. The problem was not only causing untold suffering among drug abusers and their victims, but had begun to seriously impinge on the quality of life in virtually every neighborhood of the city, especially in the parks, an important refuge for average New Yorkers looking for some relief from the daily bustle. No one could escape from it, let alone me and my family.

I live only a short distance from Astoria Park and in the summer of 1987 our neighbors were complaining a lot about the drug dealing going on there. One day Tena, who is more courageous than I am, said, "Let's take a walk through the park and check it out." Well, in the middle of the park someone had parked a huge RV with loudspeakers. On top of it stood a guy with a microphone. Surrounding it were a sea of motorcycles and a crowd of thugs with tattoos. The music was blaring and the guy was screaming obscenities into the mike. Behind the van: an open-air drug market. Tena started yelling at them all to pipe down, but I quickly escorted her out of there.

Soon after I persuaded the then deputy police commissioner, who looked and acted like General Patton, to stage a huge raid in Astoria Park. The police swept through the park and made over a hundred arrests. As it turned out, hardly anyone arrested came from the local neighborhood. Immediately my name became mud with the drug people; they found out where I lived by following one of my kids home and threw a rock through the window. It hit the back of Peter Jr.'s head while he was studying, but luckily caused no further damage. Pete tried running after the culprits but couldn't catch up. Needless to say, I was furious.

Stupidly, the drug pushers who had set up the revenge attack had made the mistake of using a local addict. A week or two later, while he was walking through one of the street fairs on Ditmars Boulevard, Pete saw the big guy who had thrown the stone. He went and fetched a cop; the perpetrator was arrested, and he gave up the two others who were in on the attack as well. The good news is that we managed to get the fellow into a drug treatment program, and afterward he went straight.

Partly because of this experience, I was always one of the biggest supporters of the mayor's "TNT" or Tactical Narcotics Team, a new technique for fighting drugs by concentrating overwhelming resources on one neighborhood at a time and cleaning that one out before going on to another. The program started out in Queens and proved such a success in my home borough that in the fall of 1988 Ed Koch decided to expand it into all five. Unfortunately, this expansion soon became ensnared in more budget and tax disputes, with the mayor asking for real estate tax increases and across-the-board service cuts in other city departments to finance the anti-drug effort. The council insisted first on a reexamination of existing expenditures and revenue sources. But without more oversight power, there was no way the council could make sure that unneeded expenditures were not made.

Meanwhile, it was important to me to find better ways than raising taxes to pay for the cost of ridding the streets of drugs. The fairest way of doing this, from my point of view, was to take it from the creeps who were making all the illegal money in the first place. So on October 26, 1988, I proposed a major package of new drug laws that would "enable the city to seize general revenues of people who are indicted on drug charges—not just assets like automobiles and houses used directly in drug transactions." Any money from the proposal would go into city coffers and directly contribute to our anti-drug efforts.

On December 7, 1988, the United States Supreme Court heard arguments in *Morris vs. the Board of Estimate.* The amicus brief submitted by the council concentrated on the city's misrepresentation of the Board of Estimate's role in the budget process, which they needed to minimize in order to stand even the barest chance of winning the case. As it was, their argument rested on a far-fetched idea. They admitted that the composition of the Board led to unequal rights for voters in the more populous boroughs, but claimed that this inequality was erased by the double weighting of the citywide officials' votes on the Board—those of the comptroller, council president, and mayor. This argument rested on the notion that these three officials voted as a "citywide" majority bloc of six that could always override the combined "parochial" interests of the five borough presidents. The argument fell totally apart in the context of votes on the city's annual budget, when the mayor was not allowed to vote (turning a supposed "majority of six" into a minority of four). Anyway, the city's complicated mathematical gymnastics could not mask the fact that they were basically defending the "degradation" of the voting rights of citizens from Brooklyn, Queens, and Manhattan.

I was there in the court on December 7, and from the judges' questions it was clear that they were buying none of the city's minimalization of the budget question. The highlight of the question-and-answer period between city corporation counsel Peter Zimroth and the justices went like this:

> MR. ZIMROTH: I don't deny that [the people from the smallest borough] have a larger voice. My — my point is how to measure that larger voice. And what is the meaning of that larger voice in the context of — this case? That is, to say what the court of appeals said —
>
> QUESTION: The meaning I suppose is that the borough president from Staten Island has the same voice as the borough president from Brooklyn?
>
> MR. ZIMROTH: Right.
>
> QUESTION: And — they represent widely different populations?
>
> MR. ZIMROTH : Yes, but — but they represent them in a context where that difference is much, much less significant than if there were a five-member body that had no citywides. . . .
>
> The reason I think this is constitutional is because I think the present system is constitutional. And the reason I think the present

system is constitutional is that this court's one person–one vote jurisprudence pays very strong attention to all of the factors that — that went into the creation of the — of the Board of Estimate. It's — it's a body which has been very successful and effective in keeping this very large city together. . . .

It has met the test of time again and again and again. Charter revision commissions have looked at this system and said that this compromise is necessary to the continued existence of the city and to the — essential to the well-being of the city.

The question that I would ask is even in terms of the democratic principles that the one person–one vote is supposed to and does further, what is to be gained by destroying this body?

QUESTION: Why do you assume the body will be destroyed?

. . .

MR. ZIMROTH: Because the voting structure is the compromise that allowed the city to get together. If you destroy that —

QUESTION: Suppose they made a compromise in Queens, women won't vote, and in — in the Bronx they will, and we'd say that's how they made the deal. It happens to be unconstitutional. Are we going to just say, well —

MR. ZIMROTH: Well, of course —

QUESTION: — it was a good deal when they made it, so it has got to be preserved?

MR. ZIMROTH: Of course not, but — but —

QUESTION: Well, what's the difference?

MR. ZIMROTH: The big differences are that this court has always said — it has to be rational.

. . .

QUESTION: Supposing I've got a successful thing where women don't vote in the Bronx, and it has worked, can you keep it?

MR. ZIMROTH: I doubt that it would work.

QUESTION: Well — [Laughter]

MR. ZIMROTH: I mean, it — I mean, in all seriousness —

QUESTION: We're limited to our past successes. We can't have any more successes in the future.

MR. ZIMROTH: Well, not —

QUESTION: Any good thing that was set up in— in 1890 — that can last, but —

MR. ZIMROTH: This is not something —

QUESTION: — that's the end of the story.

MR. ZIMROTH: — that was only set up in 1890. It was something that has been reaffirmed by every single charter revision commission since then. Every one has said that this structure is the glue that has kept the City of New York together, and don't change it. And all I'm saying is —

QUESTION: Do you think New York is going to disintegrate if you lose this lawsuit? You really —

MR. ZIMROTH: Disintegrate? I think there will be very serious consequences, yes.

I came away from the council's "day in court" proud to be a lawyer, wishing that I myself could have stood up there with Richard Emery to argue the case against the Board. As it was, I kept asking myself, how could corporation counsel Zimroth stand up there and defend the indefensible?

An important chapter in the history of New York City was being written in the nation's capital. It was exciting to be there to witness the third branch of government, in all of its majesty, fulfilling its role as conceived by the framers of our Constitution. I did not believe the high court would ignore the one person–one vote doctrine in favor of counsel Zimroth's plea for the Board's "historic role." But even if they did, I knew we had strong bases for other lawsuits, and for major charter reform based on the doctrine of separation of powers. I prepared for these legal challenges in January by hiring Richard Weinberg, one of Bob Abrams's top assistants, as our general counsel to the New York City Council and counsel to the Speaker. It had been wonderful to watch a balanced *federal* system at work. I was certain that Richard would help me realize my dream to allow a similar balance work in New York City. I would not be disappointed.

Meanwhile the campaign finance system we had fought so hard to enact was about to go into effect for the first time ever. It so happened that the date for the opening or "charter" meeting of the New Year coincided with the deadline for applying for public campaign funds, and four mayoral candidates besides Ed Koch had already done so: Dick Ravitch, Harrison Goldin, Ruth Messinger, and Shirley Chisholm (the latter two would soon drop out of the mayor's race). Several amendments needed to be made to the earlier legislation, including the unrealistically early filing date. Unfortunately the maverick chair of my Finance Committee, Mike DeMarco, decided to use this opportunity to challenge the legislation itself. It had been hard enough for me to garner the votes the first time around, since no incumbent anywhere was instinctively in favor of subsidizing an opponent. The last thing I needed was for DeMarco, the titular head of the Bronx delegation, to lead a borough-wide revolt at a time when it was crucial to continue building council unity, effectiveness, and reputation. Mike forced me to make the vote a "leadership" issue. We won the vote, 33–1. Much as I disliked the idea, I knew then that I would have to discipline DeMarco soon, before he did me permanent political damage.

In the early spring of 1989 everything that I had been working for on the council for fifteen years suddenly began to come to fruition. During the St. Patrick's Day Parade on March 17 the council and I received an ovation even greater than that of a year earlier, and less than a week later, on March 22, 1989, the ax finally fell on the Board of Estimate. On that day the Supreme Court issued a unanimous ruling rejecting all of the city's arguments for retaining the Board's peculiar "historic" status. At last, the Board had been declared officially unconstitutional.

Elated by this news, I found myself the recipient of a different sort of honor altogether the following day, Holy Thursday. That evening I was one of twelve people from the New York archdiocese invited to represent the disciples of Jesus during a reenactment of the Last Supper at St. Patrick's Cathedral, where Cardinal O'Connor washed my feet in a deeply humbling and moving experience.

Newsday reminded me of the mixed blessings of success when they ran a deprecatory article on me and the City Council three days later, caricaturing me as "the man who would be king"; in fact, they implied I was nothing but a puppet of Donald Manes and Stanley Friedman. At the same time the article ridiculed the council members as Tammany Hall lowlifes who had no business trying to "run the city." Worst of all, they published my home address, exposing my family to more attacks. In Albany for my annual breakfast with legislators, however, I found the powers-that-be almost falling over themselves in their graciousness toward me: Mel Miller, Ralph Marino, Saul Weprin, all were one better than the other, and this time I spent *forty-five minutes* with the governor, once again the old lovable Mario. What a difference the U.S. Supreme Court had made!

At the end of June the City Council conducted its last negotiations with the now officially unconstitutional Board of Estimate. Unlike earlier years, Mayor Koch's budget was approved with only minor modifications; Ed Koch declared that it was the first budget process he could remember in which "there was no harsh word expressed." What a change from the preceding years! Although Ed was quoted as saying, "There was not enough to fight over," I suspect the real reason for our shared goodwill was the revolution that had just taken place. The mayor and I knew that everything we now did was precedent-breaking. We were all under the miscroscopic inspection of the media, and we needed to be 100 percent responsible.

These months became some of the most satisfying of my life as I helped draw up the blueprint of a new government for New York City. For someone who had always been a great admirer of the Founding Fathers of this nation, there could have been no greater thrill. While I was riding high on the crest of this great reform of city government however, Ed Koch was in a tough contest to hang on to the position that had defined his political life for the past dozen years.

Personally, I did not believe Ed could win a fourth term as mayor, and I had told him so early on (I told the same thing to Mario Cuomo a few years later). He was getting the same message from many others, so he was not surprised at my candor, and did not hold it against me. Then, ten days after the Supreme Court decision, I held a "kitchen cabinet" meeting in Astoria where my closest political advisors debated whether I should run for mayor then, in 1989, if Ed Koch did not run, while my popularity was at an all-time high. Wasn't this perhaps the moment I'd been waiting for all my life?

For several hours I argued against some of the ablest minds in New York City politics, who wanted me to strengthen the powers of the mayor, an office they believed I was sure to occupy one day. I did not feel it was the right moment to change the focus of my efforts from the legislative to the executive. The twelve-member group agreed with me, 10–2, that I should forgo the race that year and just concentrate on strengthening the council. As I wrote in my diary: "Gave up 'crown' for stronger legislature." At around the same time I decided that it made the most sense to back Dick Ravitch for mayor. Dick had some personal wealth and good connections. Also, I felt my future was inextricably linked with strengthening the City Council as an institution, and it still rankled me that Ed Koch had been so nonchalant about the role of the Board of Estimate. I was sure that Dick would commit himself where Ed had been laid back.

In fact, Dick Ravitch gained the early support of the Queens Democratic Party, but his campaign never took off. I told Dick he had to get out there early and establish himself, but perhaps with his businessman's sense of prudence he saved his money until late in the race, when it was too late. In the final days of the campaign the Queens Democratic organization switched its allegiance from Ravitch and returned to the mayor's fold. I stayed behind the scenes.

In the end, the race came down to a contest between the mayor and David Dinkins. Race relations became a key factor. The voters wanted a man they believed could bring more harmony to the ill feelings created by a series of race-based crimes and incidents. Ed Koch's "in-your-face" bluntness had lost its appeal, and no one could outrank David Dinkins for gentlemanliness. To his great credit, Koch had supported the public financing of campaigns that allowed David Dinkins to compete on an equal platform. Ed Koch was not arrogant, but he really did not think he would be beaten. In fact he had been so confident that after David inadvertently overspent in the third year of the election cycle, in violation of the new campaign finance law, Ed had agreed to amend this provision to allow David to enter the program. Yet on September 12, 1989, New York Democrats voted "their hearts, not their fears," and picked the first African-American candidate ever as their mayoral candidate.

This defeat was a humbling, soul-searching experience for Ed Koch. Fritz Schwarz, the new head of the Charter Revision Commission, told me that Ed was feeling low and I should go talk to him. When I saw him he seemed lost. He asked me: "What am I going to do? My whole life has been the city."

"It still can be," I told him. "You're going to be one of the happiest people on the face of the earth."

A few weeks later when I saw him he was indeed as happy as a pig in clover. He said to me something like, "You know this morning, some guy came over and said 'I'm glad you lost, you son of a bitch.' And I told him exactly what to do with himself. It felt so good. I could never do that when I was mayor."

The four years when Ed Koch and I held powerful positions in New York City were a roller-coaster ride of thrills and disappointments I will never forget. In those first few years we probably passed more productive landmark legislation in the city's history than in any other period. Ed Koch used his power on the Board of Estimate to shift in our direction. He knew that the council was eventually going to have full control of the budget. He expected to win the mayoralty again, knowing that together we could have enormous impact on essential services in the city and its districts, from garbage collection to libraries, cops, and the homeless. The borough presidents had always zealously protected their discretionary little pots for "economic development." Economic development, yes, but what were they developing? It didn't make any difference to the man or woman on the street if he didn't see a cop or her kids couldn't go to the library.

Ed Koch is a very wise man. I still seek his counsel and advice to this day; every mayor and speaker would be wise to do the same. His enthusiasm and his verve made New Yorkers proud. He loved to invite guests to Gracie Mansion to show off the city he loved so much. This was definitely not a waste of time: no one was better at the business of making friends and influencing people. He remains a living legend, a testament to the grit, courage, and good humor of all New Yorkers. He's earned a place in history right up there with the great ones, and in this town at least, he earned the right to be called "The Greatest."

PART IV

A Real Legislature

14

A New Deal for New York City

The Supreme Court decision of March 23, 1989 that officially declared the Board of Estimate unconstitutional provided New York City citizens "a timely opportunity to restructure their government, strengthen their representation, and improve the quality and efficiency of the decision-making process that affects every area of their lives," as I declared in my *New York Times* op-ed piece of March 27, "No More 1 Person, 1/4 Vote for NYC." I tried to allay the concerns expressed by some Staten Islanders about losing voice in city government and strongly urged that the Charter Revision Commission turn over to the city council "the full legislative powers enjoyed by its counterparts in Albany and other cities elsewhere in the country."

The Supreme Court decision had thrust the charter commission, under the new leadership of Frederick A. O. Schwarz Jr., into the spotlight. Because of mandated municipal elections scheduled for the fall of 1989, it would be necessary to come up with proposals for totally overhauling New York City government within about six months—otherwise officials would be elected to offices that no longer existed. Koch had appointed Schwarz back in mid-November, when Ravitch told him he would not continue because he planned to run for mayor. Until recently Schwarz, as city corporation counsel before Peter Zimroth, had been instrumental in formulating the city's argument *against* eliminating the Board of Estimate, and although I knew and respected him as an extremely intelligent lawyer he, unlike Dick Ravitch, was largely an unknown quantity. For months Dick Ravitch, the commission's counsel Eric Lane, and I had discussed the issues of how to reshape city government; the last thing I was interested in was a "fresh new approach." Several factors spoke well for Schwarz: he had codified the laws of one of the newer African nations, which I knew from visiting him once while I worked on the New York City codification; also, Richard Emery, who had argued against the Board before the Supreme Court, was satisfied that the appointment had gone to a legal expert rather than a political figure.

Luckily, it quickly became clear from comments of members of the charter commission that Ravitch's nearly final proposals from the year before would probably still be the basis of the commission's first recommendations. Those proposals included expanded power for the City Council over the budget and many other areas, even perhaps awarding franchises.

Zoning and land use powers, however, were potentially more complex. Borough presidents would probably be retained and given some role in city planning, but otherwise would fulfill a largely ceremonial or cheerleading function for their particular borough.

In early April I testified before Schwarz's commission, urging them to continue along the course established by Ravitch. Two weeks later when Fritz Schwarz and Eric Lane outlined the proposals they would make public a few days later, I was satisfied that the council stood to gain much of what we were looking for on the major issues. The only part they mentioned that struck me as cumbersome and unnecessary was one entertaining the idea of a bicameral legislature with an "upper" legislative house that would probably include the borough presidents.

The presidents themselves, however, expressed little interest in condescending to become "legislative." Most of them criticized the commission's ideas as tantamount to a mayoral power grab, although David Dinkins expressed worries about the new powers about to be granted me. Together the group proposed an unworkable and clearly unconstitutional scheme granting them executive control with the mayor over the budget.

To assuage their concerns, the commission soon gave the borough presidents a controlling voice over 5 percent of capital and discretionary operating expenses. It also reversed itself on its first-draft effort to create an "apolitical," appointees-only land use and zoning commission. A few weeks later Fritz Schwarz called me the "George Washington of New York City" who would "set the precedents for leadership into the next century." Yet as the commission was pushed and pulled by various interest groups over the next month, they floated options and refinements—an independent budget office, enlarging the borough president–appointed community boards' influence on land use and zoning—which undercut their earlier resolve to give the council the real power to counterbalance the mayor. My frustration with this vacillation became apparent at a mid-June meeting where I told the group I wasn't sure whether I should "shake or break" their hand, and that it was "important to be consistent and true to your word." The group was soon back on track, and three weeks later, on July 7, I received word that if the proposals passed in the November referendum, the council would gain most of the new powers we wanted. Also, I would get the new title I had asked for as "Speaker" of a newly expanded City Council. (Only the first Dutch "Common Council" in New Amsterdam could have known that a "Vice Chairman" was supposed to be the legislative leader.)

Voter approval of the charter proposals was by no means a certain thing. Opponents organized an aggressive television campaign to defeat them, including a clever "can of worms" commercial that tried to portray the changes as a Pandora's box of destabilizing innovations. Among the most vociferous naysayers regarding the new form of government were borough presidents Howie Golden and Freddy Ferrer. On the other hand their fellow presidents Claire Shulman and David Dinkins, the victor over Ed Koch in the Democratic primary for mayor, adopted a milder opposing view.

Dinkins's victory over Republican and Liberal Party opponent Rudolph Giuliani was no more certain than that of charter reform. The reputation Rudy had gained during his successful investigations and prosecution of the scandals involving Donald Manes, Stanley Friedman, and the Parking Violations Bureau provided him a reservoir of support from law-and-order-minded outer borough residents. It also gave him a halo of incorruptibility for some good-government types. Also, revelations about David Dinkins's sloppiness in failing to file income tax returns two decades earlier created doubts about his management style.

In the end, Rudy's hard-edged manner and lack of experience (he had never before held elective office) were unappealing to a bare majority of New Yorkers. They took to heart David Dinkins's promise of healing and unity. Ed Koch's wholehearted show of support for the Democratic candidate who had defeated him in the primary helped overcome a last-minute surge in support for Giuliani among more conservative Democratic voters, enough to elect Dinkins New York's first African-American mayor by a narrow 1 percent margin. Luckily, skepticism about both candidates did not carry over to the charter referendum, which was approved by a strong 55 to 45 percent vote. This result made me happier than my first electoral victory in 1974. (Though I was still perplexed how 45 percent could have fallen for the "can of worms.") The victory over the charter was sweetened even further when Mayor-elect Dinkins came to see me in my office with hordes of television and press in tow (Ed Koch had visited me there only once in twelve years). In our private discussion we vowed to work together for the betterment of the city.

Alas, it became clear from the moment David Dinkins took office that, far from bettering the city, the best we might do is avoid a rapid deterioration. A serious financial downturn on a national and statewide level quickly tied the hands of the new mayor. In January of 1990 Governor Cuomo announced that the state had to cut its budget by $1.2 billion—

which meant the city would have to cut its spending by the same amount in less than a month to keep pace with the loss of matching funds. This represented one of the biggest cuts the city had ever faced. Together David Dinkins and I had to make painful choices about where to cut, while at the same time facing an increasing wave of crime, racial unrest, and myriad other problems.

The budget crisis of 1990 aggravated a breakdown in law and order that seemed to climax during the summer of 1990 with the death of several children from stray bullets. Beginning in the early 1980s Mayor Koch had promised to restore police staffing levels to pre–New York City fiscal crisis (1974) levels, but had been forced to delay these increases because of budget shortfalls. In his 1989 campaign Dinkins himself had made an issue of the need to hire more police officers, but once he came into office he delayed the hirings because of the severe budget crunch and because to do so would mean sacrificing many of the social service programs which to him were just as or more important than additional police officers.

Dinkins's top priority was to rebuild the city's social services, a legitimate concern, but a difficult priority to stick to during the hard financial times we were enduring. Since we had already agreed upon a budget before the summer's crime wave and the mayor was still the only one with the power to propose a "budget modification" during the course of a year, despite the charter reforms, we were powerless to act without him. Unfortunately, dealing with the mayor and his staff was not always easy. Every mayor likes to appear in charge and hates having to go through a legislative body to approve his initiatives. Under the old system, the mayor had usually been able to mold a consensus in the Board of Estimate and effectively bypass the City Council. That, of course, is one of the reasons we had wound up with an understaffed police force in the first place: borough presidents' priorities were always the economic and cultural development of their boroughs. They figured the mayor and the council would "take care of" the cops.

The new system was only months old and largely untested. During the charter hearings David had complained about the power the proposed charter reforms would bring to me, the new Speaker. So he was bound to be sensitive to any appearance of "giving in" to legislative pressure from our side. The random shootings of children by stray bullets during the summer of 1990 brought a new level of nervousness to the city. During August Mayor Dinkins at first dismissed our council proposal to increase police levels by 500 as fiscally impossible, then later proposed upping the increase to 1,000.

David Dinkins had come to office promising to soothe racial animosities, but for over six months the mayor's office had proved unable to put an end to a racially based boycott of a Korean greengrocer in Brooklyn. The outbreak of random violence in the summer was aggravated by poor relations between minority populations and a largely white police force, by Dinkins's own unpopularity among the cops and other uniformed workers, and by the repeated absence of his police commissioner because of his wife's health emergency. The slaying of twenty-two-year-old Brian Watkins in a Midtown Manhattan subway station by a roving band of teenage robbers was the last straw for many New Yorkers. It wasn't enough that the gang had robbed the tourists from Utah on a visit to attend the U.S. Tennis Open, but they had started punching Brian's mother. When Brian came to her defense, they had stabbed him to death.

After this senseless killing we on the council felt we were faced with a make-or-break decision to restore law and order to the streets of New York. The question was, what could the council do if the mayor did not take the initiative? By proposing and passing a law requiring the mayor to hire police and garnering editorial and some political support, we hoped to force his hand.

But we would also need the mayor's cooperation. We might pass laws, but the mayor would have to sign them. And as far as raising taxes to pay for the new cops, the only taxes over which the City Council had sole discretion were the real estate tax, the least popular tax of all, and the archaic commercial rent tax. To increase any other tax, including the city income tax, we would have to get permission from the state legislators in Albany, who had a history of being reluctant to grant the city the power to tax itself. Certainly we risked the wrath of voters tired of empty promises and higher taxes, but the very survival of the city was at stake. My staff and I realized that this was the opportunity—and responsibility—we had been seeking for all these years. I would have to convince at least two-thirds of the council members to swallow their best instincts against raising taxes and to stand with me.

The City Council proposals garnered enthusiastic support from editorial pages and the governor's office. When I announced at our September 6 press conference that "we don't think we can wait even a day. . . . We have to do something to take back the streets," I sincerely was not trying "to steal the mayor's thunder." But I was aware that if we failed to jump-start Dinkins out of his sometimes overly deliberative approach, we would never see the moment when "both sides of City Hall strike lightning together.'"

To me, the press conference that day was just as important for the eventual "reclaiming" of New York as a safe and secure city as the impressive measures for which Mayor Giuliani received credit several years later. I cannot repeat how often I heard in those days the sentiment that, finally, something was being done. We knew we were taking a big chance. For years press conferences at City Hall had proclaimed the imminent hiring of more cops, only to see those hirings quietly killed in backroom budget negotiations. We were determined that this time would be different. It was.

After several months of inconclusive back-and-forthing, the Dinkins administration and its distracted police commissioner, Lee Brown, finally took up the basic outlines of the City Council proposal and drafted the bill that became known as "Safe Streets, Safe City." This landmark legislation mandated the hiring of enough new police officers to increase the minimum troop strength of the police force to pre–fiscal crisis levels. Funding would come only from a dedicated source of revenue created by whatever tax increase we could push through Albany.

David and I then went hat in hand to Albany. There, Mayor Dinkins proved instrumental in drumming up support for the bill not only with the minority legislators who were his natural constituency, but in placating a multitude of condescending state assemblymen and senators who insisted on having their petty parochial demands met before agreeing to allow us to tax ourselves. For the first time I knew of, Albany agreed to our request to earmark billions of dollars to rebuild our criminal justice system by way of a surcharge on our personal income tax and a slight increase in our real estate tax. On that legislation, Mayor Dinkins's signature and mine appear alongside the signatures of Governor Cuomo, Senate Majority Leader Ralph Marino, and Speaker of the Assembly Mel Miller.

This bill is the best example of the city and state executive and legislative branches working together to change policy. The historic document was amended again in June 1993 and in January of 1997. As promised, the City Council returned the income tax surcharge in 1998, by which time the magic number of 38,310 police officers had been reached. By 2001 New York City was the safest large city in the country, with a combined police force of 40,710. It is now the duty of any mayor and council to make sure that fiscal woes do not ever again undercut public safety. What is the magic number of police officers needed to keep our city safe?

No one knows for sure, but we do know that the historic Memorandum of Understanding (MOU) between the city and the state sets forth a 1997 level of 38,310. I am not one to argue with success, and it makes no sense to go below that number. Unfortunately, because of attrition we have fallen below the MOU standards of safety to the point where, in 2005, the number was 37,038. Although so far crime has continued to decline, the low figure should be a major cause of concern for both the mayor and the council, and for New Yorkers in general.

By the time of our success with Safe Streets, Safe City, the city council had made tremendous strides in becoming a full partner in New York government. None of this could have been accomplished without the superb professional staff we were able to assemble in these years. Because of my narrow margin in 1986, I had agreed to let every employee then on the payroll keep his or her job, although I knew all too well the inadequacies of the staff I was inheriting. When I asked our then finance director for his opinion on a particular budget question, for example, he would regularly say, "Let me think about it a few minutes, I'll be right back," then take a stroll across the hall to talk to the mayor's budget or finance director. Likewise, our lawyer would go to the city's corporation counsel. That's not what I wanted. I wanted independent staff of equal excellence.

Fortunately, our new finance director, Marc Shaw, had been in place for over a year by the time of the Brian Watkins tragedy. We hired him when he was only an assistant to the Republican senate's finance staff in Albany, as well as a registered Republican. But his enthusiasm and imaginative ideas together with terrific references and background won over Joe Strasburg and me completely. Besides his budgetary prowess, Marc had a keen sense for which taxes the state was likely to pass, and which they would reject. He proved a steadying hand during months of terrible financial news. He was even quoted by the *New York Times* as declaring cheerfully: "If one likes chaos, this is the place to be."

Marc's skills had proved essential during our first one-on-one budget negotiations with the mayor's office. With the Board of Estimate now defunct, we had to take full responsibility—and we did. Right before the deadline, we agreed on the most difficult budget I had seen in sixteen years, one that led to the largest tax increase in city history as well as the hiring of more police officers and cuts in services. It was a trade-off, with both sides getting some of what we wanted and losing some—the Staten Island Ferry ride, for example, which had been a quarter, went up to fifty cents.

As Dave Dinkins said, no one was "fully satisfied . . . there is still much more that we would like to do." Most important, however, the council and mayor had pulled together, not apart, in their first test of the new system.

Richard Weinberg, who became the counsel to the council as well as to my office, put together an excellent cadre of young and enthusiastic lawyers to staff the committees and help the individual members of the council introduce and pass legislation. And even though later he both defended the council against suits brought by Mayor Giuliani and actually sued him, Rudy was extensive in his praise of Richard when he appointed him criminal court judge at the end of his and my term.

Telling the truth and establishing credibility was most important in dealing with the media, and no one has ever done it better than Peg Breen, whom Joe Strasburg and I selected to be in charge of the council communications office. Peg was able to absorb and accurately explain to the City Hall press corps any issue that ever came up in the council, whether legal, financial, or political, no matter how complex. Peg also taught me everything I know about handling the media, and that was a great deal.

Jonathan Drapkin became the head of our new Office of Oversight and Investigations and did an incomparable job assisting all twenty-two standing committees perform their oversight functions over scores of different mayoral agencies.

Finally, once it became clear that the City Council would have final say over any change of use or zoning approved by the City Planning Commission, we embarked on a countrywide search for the best person to head up our land use office and found her right on our doorstep in Gail Benjamin. An urban planner by trade, Gail had represented Comptroller Jay Goldin at the Board of Estimate, and was head of the city's environmental review process when she started working for the council in January 1990. She and her deputy Andy Lynn, who came to us from the Charter Revision Commission, went out and in turn hired thirty-five of the best land use staff to investigate every land use matter that comes before the council.

Joe, Richard, Marc, Peg, Gail, and Jonathan—these were the principal staff members who would gather at eight every morning in my City Hall office to discuss the day's events. I don't know how I could have managed without them. As the months and years went by other top staff and kitchen cabinet included my former intern and brilliant lawyer Ralph Miles and successive chiefs of staff Kevin McCabe, Bruce Bender, and John Banks; also successive communications directors Dick Reilly, Michael

Clendenin, and Michael Regan. Finally, the one person who was always there when needed, Gary Altman, counsel to the Speaker's office, prepared the agenda for the stated meetings and was always my "go-to" guy when I wanted to know the status of anything in the nearly four-century history of the city. I don't think Gary ever even told a "white lie" in his life, and he is a model of veracity and integrity. He still works at the City Council and teaches government classes with me at Fordham University and now at Baruch's College of Public Affairs.

Once my staff was all in place, I could not function as an effective legislative leader in the new system without bringing the borough delegations together. I asked each delegation to elect a borough representative to meet with me at least once a week to share leadership decisions. We called this the Steering Group, avoiding, as Richard Weinberg suggested, the use of the word *committee.* (A committee must always be open to the public and the press.) This group became critically important in governing the council. There was Deputy Majority Leader Archie Spigner from Queens, who did so much to heal race relations during some very turbulent years; new Finance chair Herb Berman from Brooklyn, whose boundless energy and unfailing good humor were always there when needed; majority whip and chair of Youth Services and later Health Victor Robles (now city clerk), one of the most dynamic chairs in the entire history of the council, who remained loyal to the very end and never failed to round up the necessary votes when we really needed them. And then there was the hardworking chair of the Land Use Committee, June Eisland from the Bronx, who together with her distinguished and scrupulously honest predecessor Jerry Crispino had an unblemished record of achievement in a difficult and complex area; also Stanley Michels, chair of the Environmental Committee from Manhattan, who somehow always managed to get the Manhattan delegation together when it counted and fought hardest to keep rent regulations in place; and finally chair of Economic Development Jerome O'Donovan from Staten Island, who brought equal stature to a borough that had been too long forgotten. During budget negotiations we expanded this group to include Mary Pinkett, chair of Government Operations; Wendell Foster, Parks Committee chair; Morty Povman, chair of the Rules Committee; and Priscilla Wooten, chair of the Education Committee.

All of us developed lasting friendships and bonded for the good of the council and of the city. So that the remaining members of the council did not feel left out, the "borough reps" met with their respective delegations to pass along what went on in Steering Group meetings. Top staff was made available to each member as requested. Further, I never refused to meet with any member, including after the council was expanded to fifty-one members in January of 1992. I made it my policy to share every official piece of paper I received with every member of the council: I was determined that there would be no council secrets during my tenure. This open process represents (and remains) a huge difference from the closed deal making that rules Albany. Indeed, one of the main reasons I ran for governor in 1998 was to open up state government in a similar manner. I firmly believe that the more you open government to its elected representatives and the public, the more you are likely to receive the support and cooperation necessary to succeed. This is especially true in bad economic cycles.

The glue that kept this new and empowered City Council together was the trust we developed in one another and in our staff. By and large we always came together on budgetary matters and on important citywide issues. The norm we all agreed upon: anyone who wanted to become a committee chair and part of the council leadership was obligated to stick together on so-called leadership votes. This was broken into two parts: (1) budgetary votes, and (2) institutional matters.

On budgetary matters we had six months to argue how to fairly allocate the expense and capital budgets for the entire city. Since only the mayor could set the revenue estimates and about 95 percent of the expense budget was already fixed in salaries and other mandated costs, the room we had to maneuver, even in a budget that had grown to $40 billion by 2000, was only several hundred million dollars. The mayor would come out with his priorities in the middle of January, and we had until June 5 to examine, negotiate, amend, and finally adopt the budget by a majority vote. If the mayor vetoed the budget, it would take a two-thirds vote to override the veto. State law held that if both the city and state comptrollers certified that the budget was in deficit by more than $100 million, the Financial Control Board could declare an emergency and take over city finances, as almost happened in the mid-'70s. If this happened again so many of the programs we had fought so hard to implement—such as Safe Streets, Safe City, senior citizen services and social programs, youth centers, libraries, cultural institutions, and nonprofit organizations throughout the city—would be the first items to be cut. We therefore agreed to work together, around the clock if necessary, until we all agreed on a budget. This helped immeasurably when it came to dealing with three very different and forceful mayors.

They knew how difficult it was to get a majority of legislators to agree, and so the final face-to-face between the mayor and me as Speaker usually went smoothly. For the most part the council acted responsibly, never exceeding fixed revenue estimates without making corresponding cuts. Ed Koch, David Dinkins, and Rudy Giuliani remain good and close friends of mine until this day. While we had many disagreements and even sued one another, we never lied or deliberately misstated a fact. Truthfulness was the bond that kept us going during the many crises that occurred in each administration. Further, the council was never late in adopting a budget before the start of the next fiscal year, unlike most other state and city legislatures throughout the country.

I was criticized for recommending that the full council vote to strip several council members from their committee chairs because they voted against the budget. They preferred the publicity and the mantle of "hero" for their actions. This happened only on three occasions over the course of my sixteen-year tenure, but it never happened without the council member knowingly breaking his or her word and knowing in advance the consequences. Contrary to press reports, the districts they represented never lost funding. It was not a question of punishment, but rather the removal of a reward. A member who could not vote yes on crucial leadership issues was violating the consensus agreement that was a condition of that reward. My successor, Speaker Gifford Miller, is bright, honest, and articulate. He and his successors must find their own way to keep the council an effective and united legislative body.

Furthermore, the door was always open for the three "stripped" council members to regain a chair if they renewed their commitment. The best excuse I received from one of the three who voted against the budget after participating fully in the budget process and agreeing it was fair and equitable was, "I can't stand the mayor and want to send him a message." What would happen to our city if all council members voted "to send a message" rather than do what was best for the people?

One of the most difficult votes for council members came in 1991. In order to implement the Safe Streets, Safe City plan, we had to vote in a modest real estate hike amounting to about $20 for the average city homeowner, and a temporary income tax surcharge of about $100 for the average wage earner. Because of redistricting and expansion of the council, a special election was called, and members were running that same year. Some had pledged never to vote for another tax hike. The tax increase was particularly difficult for members of the Queens delegation, who represented mostly homeowners, so if other delegations were to fall in line I would first have to make sure that the Queens delegation was unanimous. Walter Ward, the dean of the Queens delegation, had represented the Rockaways for over twenty years and had never previously voted for a real estate tax hike. Walter was tall and handsome—in looks he reminded me of Gary Cooper or Walter Pidgeon, the stage and screen stars of his era. This would be a very painful vote for him, he told me: he was certain he would lose his seat if he broke his promise and voted for a real estate tax hike. I said to him, "Walter, you are such a fixture of stability in your district, you could never lose!" After much persistence on my part Walter finally gave in, the last Queens member to so agree.

The only member of the Queens delegation who faced an imminent primary from a prominent opponent was Karen Koslowitz. Karen had recently replaced Arthur Katzman, who had retired in mid-term, and her special election was only a month away. Since she stood a real danger of losing, I had told her that she was "off the hook" and did not have to vote for any tax increase. Nevertheless she said she would support it, and indeed, when it came to the roll call, she stood up and courageously voted "Aye." At almost the same moment, the tall figure of Walter loomed over me. He said he had changed his mind and would vote no. I immediately stopped the roll call and took a five-minute recess.

If Walter voted no, the commitment I had made to the other delegations would be breached. I brought Walter over to Karen and said, "Karen, all bets are off. Walter has just informed me that he will not vote for the real estate tax. There's no way you can win in the adjacent district if he votes no, so you may want to change your vote. As a matter of fact, quite a few members may do likewise."

To her great credit she answered, "I will not change my vote. It's more important to have cops on the street and make this city safe again than it is for me to win an election."

After a brief pause that seemed like an eternity to me, Walter changed his mind again and said, "Okay, if she can do it I guess I can, too."

The rest is history. The only two members who voted against Safe Streets, Safe City were two of the "stripped" members.

It also turned out Walter was right. He lost the election the following year to his Republican opponent, Al Stabile, while ironically Karen won. Walter died of natural causes a few years later, and his grateful community successfully lobbied to name the local public school after him. The council followed suit with a local law renaming a playground in his honor, and thereby ensuring that he will forever be remembered.

The other kind of critical leadership vote—on institutional matters—involved votes on questions that affected the council when it was under attack from the powerful office of the mayor. These occasions were infrequent, but usually involved the mayor attempting to break off individual members from the leadership.

One such instance led to the dismissal of Mike DeMarco from his long-time position as chairman of the Finance Committee. From the first moment in 1986 when I had agreed to take on DeMarco as finance chairman one of my conditions had been that he curb his tendency to undercut my authority. I had been forced to read him the riot act about this several times, but the straw that broke the camel's back came in 1989 in a dispute between the council and the mayor's office over whether or not to reimburse seniors for Medicare Part B charges.

Koch's staff had been working furiously to peel away individual members from the united "leadership" position in favor of reimbursement, applying pressure in the form of promises to include specific member items in the expense and capital budgets. In the face of such inducements it was even more important for the council to stand firm on our position. The mayor actually convened a meeting in the Board of Estimate meeting room to have a hearing on the question, raising the relatively simple dispute to an institutional tug of war. When I entered the meeting room that day with my chief of staff and a couple of aides, the first thing I noticed was that Mike DeMarco and Ed Koch were sitting together and smiling at each other. I knew at once what had happened.

In fact, the council had its way with reimbursement despite the defection of its Finance chair, and ten months later I summoned Mike, ran through the litany of instances in which he'd been out of step on important "institutional" matters, and told him he was being switched from Finance chair to chair of the newly-created Committee on Committees, a powerless position.

Mike was a big brusque guy who could sometimes sound threatening, and my security guards had not wanted me to face him alone. He was very upset, but I reminded him of my repeated warnings and pointed out that he had brought it on himself. Mike never challenged the council as an institution again. And as soon as a vacancy occurred in the important State

Legislation Committee, Mike became chair and the Committee on Committees went the way of the Board of Estimate. Ironically, Mike, one of the original "sure" votes for me in my one-vote victory in 1986, was replaced as Finance chair by Herb Berman, the very man the Brooklyn and Manhattan delegations had been maneuvering to place there in their failed cabal that same day.

The only other unwritten rule I insisted on as Vice Chair and Speaker was that every member was free to vote yes or no on any issue, but please, no surprises—at least have the good sense to familiarize yourself with the issue and advise the chair of the committee in question the reasons you will vote no. Nothing ever came out of a standing committee without debate and necessary changes, and every member was free to contribute. On one occasion a member voted no on a gun control bill thinking that 22-caliber pistols were not included; if he had asked beforehand, he would have learned that they were indeed included. This was not a leadership vote, but it was an important issue and deserved more attention.

A casual observer of a "stated meeting" (a regular, full session of the council) might think that little debate is taking place there, but in truth these "intros" have been the subject of from one to a dozen committee hearings before they ever reach the floor of the council. These committee hearings, which are open to the public, are the forum where extensive debate takes place. By the time the whole council gets to vote on an intro, it has already been passed out of committee. Because of this, the time for debate on the floor is limited to two minutes unless the intro is "set aside" and the time extended to ten minutes. If every intro were set aside, nothing of substance would ever get done. Dozens of routine land use matters are on a time clock and must be acted on expeditiously. Members learn quickly to focus on and debate only important matters on the agenda. The only items on an agenda that do not go through committee are certain resolutions, usually ceremonial in nature, which require a unanimous vote. Even one negative vote on these sends them to the appropriate committee.

For loquacious members, time is set aside to discuss any matter whatsoever, but only after the roll call of votes is finished. Because no one is thus forced to hear endless orations, council meetings are timely and efficient, and attendance is usually nearly unanimous. This is not true in Albany or Washington. I am convinced this is because representatives sleep over at least a few nights per week and are really trapped a great distance from home. Why not drag the meetings out? They have few other places to go.

In the city, the council members are only a few minutes from their local offices, where they are needed to handle local matters. They are not looking to hang around City Hall. Priority of time is reversed during budget time, when members spend long hours at City Hall and in frequent finance and state legislation meetings. This is also true when important land use matters are discussed, such as the future of Yankee and Shea Stadiums, the train-to-the-plane extension to JFK airport, banning sex shops from residential areas and cleaning up Forty-second Street, or the "Potty Parity" law (more toilets for women in public restrooms), passed in June of 2005.

15

David Dinkins, Heart of the City

In January 1990, shortly after Mayor Dinkins's inauguration, a Haitian woman named Giselaine Fetissainte entered the Korean-owned Family Red Apple grocery store in the Flatbush section of Brooklyn and became embroiled in a dispute over a couple of peppers. At the end of the argument she wound up on the floor of the store. She claimed she had been insulted and assaulted; the Korean owners of the store claimed she had refused to pay the full amount for her purchases, threatened and spat at them, then collapsed when they attempted to restrain her. The woman brought charges against the grocers and at least two separate African-American-led community groups initiated a boycott of the store where the incident took place, targeting as well another Korean store across the street, which organizers claimed was linked to Family Red Apple.

The boycotts attracted a great many black people who felt they had been insulted or demeaned by Korean store owners at these and other stores throughout the city. Protesters descended upon Flatbush. A climate of intimidation and fear was created by radical organizers, including a black activist named Sonny Carson. For their part the Koreans were determined not to cave in. The store owner in this case was a relatively young Korean who had invested his life's work in building up the store and, though he had been charged with the assault, had not even been present when the incident took place. The facts had little effect on the passions aroused by the symbolism of the incident. The boycott gained momentum in the black community, and among some of Mayor Dinkins's own supporters, that was hard to stop. The Korean community throughout the city, feeling unfairly accused of bias, also became aroused.

His reputation as a healer of race relations was one of the biggest pluses Dinkins had brought to the mayor's office. His low-key manner was the opposite of Ed Koch's bravado, which sometimes inflamed race relations rather than calmed them. In his recent past as borough president Dinkins and his staff had successfully negotiated an end to similar conflicts between blacks and Koreans in Harlem—usually by the owners selling the store or making some form of symbolic amends or reparations. In this case, however, the behind-the-scenes efforts of Deputy Mayor Bill Lynch and other members of the new administration got nowhere. Nor did the mayor's carefully calibrated declaration that he saw the boycott as economically rather than racially motivated, and was opposed in principle to boycotts as a way of achieving economic justice. Ed Koch and others called on him to go to the scene, confront the boycotters, and work with the Korean owner. Many minority council members had sympathy for the protesters because of their own experiences. By and large, however, they sided with majority opinion in the council that we should not let the boycotters put the Koreans out of business. No elected official wanted to heighten racial tensions, but matters got worse as time went on. The mayor's refusal to be anything but a gentleman began to look ineffective.

The Korean community appealed to Dinkins to become actively involved in settling the dispute. After a few months this became a question of halting the boycott. Its organizers were willing to settle for only one thing: the closing of Family Red Apple. The mayor appointed a special panel to look into the merits of both sides. Unfortunately, some members of the panel had ties to the boycott supporters, and ended up issuing a report that did nothing to resolve the questions raised.

After more than eight months the boycotters began to lose public support, even in their own community. Frustrated by the lack of progress, the City Council decided to hold hearings on the situation in September. At those hearings state assembly speaker Mel Miller, who lived near the scene of the boycott, condemned the boycott as racially motivated. Like Ed Koch earlier, he called on Mayor Dinkins to break the boycott by shopping at the store. About ten days later, after courts had severely restricted the boycotters' tactics and public opinion turned strongly against them, Dinkins put in a public appearance at the store and made purchases of about $10. The boycott was over, but the mayor's reputation as a healer had been seriously compromised.

Concurrent with the Korean boycott, Mayor Dinkins's racial sensitivities were tested by the ambiguous results of the "Bensonhurst trials." These stemmed from the 1989 killing of a black teenager, Yusef Hawkins, in the predominantly white neighborhood of Bensonhurst. That killing had been seen by many as a tragic symbol of the racist dangers that confront any young black male in white America; others saw the attempt to draw lessons from the tragedy as a politically correct attempt to impose shame on an entire neighborhood for what was not a racial killing, but a tragic case of mistaken identity. Of thirty youths the prosecutors identified as having participated in the confrontation, only eight were charged and one convicted of murder; four others were convicted on lesser charges and three acquitted. As the trials dragged on, African-American activists like Al Sharpton conducted marches through Bensonhurst. Sharpton was attacked and stabbed during one such march, confirming to his supporters the neighborhood's usefulness as a symbol of racism.

Even worse racial tensions arose in August 1991 from a tragic series of events in yet a third Brooklyn neighborhood. Crown Heights had long been the site of seething tensions between the predominantly black Caribbean populace and an active community of Hasidic Lubavitcher Jews. The Hasids are extremely self-reliant. Many African-Americans felt that their determination to defend themselves, including formation of their own neighborhood patrols, was too much like taking the law into their own hands. This resentment was exacerbated by the apparent cooperation between the Hasidic groups and the city police.

On Monday night, August 19, "these tensions spilled over," according to the *New York Times,* "as the Lubavitcher Grand Rebbe Menachem Schneerson was returning from his regular weekly visit to the grave of his wife at Montefiore Cemetery, accompanied by the unmarked police car normally sent along with him as both a courtesy and a security measure." In the same group of cars was a dark blue station wagon. The driver was one of Rebbe Schneerson's followers. The station wagon found itself trailing behind the other cars somewhere around President Street, and ran a red light to catch up. In the process it hit another car, which sent the station wagon careening onto the sidewalk. There, seven-year-old Gavin Cato and his cousin Angela were playing not far from their apartment. According to the *Times,* "The station wagon plowed into them, pinning them against a steel grate, killing Gavin."

The tragedy was compounded when young black men attacked the driver of the station wagon just as two ambulances arrived almost simultaneously at the scene. One was the city's regular emergency vehicle. The other was a private, Hasidic-operated ambulance. The police told the Hasidic ambulance, whose crew also came under attack, to take the driver and leave the scene, to help preserve the peace. Rumors quickly spread among the crowd of black youths, enlarged by several hundred who had just left a nearby B. B. King concert, that "the ambulance" had given preferential treatment to the driver rather than to the dying child and his injured cousin. Within an hour or two, according to the same *Times* account, "hundreds of black youths began running through the streets, smashing windows, turning over at least one car, shouting 'Jew! Jew!'"

Mayor Dinkins arrived in Crown Heights within a few hours of the accident and visited the injured girl in the hospital, where he also called for peace and that "no more be hurt." He could not know then that the young black men prowling along President Street had already exacted their "revenge" for the accidental death of young Gavin Cato. A group of them crowded around the car of a young Yeshiva student visiting from Australia. When he tried to get out, they stabbed him and left him bleeding on the hood of the car. He died a few hours later.

Yet more tragedy followed. The next night Crown Heights was swept by disorder. As African-Americans and Hasidic Jews each mourned their victims, swarms of hot, angry black youths looted and set fire to stores, burned vehicles, and rioted against the "white Jew murderers." Mayor Dinkins, trying to avert a full-scale race riot, attempted to apply salve to the raw emotions on both sides by returning to Crown Heights to visit Hasidic leaders and meet at a school with a group of skeptical young blacks. While the hotheads on the street vented their rage that the driver of the station wagon was not in custody, Police Commissioner Lee Brown issued public statements asking that police officers show respect for "the community's feelings."

The mayor's and his commissioner's appeals for peace again failed to calm the disorder. Instead a protest march called by Sonny Carson, Vernon Mason, Al Sharpton, and others escalated out of their control. Just a few minutes after Commissioner Brown assured the press that his officers had the situation under control, a group of reporters and police that included his own security detail were confronted with a rock-throwing crowd of some two hundred youths and forced to take refuge inside the school Mayor Dinkins was about to visit. After the inconclusive school meeting, the mayor was trapped for some time by a jeering mob inside Gavin Cato's family's apartment.

On this fateful second full day of disorders the "hold-back" policies of the police commissioner and New York's most compassionate mayor nearly got the better of them. Police union officials were criticizing the mayor for not letting the cops loose against the youthful rioters. Hasidic groups, which had offered to assist the police by "going after" young men throwing rocks from apartment buildings, began to talk about a "pogrom." My former aide and political advisor Ralph Miles, who served as a board member on the Jewish Community Relations Council, came to see me with several others, including Judah Gribetz, former counsel to Governor Carey and Mayor Beame. These men were in touch with Jewish groups in Crown Heights and monitoring the situation carefully. They told me that they had been overwhelmed by calls from reliable people complaining about an atmosphere of terror; that Jews felt "under siege"; that some Jews had been beaten up; that police officers were under orders to exercise restraint and were in effect doing nothing to bring order to the streets, no matter how many times the police commissioner declared the situation was under control.

I had been reluctant to get publicly involved in this ugly standoff, but my friends Ralph and Judah had 100 percent credibility, and when they told me I should not accept the mayor's public assurances, I decided I had to send David a handwritten note asking him to get tough on the rioters immediately, and that I would back him all the way. The next day he did precisely that, establishing a major police presence under orders to stop any more outbreaks. Order quickly returned to the streets of Crown Heights.

At Gavin Cato's memorial service a couple days later Mayor Dinkins continued to try to ease tensions, stating: "Two tragedies. One a tragedy because it was an accident. The other a tragedy because it was not." A little later he equated the killing of Yankel Rosenbaum with a "lynching." However, a year later the young man police identified as the seventeen-year-old assailant of Yankel Rosenbaum was acquitted of first-degree murder, despite having been captured soon after the killing with the bloody knife in his pocket. Council member Noach Dear introduced and tried to pass a resolution condemning the acquittal in terms similar to those the New York City Council had used in a resolution condemning the acquittal of the white police officers in Los Angeles who had almost killed Rodney King a few months before. The issue was still too raw; tempers frayed, and white and black council members, usually civil to one another, exchanged insults and nearly came to blows.

After Crown Heights the reputation for healing that had won David Dinkins the mayor's job in 1989 suffered permanent damage. His mayoralty never quite recovered. His approach in this instance—to offer inspirational speeches aimed at making the city come together—was heartfelt, sincere, and in other circumstances might well have been the perfect antidote to crisis. But it offered little in immediate reassurance to a traumatized city.

In his first two years David was also hurt by a bad economic situation and from having to adjust to the new city government that went into effect in 1990 and gave the City Council much more power than before. The final step in the city's restructuring took place that same autumn of 1991, when a rare "midterm" vote was held to elect a new fifty-one-member City Council, enlarged and redistricted to ensure better representation for minority groups.

The redistricting plan governing the election of the new council members in 1991 was neither the best nor the fairest redistricting plan that could have been drawn, but it accomplished its purpose. It raised the representation of blacks and Hispanics on the council from around 25 to 40 percent of the membership, still short of their approximate 50 percent share of the population, but nevertheless "a stunning result," according to the U.S. Justice Department's civil rights division. (By 2001 black and Hispanic representation had increased to 50 percent, although Asian-Americans, with only one council member, were still underrepresented.) During the same election, Republican representation on the council went from one to five seats. This blossoming of the two-party system, while it did not bode particularly well for the Dinkins administration, was a healthy development for the city's politics. Moderate centrists prevailed. As I said at the time, "The real message is that we can't just be raising taxes and spending. People want to downsize government."

Philosophically, the differences between Mayor Dinkins and me were more matters of emphasis and means. David liked to talk about the "gorgeous mosaic" of different ethnicities and races in New York, and I preferred the older idea of the "melting pot." I always felt the council needed to adequately represent the bedrock of the city's population, the middle class in all its racial and ethnic varieties. Our priorities emphasized basic services like schools, libraries, and transportation as opposed to complex social services programs for the poor. I was in favor of some such programs, but I knew that the city could not afford to pay for them on its own without driving its taxpaying citizens to the suburbs. The federal government, not the city, should be funding them. I also favored commonsense laws like the one we passed to allow homeowners to do construction work between 10 A.M. and 5 P.M. on weekends, despite the city's anti-noise ordinance. Out of budgetary necessity, and with the opportunities presented by a Democratic Congress and later a president in Washington, David Dinkins came to accept many of my positions. By the time of the 1991 council elections, the mayor and I were better able to emphasize our common political ground and accommodate each other's different political personalities.

Personally, David and I had dramatically different operating styles. It's true we were both known for our integrity and good manners. I, however, am a direct, can-do kind of guy, impatient to take whatever action is possible. In 1990 I was determined to bring the City Council forcibly and immediately into the late-twentieth century. David, on the other hand, was the picture of a thoughtful gentleman. He is cautious, meticulous, happy to delegate responsibilities, and hates to be rushed. Having recently been a member of the Board of Estimate, he was also used to getting things done by speaking to only seven people.

Our first couple of years working together were marked by normal friction and growing pains. While his deputy mayor Bill Lynch was largely an effective behind-the-scenes operator in the political world, his deputy mayor Norman Steisel, despite unquestionable management savvy, created antagonism wherever he went. Steisel had come into the Dinkins administration with superb credentials, having served under Mayors Lindsay, Beame, and Koch. As sanitation commissioner during the first two terms of the Koch administration he completely turned around the lackluster performance of that department. Steisel was undoubtedly brilliant, but his abrasive personality made him an odd representative for such a courtly mayor. The bare-knuckle methods he employed as the central executive power in the Dinkins administration led to repeated clashes between mayoral and council staffs. David loyally defended Steisel, but more than once I was forced to warn him that if Norman didn't watch his mouth, someone was going to pop him one.

My one-on-one conversations with David were invariably pleasant, but circumstance and personal habit combined to make them less frequent than desirable. We were both avid tennis players, but he played his game first thing in the morning, which was my concentrated working time. I tried to leave City Hall on quiet afternoons so that I could stay in touch with my home district and the city at large. As a result our schedules matched only infrequently, and we rarely used the "hot line" connecting our offices. Miscommunication sometimes resulted.

For example, at one point David called John Cardinal O'Connor to ask me to "back off" on the pressure I was applying for more cops at a time of diminishing funds for essential social services. When I received a call from the cardinal's secretary saying that he wanted to put me through to the cardinal at the request of the mayor, I became about as mad as I have ever been in my years of public service. I had been brought up to believe that you don't mix religion and politics. I had never even heard a politician or elected official speak in a Roman Catholic church. Though the cardinal and I were good friends and had frequent breakfasts together, I told his secretary to tell him that the dispute was between the mayor and me and that I would not talk to him about it.

I then headed straight for Gracie Mansion. David was having a staff meeting in the basement; I entered unannounced and asked to see him privately upstairs. There, I heatedly told him, "Mr. Mayor, do not ever call the cardinal or my wife on any political or governmental matter that is between you and me! I am outraged that you would think that the cardinal, or even the Pope, would change my mind about hiring more cops or any other issue between you as mayor and me as speaker!" David apologized, and I soon calmed down.

To the mayor's credit no such incident ever happened again. Years later when I was running for governor I realized that David had meant no disrespect in calling the cardinal, and that it was primarily the Catholic Church that keeps the rule about no politicians in its public pulpits. Elsewhere it seems perfectly acceptable to mix religion and politics, even if it means skirting the tax exemption.

During our second two years of concurrent office David and I had a much better working relationship. He came to understand I wasn't being personal when I had critical words about his actions as mayor, and we were able to enjoy a cooperative relationship as both friends and political allies. The fruits of this working relationship became visible early in 1992 when the mayor and the council worked together to pass major recycling and energy legislation and also reached a budget accord ahead of time, with little discord and wrangling.

My interest in energy issues can probably be traced back to the neighborhood I grew up in, sandwiched as it is between two of the largest power plants in the world and sitting astride a crossroads of airports, water, bridges, and tunnels. My first entry into public life came when I led a protest against the Lindsay administration's proposal to double the coal-burning capacity of Big Alice, the power plant in Long Island City. By the mid-1980s it had become clear to most council members that the city faced an impending garbage crisis: we had run out of room to store our waste.

The poisonous effects of dumping it had become clear. Historic methods for burning it had produced unacceptable levels of pollution and noxious waste. And shipping it out was becoming expensive and more and more difficult. For these reasons the council had passed and funded recycling laws over the objections of both the Koch and Dinkins administrations. Finally, in the early spring of 1992, the council was able to pass the largest recycling bill in the world, one that promised to handle a good 25 percent of the city's garbage within five years.

Recycling of a different sort would soon become even more important to the city's garbage management plans: namely the conversion of some of the city's garbage into energy through new, environmentally sound burning technologies. For several years a plan had been floating around to build a major garbage-to-energy incinerator at the largely unused Brooklyn Navy Yard. Environmental and neighborhood groups had expressed legitimate concerns about the possible polluting effects of such a plant. David Dinkins had opposed the building of the plant in 1989 when he ran against Ed Koch—under the conditions and with the technology then proposed. By the middle of his administration, however, David, like me, had become convinced that in a city our size even the most ambitious recycling plan would never dispose of all our waste, and that some incineration was inevitable. I did not support waste-to-energy "incinerators" until I personally visited two such efficient and environmentally safe plants in Connecticut and Massachusetts and my staff and experts had convinced me that they were as clean as those that burned low sulphur oil.

While the technology had been improving, the opposition to building another incinerator anywhere had been growing for several years. The mere use of the word "incinerator" was used by some demagogues to elicit images of toxic, cancer-producing gases descending upon helpless neighborhoods. Still, something had to be done about the old-fashioned, pollution-spewing incinerators that were currently in use. It would have been much easier to duck the issue altogether. But the garbage problem was not going to go away.

By the early summer of 1992 the Dinkins administration and the City Council had jointly introduced a comprehensive solid waste management plan that called for increased recycling, the upgrading of three existing incinerators, and the building of a state-of-the-art incinerator at the Brooklyn Navy Yard. Although most of the council leadership and I favored the basic outlines of the bill, the proposal aroused intense opposition from several organized public groups who were applying pressure upon individual council members to vote down the proposal. In fact, nearly two-thirds of the council members stood on the steps of City Hall in early summer and vowed to defeat the measure.

Recognizing the legitimate concerns of some of these opponents, I was able to head off this open "revolt" of council members on July 9 by getting them to agree to postpone the council vote for six more weeks. During that time the council's environmental protection committee held public hearings throughout the five boroughs and at City Hall. These hearings were not just for "show," but meant to give the boroughs and their representatives a real chance to improve the bill. I spelled out the guidelines the council leadership was following in my radio address of August 11:

1. The council is pushing for citywide recycling at a significantly earlier date than originally proposed.
2. Even at the highest realistically achievable level of recyling, some incineration will be necessary.
3. All incinerators are not equal. While older ones are dinosaurs, today's technology is safer and cleaner. The council will make sure that the technology meets environmental concerns and will never agree to a plan posing unacceptable health risks.

At the same time I made sure to remind my listeners of the purpose underlying the legislation in the first place. We already incinerated oil, natural gas, and coal to make energy. We even burned dirty coal in our schools. If we had to burn anything at all, it made much more sense to incinerate garbage, since for every ton of garbage burned, we did not have to incinerate one barrel of expensive imported oil. As I said, "We cannot, and will not, drown in our garbage. We must act."

The next several weeks were frantic as Mayor Dinkins's political wizard Bill Lynch and I went about persuading recalcitrant council members to support compromise legislation that involved shutting down two of the city's incinerators and upgrading a third. (True to form, Deputy Mayor Norman Steisel nearly torpedoed the accord by stating publicly near the end of our delicate negotiations that the plan did not guarantee that other new incinerators would never be built.) The bill that emerged accelerated recycling, going so far as to make construction of the Navy Yard incinerator contingent upon it. The discussions on the final day continued around the clock, with the 7:30 A.M. vote to approve the measure registering 36 in favor, 15 opposed. This was a great triumph, given that earlier in the summer thirty-four members had been publicly opposed. The *New York Times* made a telling remark about the institutional sea change in city governance made evident by the intensity of this political process: The "intense brokering . . . reflected just how much the Council has replaced the board [of Estimate] as the center of municipal affairs." When Mayor Dinkins signed the bill two weeks later I felt the *Times* had been right to call our leadership "clean and courageous," and the legislation a "New Dawn for the City."

Alas, we were too far ahead of our time. David Dinkins's support for the garbage-to-energy incinerator in the Brooklyn Navy Yard possibly cost him the election a year later when Rudy Giuliani gained significant political mileage by opposing it. The facility was not built, recycling languished for a decade, and once again, New York City is drowning in its own garbage. The vision of creating our own energy by using some of the city's waste has since become part of the unfortunately as-yet-unrealized legacies of the Dinkins years.

David Dinkins and I worked with noted success in two other areas during the later years: on legislation reestablishing the Civilian Complaint Review Board (CCRB) as an independent civilian-member body with subpoena and investigative authority, and in establishing a procedure for responsible review of land use change in the city.

Mayor Dinkins knew something needed to be done to reestablish better relations between the largely white city police force and many of his minority constituents. Early in his term he proposed establishing a civilian board with no ties to the police as a board that could review controversial actions of officers. For years I had been convinced that the uniformed officers had been largely effective and fair in policing themselves and that more communication, rather than another agency, could accomplish David's purpose.

What happened in the fall of 1992 changed my mind. On September 16 a police union rally near City Hall, addressed by Dinkins's expected antagonist Rudy Giuliani, degenerated into chaos. A crowd of unruly off-duty police officers were so frustrated with the Dinkins administration that they shouted epithets about the mayor, including racial insults, knocked down their own police barricades, and, effectively unrestrained by their uniformed colleagues, took over the Brooklyn Bridge, shutting it down for an hour. The poisonous after-effects of that rally changed my mind about the independent review board and significantly changed the political climate as well. I had always been a supporter of the police, if not of their union. However I could not countenance, even implicitly, the breakdown of law and order among those sworn to uphold it.

The mayor, who had signed into law the biggest boost for the police force in two decades, was visibly outraged by Rudy's continued defense of the police union and its leaders, despite the moblike behavior. For his part, Giuliani was unrelenting in his criticism of Dinkins. The racial divisions aroused by the Korean boycott and Crown Heights tragedies, as well as recent unrest between police and neighborhood residents in Washington Heights, was coming home to roost. Tempers were high on all sides, and nothing good could come out of further racial division in the city. In an effort to bring back some sense of comity, I helped fashion a compromise that would establish a police review board with members designated both by the mayor and the council, excluding police employees. Although it hurt me to find myself allied with Al Sharpton and attacked by many of my former police supporters, the legislation we passed succeeded in lowering the temperature of the debate.

Meanwhile, the council's record on land use after two or so years of exercising its new powers had proved its capacity for favoring the city's overall interests rather than the parochial interests of local neighborhoods. Real estate being an eternally contentious issue in New York, there had been real fears from the Charter Revision Commission that the council might adopt a small-minded attitude against development, but this did not prove to be the case. For example, the council as a whole overruled Mike DeMarco's objections to the building of a small condominium on City Island that was favored by his borough president and had passed a review from our land use office. Where once council members might have given the local council member final say, this time we decided that because the project was good for the county and the city, we would approve it despite Mike's objections. A small condominium, we reasoned, would not significantly alter the character of the City Island neighborhood of mostly single-family homes. The council's approval of the Brooklyn Navy Yard incinerator and of Riverside South, Donald Trump's housing development on the Upper West Side, are other examples of our ability to forge a consensus based on what's best for the city overall. When a top political consultant like Howard Rubenstein told me in February of 1992 that "real estate developers now know that decisions will be made on the merits," not just politics, it was truly music to my ears.

In the 1993 election rematch between David Dinkins and Rudy Giuliani, David was unable to capitalize on the solid achievements of his administration. He had a reputation, fueled by the city's cutthroat press, as hapless and inept, and for months Rudy had been trampling him in the opinion polls. Then, in the summer, the really bad news hit; a New York State report issued in late July about the Crown Heights debacle included a harsh indictment of several members of the Dinkins administration, including former Police Commissioner Brown, for failing to appreciate the severity of the situation and doing little to stop the rioting. It also criticized the mayor for not asserting his authority earlier. The timing was terrible for David's reelection efforts. As I wrote in my diary: "Giuliani should feast on it." A month later David suffered another political headache he should not have had to worry about, when members of his administration resigned for ethical violations.

Nonetheless, I endorsed David for mayor at the end of August and loaned him my then chief of staff, Kevin McCabe, to help with the campaign. Sure enough, the race tightened, this time with Democrats mostly coming back to Dinkins. It was not enough, however, and Rudy won by 45,000 votes—about the same spread by which David had beaten Rudy four years earlier. It was a small margin of victory but David, ever the perfect gentleman, did not even consider calling for a recount. He went out as he came in: with class. He delivered a well-spoken, elegant, and gracious concession speech, refused to engage in bitterness or throw fuel into the fire of racial tensions by calling attention to Rudy's questionable use of the cops against their own mayor.

David's prime concern throughout his four years of turbulence had always been to make sure that children's services were not cut—so much so that at first he even wanted to name our police buildup "Cops and Kids." His love for children was evident from the photographs he kept on the walls in his office, including not only his own children and grandchildren but also those of his many friends and associates. Just as Ed Koch represented the spirit of this indomitable city, so did David Dinkins represent its heart.

A major priority of mine during David's tenure—which he wholeheartedly supported—concerned the teaching of old-fashioned values to our public school children. We both knew that ultimately the only way to prevent racial conflict was through a long-term educational process. In recent years we had experienced too much misunderstanding and hatred to remain passive about seeing that our youth learned the fundamental values of getting along in a multicultural society.

As part of this effort I met with then Schools Chancellor Joseph Fernandez and School Board president Carl McCall in January of 1992 to publicize the fact that "release time" still existed for parents who wanted their children to receive religious instruction. They agreed that such instruction could be a valuable tool in teaching nonviolence, tolerance, and other important values, just as it was for me and my generation years ago. I still remember that as a student in PS 122, I used to walk under supervision with my fellow Catholics to the nearby Immaculate Conception School eight blocks away. Other classmates would go to their local Protestant church or synagogue, which were just as close. These Wednesday afternoon excursions became a veritable ecumenical march along Ditmars Boulevard in Astoria. It was a sure way to remind everyone that the word *Creator* meant getting along with and respecting one another no matter how different we were.

Religious instruction cannot, of course, reach everyone. So I also worked with my local School Board 30 in Northwestern Queens to develop and fund a pilot values program that came to be called LIVE, or "Lessons In Values Education." I asked superintendent Angelo Gimondo and his former assistant Anthony Petrocelli to construct a curriculum based on Micah's admonition to "do the right thing," and add to it the values mentioned in the following passage from the Eighty-fifth Psalm:

> *Kindness and truth shall meet,*
> *Justice and peace shall kiss,*
> *Truth shall spring out of the earth,*
> *And justice shall look down from heaven.*

The LIVE curriculum they developed is now taught throughout the public school system. It is based on six core values derived from a consensus of educators, parents, community leaders, and experts in moral education: respect, responsibility, honesty, kindness, freedom, and nonviolence. According to the curriculum's introduction, these values are to be fostered through a series of lessons and interdisciplinary activities drawn from "literature, fables, folktales, original stories, music, art, current events, and historical data."

If Mayor Dinkins attempted above all to be a mayor for children and youth, it was a job made all the more difficult by the state legislature's discriminatory treatment of New York City. For years Albany had cheated New York City schoolchildren out of hundreds of millions of dollars by not counting them the same way it does "upstate" schoolchildren. Several years ago the state's discriminatory educational funding was thrown out by the courts—a judgment repeatedly upheld despite appeals—yet as I write we are still awaiting the city's fair share. Another glaring example of Albany's financial discrimination against New York City: we are the only city that pays more than three billion dollars in Medicaid charges that in every other state are paid by state authorities. In truth, New York City is a city held hostage by upstate political powers.

Given these circumstances, David's contribution to the city's well-being was far from merely inspirational. He never gets the credit he deserves for helping to make this city safe. Because so many minorities resented the police, I doubt that anyone but David Dinkins could have "sold" Albany on the necessity for Safe Streets, Safe City—certainly not Ed Koch, Peter Vallone, or Rudy Giuliani. A white face would not have engendered the sense of necessity that Dinkins's did. Up in Albany, he went from minority member to minority member personally convincing them to vote for the bill. He and I were forced to eat humble pie just to get the resources to make this city safe. Together we had to beg, plead, and cajole the skeptical state legislature to allow us to tax ourselves—a legislature that can't even adopt its own budget on time. One senator from Queens insisted he would not vote for the bill unless we committed to providing a specific number of cops in his precinct. Unflappable, David proceeded to provide a guaranteed number for each and every precinct. Such humiliating treatment did not stop Mayor Dinkins, who deserves the respect and admiration of every New Yorker.

16

Rudy Giuliani, Brain of the City

On July 7, 1992, two months before he addressed the police union's anti-Dinkins rally on the steps of City Hall, Rudolph W. Giuliani invited me to lunch. It was the first time we had met. Although he knew I was going to support Mayor Dinkins's reelection, it was a remarkably friendly occasion. Far from the hard-nosed prosecutor I had come to think of, Rudy could not have been more genial, rising to vigorously shake my hand and complimenting me for my work in the council. Apart from his detailed knowledge about me, I was impressed with his understanding of the ins and outs of the city budget and upcoming legislation. My diary for that day reads: "Rudy could turn out to be A-OK."

A few days after Mayor Giuliani's inauguration on January 1, 1994, I arrived at the Speaker's office in City Hall as usual. I was anxious to get back to the drawing board on the Horse and Carriage Bill that Mayor Dinkins had vetoed as one of his last acts in office. I was determined to balance the necessity of treating horses humanely while doing the most to keep the tourist-friendly carriage horse industry (and its unions) in business. Extremists on both sides of the issue were attacking me, with some animal advocates seemingly satisfied at nothing less than having humans carry horses on their backs, and some horse owners ridiculing as outlandish regulations to keep horses out of serious weather and traffic. I believe that cruelty to animals is followed by cruelty to people, and I also believe in the right to work, so I was determined to find a way to "do the right thing" for both sides.

Much to my surprise Rudy Giuliani walked into my office at about 8:05 A.M. that January 3 to ask me a couple of questions: (1) Why is your side of City Hall so clean and my side so dirty?; and (2) What are you so busy working on? It was the first time I had ever heard of a mayor walking over to see the majority leader to consult on our mutual business (it had always been the other way around, and by invitation only). I told him so, and gave him a plaque inscribed with part of the Eighty-fifth Psalm, the part about "kindness and truth" that I had suggested as inspiration for the LIVE curriculum. I then explained to him that I was a bug about tidiness and had a good rapport with the cleaners at City Hall and was sure they would keep his offices just as clean if he asked. As for the work I was doing, I invited him to read over the proposed bill if he was really interested.

Lo and behold, he took copies of the mass of reports and testimony that had already gone into the first version of the bill and actually sat down and read them. I said to myself, I finally have a lawyer who understands something about legislation! Rudy then worked with me at creating a responsible, balanced bill, and the compromise Horse and Carriage measure, Local Law 2 of 1994, was the second piece of legislation he signed. By then I had realized that our new mayor was not only a "brain," but someone who was willing to work hard and ignore criticism when he thought he was right. This extraordinary self-conviction would prove to be both his strong and weak point over the next eight years.

For example, he was convinced that the Dinkins administration "did not have clean hands" when it came to the arrangement they had made with the U.S. Tennis Association to build a new tennis stadium near Shea Stadium in Queens. He thought Dinkins had been overly influenced by Sid Davidoff, the lobbyist for the USTA; coming from his prosecutorial background, he was always distrustful of any deal that involved people making money. He wanted us to use the council's powers to undo the negotiations.

"Why?" I asked.

"Well, I don't like the way it smells."

But my staff and I had worked hand in hand with Dinkins on this, and we monitored every section of it, I told him. Dave Dinkins is an honest man, and Sid Davidoff is a respected lobbyist. There was no wrongdoing, I assured him. Furthermore, the stadium would prove to be a tremendous shot in the arm for our ailing city—financially and otherwise.

As the stadium prepared to open in August of 1997, a few months before Rudy faced reelection, he decided to reopen the issue. He criticized the original agreement, especially the provision that called for planes landing at JFK and La Guardia airports to fly over a different section of Queens during the two weeks a year of the U.S. Tennis Open (those two weeks of tennis produce more revenue for the city than any other sporting event). The mayor even boycotted the opening ceremonies. However impassioned Rudy later became about building a new facility for the Yankees, I doubt that to this day he has ever gone to the new Arthur Ashe Tennis Stadium, named after the great black tennis player and AIDS activist. (In any event Rudy, unlike Dave Dinkins and me, plays golf, not tennis.)

Despite our excellent personal rapport, there was plenty about the art of governing a city that Rudy needed to learn before we could work together effectively. Kevin McCabe had replaced Joe Strasburg as my chief of staff soon after Rudy took office. Kevin came to me shortly thereafter and complained that, contrary to protocol, Rudy's aides had been scheduling meetings directly between council delegations and the mayor. Immediately I was reminded of Mike DeMarco sharing that secret smile with Ed Koch a few years earlier! This was no way for Rudy to start out our years together—peeling off council members to do the mayor's bidding. So Kevin walked over to the mayor's offices: "Are you out of your mind?" he asked them. "If you fractionalize the legislature, you'll never have a budget, you'll never have anything." I laid the episode down to the mayor's new staff, many of whom were prosecutors and used to having their own way.

The first substantive disagreement that arose between the new mayor and the council involved his ambitious plans for privatizing many city services. I've always been in favor of privatization, but only if it helps the people of New York, not for its own sake. Take sanitation. Of course, it's possible to find people who will pick up garbage more cheaply than our sanitation workers, but they won't clean the streets and clear the snow, too. When Rudy attempted to contract out a whole range of city services, the council passed a law stipulating that, before any such privatizations take place, hearings had to be held showing how the private business could provide an equivalent or better quality of service for less money. Rudy vetoed the bill, the City Council overrode his veto, and our law stands. Later, he came up with a cockamamie scheme to charge homeowners when the Sanitation Department removed bags of leaves and grass collected from their lawns. I buried this idea where it belonged.

Perhaps most significant was our successful effort to halt Rudy's attempt to privatize several of the city's public hospitals by selling them off. The City Council sued and was vindicated when the courts rejected the legality of the sale. In the process we were able to prevent the dismantling of the best public hospital system in the nation.

While the city's Republican mayor may have been overenthusiastic about some ideas for running the city like a business, his support for chipping away at other city practices that had outlived their usefulness was a real help. One such nonsensical sacred cow were the rent limits on a certain class of luxury apartments: those being occupied by the well-to-do.

In March 1994 the council moved to break this stranglehold on the city's housing supply by passing a law decontrolling apartments for occupants with annual incomes exceeding $250,000 where the controlled rent exceeded $2,000. Even this small effort to modify incongruous aspects of our rent laws that were mostly hurting the middle class and the poor was interpreted by some tenant interest groups as the opening salvo in a conspiracy to destroy rent control and rent stabilization.

The first big test between the mayor and the council—particularly for me—involved the budget of 1994. A sizable group of Democratic politicians, especially those in the minority caucus, would never forgive Mayor Giuliani for standing on the steps of City Hall and rallying the mostly white, off-duty cops against Mayor Dinkins. Rudy and I liked each other personally, which usually made our negotiations easier. During talks that first year, at a time when the city economy was still far from recovery, he was as generous about the council's top priority—education—as any mayor could have been, offering an additional $75 million for building desperately needed new schools, as well as a promise to get rid of the Board of Education. I would bring in senior council members like Archie Spigner and Victor Robles one at a time and explain to them that however many things about the new mayor they disliked, we still had a city to run, and he was offering us many of the things we had asked for. It was a hard argument to get across, especially with so much hostility carried over from the election a few months earlier. Most of them wanted to bring the whole house of cards down on Giuliani's head, just to send him a message. Their sense of politics said to them: "Oppose the guy!" I have always felt that government is more important than politics, that we Democrats should oppose Rudy as mayor when he ran for office, but not interfere with running the city. I pointed out that if the wheels of government came to a halt, senior citizen programs and other important social benefits would be the first to go.

In the end I was able to persuade a sizable number of Democrats to go along, and we adopted a budget, 43–8, "without racism or rancor," as I noted in my diary. Luckily I had a little helping hand from our congressional delegation in Washington, who arranged for $75 million of federal aid for council projects that Rudy had attempted to cut out of the budget. With Daniel Moynihan as chairman of the Senate Finance Committee and Charlie Rangel heading up the House Rules Committee, we had a good connection that, when it worked, was a real godsend.

But the budget wars were not over. By early fall of 1994 a $1.1 billion gap emerged between projected revenues and expenditures. In October Rudy imposed several unacceptable cuts in the spending plan we had so painstakingly negotiated together a few months earlier. When the council objected, he asserted that whatever reforms the 1989 city charter had introduced, he as mayor had the unilateral power to cut programs when revenue faltered. He then refused to bargain with us. In response the council, using the mayor's new revenue figures, passed an alternative budget modification. Rudy denounced our action as fiscally irresponsible, vetoed it, and again rejected our authority to change his cuts.

Perhaps Rudy had underestimated me, thinking that because I had tried hard to get along with him in the first budget process I would just go along and get along with whatever he did. It's easy to get along with me, but when it comes to what's best for the city, there are certain principles I will not compromise. I had fought my entire political career so that the council could have authority over the budget.

At this point it became an institutional fight. The council refused to accept the mayor's argument that he had the unilateral power to alter the budget we had agreed upon as equal partners. With all but one of our seven Republicans joining in, the council overrode Giuliani's veto of our budget plan, 47–1. Simultaneously, we brought a lawsuit demanding that the executive implement *our* budget, not his.

Such a situation, with two separate New York City budgets, each of which could claim to be legally valid, was unprecedented. As I had pointed out to my fellow legislators back in June, the last thing I wanted to do was throw the machinery of government into disarray. I hoped that a court decision would clarify the contradictions inherent in the budget process outlined by the 1989 charter revisions. Rudy at first tried to overpower us through sheer insistence. He ordered city agencies to make his cuts, as if the council's budget did not exist. He claimed that even if the court ruled in our favor he could circumvent the decision by declaring a fiscal emergency and impounding the funds we wanted to spend. "What that all tells you," he declared, "is that we're going to get to the result of these reductions one way or another."

The judge who was supposed to rule on our lawsuit apparently decided our disagreement called for a family court kind of approach. In her first ruling she instructed both parties to stop squabbling and reach a compromise. A week later, to reinforce her point, she threw out both budgets. We were back at square one, except by that point it was mid-holiday season, 1994. At the council's Christmas party on December 21, I decided to inject a little humor into the dispute by serenading the mayor with a version of "Rudolph the Hard-Nosed Reindeer." Rudy took it in good spirits, and soon dropped his confrontational attitude.

A few days later, I found out that the mayor had offered the council's former financial whiz Marc Shaw the job as his new budget director. It had been terrible to lose Marc a year earlier (when he had accepted a position as the Mayor's finance commissioner), but a move to the mayor's office was a step in the right direction for him. Marc was succeeded for a brief time by his deputy, Tom McMahon until the energetic and effervescent Haeda Mihaltses took over. Most important for future budget cooperation between the mayor and the council, Marc understood the council's priorities and he understood me. Picking him could not have been a clearer sign that Rudy meant business when he said in his January State of the City speech that he would work together with the City Council to close the budget gap, rather than in confrontation. Indeed, we worked together during the first months of 1995, as the fiscal situation worsened, in ironing out a solution to the city's groaning budget gap. The bonds formed then were the seeds of a lasting friendship.

Rudy and I are good friends to this day, but we are very different people. Perhaps because of his intelligence, Rudy has little patience for what he considers stupidity in others, and sometimes even for those who just disagree with him. We both have Italian tempers, but in those days he sometimes became too personal. If he didn't like you, it might seem he wanted to kill you. This tendency to bear a grudge may have had something to do with his background as a prosecutor. He had a lifetime of experience with criminals who were trying to get away with things, and was suspicious of anything he didn't think was right. One reason we formed such a good partnership is that he tended to see the dark part, and I tended to see the light part of human behavior. Together we hit the balance pretty accurately.

Rudy's "mean streak" was on frequent display during the first five or six years of his tenure as mayor. He blamed earlier Democratic administrations for the financial straits the city was confronting and picked public spats with Ed Koch, who was more than happy to respond on the platform readily offered him by the city's media. At the unveiling of the official portrait of Rudy's predecessor, Rudy pointedly refrained from inviting mayors Koch and Beame onstage. So after my speech honoring Mayor Dinkins, I invited the other former mayors to come up as well. Beame, who was elderly and not in the best of health and wanted above all to avoid shaking hands with Giuliani, grabbed my arm and would not let go. I was scared stiff that he would collapse, especially since there was no chair for him onstage.

Rudy found it difficult to reach out to legislators, whether in the City Council or in Washington, and once when I was in D.C., Charlie Rangel complained, "This mayor has never met with us." But the Giuliani feuds that captured the most public attention were often with fellow executives. Whether it was school chancellors Cortines or Crew, or Police Commissioner William Bratton, Rudy could not abide administrators who, in his opinion, took credit for achievements without being accountable for their performance. Rudy's biggest pet peeve was the city's Public Advocate, Mark Green. Sometimes Rudy seemed to carry this campaign so far that the top priority of his administration seemed to be how to thwart the future mayoral candidate. For example in June of 1994, a few hours after he and I shook hands on the first budget we had negotiated together, and while the budget itself was being printed, Rudy called me up on the "hot line" connecting his office to mine.

"I forgot something," he began. "We have to de-fund the Public Advocate's office."

"What are you talking about? Every agency has already taken a cut."

"Well, cut Mark Green more—don't you realize he's going to run against you? This is a good time to get rid of him." Rudy was already predicting the likely candidates for mayor in 2001, after his terms were up.

"Rudy, you can't do that, you'd be decimating the staff. And we already shook hands. Besides, even if he does run against me, it would be wrong."

Rudy would not be placated, so I had to call Kevin McCabe to get in touch with Rudy's first deputy mayor, Peter Powers, and threaten to bring back the whole council to write our own budget.

One of the few things on which Ed Koch and Rudy Giuliani agreed in those years was their dislike of Mark Green. Partly this was due to the do-nothing nature of the Public Advocate's office, the new title given by the Charter Revision Commission to the former office of City Council president. Like the borough presidents, the Public Advocate has no responsibility for raising money, but is free to criticize as he or she wishes. Worse, although the position is voted for independently of the mayor, whoever holds it stands next in the line of succession should the mayor die or be disabled. Although I understand the position of those who argue for the usefulness of having an institutional critic within government, I myself don't believe it is necessary. Instead I favor an office of vice mayor, to be elected on the same ticket with the mayor. As Rudy said: "Why fund the guy? We do the work, he gets all the publicity!"

After Mayor Giuliani gave up on getting rid of Mark Green by de-funding his office, he began appointing charter commissions meant to abolish the office. I would have been happy to do away with the Public Advocate's office in the context of a legitimate governmental review—but not as part of a political vendetta. The way Rudy went about it, I was forced to defend an office I personally believed was unnecessary. Meanwhile the controversy Rudy's fixation engendered was a political bonanza for Mark Green in his campaign for mayor.

Rudy and Ed disliked Mark for both his politics and his personality. I myself have little use for some of Mark's liberal crusading, but personally I like him a great deal. First of all, he has a great sense of humor. He's also one of the smartest politicians I've ever known—which may be why he often comes across as arrogant and talking down to people. Long after Mark Green was defeated for mayor, I had breakfast with him. His question to me: "Can you tell me now why Giuliani hated me so much?"

Rudy's zeal to prosecute everyone who ever thought about disobeying the law was certainly valuable in some situations, as when it came to ridding the Fulton Fish Market of criminals. When we tried to work together to do the same thing for the Hunts Point Market in the Bronx, however, he went overboard and tried to get the council to amend the law so that innocent and unknowing employees who happened to be working for an allegedly criminal employer would suffer the same penalties as the employer.

If you ask me, an alert and thoughtful staff is usually just as effective in rooting out corruption as an aggressive cadre of investigators. Take the celebrated case of the council's "fallen angel," Angel Rodriguez. Angel had been a breath of fresh air when he first arrived at the council because he was a certified public accountant with tremendous expertise in finance. I immediately placed him on the Finance Committee, where he made several valuable contributions. Shortly before the end of my term, however, Angel ran afoul of our procedure on land use. Under my tenure, the rules for approval of any land use or zoning matter were quite simple. If it was the right thing to do for the city, the local council member's opinion was to be sought and respected, as well as the affected community boards' and the borough presidents', and of course the city planning commission's, representing the mayor. In the end, however, no council member or single entity had veto power, and the final decision would be what was best for all the people of the city.

On the day in question my brilliant and amiable chief of staff, John Banks, came in to say that Angel Rodriguez objected so strongly to a particular land use matter in his district that he was threatening to vote against an important year-end budget modification if we didn't vote it down. This kind of threat was unlike Angel, who up to this time had always seemed reasonable. In fact, I only had a few more months to go as Speaker, and Angel was emerging as the likely choice of Brooklyn's delegation to succeed me.

After John left my office I called in Angel, whose only justification for opposing the zoning question at hand was something like "they should have come to me first." Then he angrily repeated his threat to vote against the "budget mod."

"Angel," I told him, "you have just done the worst thing you can do: threaten me. By placing your interests against the city as a whole, you have seriously injured your chances to become the next Speaker. As a matter of respect for you, however, I will call in staff and see if there is any merit to your objections." I then called in the head of our Land Use Division, Gail Benjamin, along with her most capable deputy Christopher Collins. We reviewed the matter together and agreed that Angel's objections were groundless. June Eisland, the chair of the land use committee, also agreed with us. The project went ahead without Angel's vote. It also cost him my neutrality in the contest as to who would succeed me. A few weeks later Queens county leader Tom Manton told me that the Queens delegation was going to recommend Rodriguez as my successor. I told him he should not do that. I knew nothing about any criminal behavior on Angel's part; I only knew that I would actively oppose him or any other candidate who did not put the city's best interest over his own. I reminded Tom that my son Peter Jr. and other soon-to-be-voting members of the council both in Queens and citywide would not support Angel. There was something fishy about him. Gifford Miller was far and away the best candidate, and with the support of Queens he was elected the new Speaker.

A few months later the FBI interviewed Gail Benjamin, John Banks, and all my top staff about what they knew concerning a similar project in Angel's district. What marching orders had I given in reference to this or any other matters in Angel's or any other member's district, they asked? All of them said, under oath, "The Speaker said we should always 'do the right thing.'"

In 2003 Angel Rodriguez was sentenced to more than four years in jail for extorting money from a builder who was seeking land use approval for a project in Angel's district.

When it comes to education, the city can only do what the state allows because education is primarily a state obligation. Even though the council has no direct jurisdiction on education, we learned early on in the 1970s, when Frank Macchiarola was schools chancellor, that by agreement we could freeze city money in the Board of Education's vast and unaccountable budget to be used only for the purposes we intended. Thus, we were able to introduce security guards into each school, reduce classroom size, provide kindergarten and early childhood education, enhance teacher education, provide computers and computer training for teachers and students, and much more. No matter what we did, however, education kept slipping as student achievement levels fell in comparison to students across the state and country. Instead of concentrating on this fundamental failure, the members of the board seemed to spend most of their time selecting a never-ending succession of school chancellors.

The New York City Board of Education was composed of seven members. The borough presidents appointed one each and the mayor appointed two. This composition reflected, in essence, a vestigial remnant of the undemocratic and unconstitutional Board of Estimate model of running the city. Worse, the state's supervisory role meant that individual state legislators could and did bring their influence to bear directly on the chancellor and on members of the board rather than dealing with the mayor or City Council. The chancellor, and the board members who selected him, reported to multiple bosses and were accountable to none. This setup guaranteed a constant power struggle among the mayor, the board, and Albany.

After I became Speaker I tried over and over again to get the legislature to reform the makeup of the board. By giving the council two board appointments I believed we could at least create a board with a less parochial, more citywide emphasis. Later, Mayor Giuliani and I joined together to call for abolishing the board and giving total control and accountability to city representatives "rather than to a legislator in Plattsburgh, which is closer to

Kentucky than it is to the city." Albany, however, where ultimate authority lay, did not want to cede any power to city authorities, whether the mayor or the council. It would take a few years into the new century and the advent of Mayor Bloomberg for them to finally hand over authority where it belonged.

As was usual with Rudy, he was implacable when he believed he had a good cause—and in this case he did. However, the political realities were stacked against him. Four of the five members appointed by the borough presidents—all but Staten Island's member—were determined to resist granting the mayor additional power over the city's educational system. Adding Staten Island's member to his two members still meant that Giuliani would always come up short. Rudy could not fire the chancellor, but he could make life so difficult the chancellor would either be intimidated into paying him heed, or leave.

I agreed with Rudy that we should speak out in favor of abolishing the Board of Ed. The board was a morass of inefficiency, and until it was gone much of the money spent for education would not go where we wanted it to go. But driving the chancellor crazy in the meantime seemed counterproductive to me.

Indeed, Ramon Cortines resigned after enduring two years of nearly constant battles with Rudy. Rudolph Crew, who came in during October of 1995 and was acceptable to Rudy at the outset, lasted three years. When Rudy Crew called me from his home in Tacoma, Washington, after accepting the job, I had three things to tell him: 1) the council and I would do everything we could to help him, no matter how the mayor treated him; 2) he should come visit my local Astoria diner to get a feel for a typical New York city community; and 3) I would pray for him.

My first effort to help Rudy Crew and the kids of New York came within weeks of his appointment. On October 23, 1995, I issued a plan to replace the Board of Ed with a Superintendent of Schools to be appointed by the mayor and the council, while simultaneously creating school-based councils of parents and community members that could hire and fire principals. While the plan echoed Mayor Giuliani's call for mayoral control over the system as a whole, it offered grassroots empowerment of a kind advocated by Assembly Speaker Sheldon Silver, without whose support no overhaul would ever take place. Chancellor Crew wisely refused to comment on the plan, saying he would concentrate on education rather than questions of power or control.

Then, in January, I proposed a major new educational initiative. My idea was to do for the city's schools something similar to what we'd done for the city's streets: dedicate part of our tax money to saving the school system. My initial proposal involved extending the income tax surcharge used for Safe Streets, Safe City, but this time as a fund dedicated to building new schools to end overcrowding; renovating existing schools; and purchasing up-to-date textbooks and other educational materials. Albany might not yet be ready to grant us accountability over the system as a whole, but why not take over what we could?

I started referring to my educational initiative as "Smart Kids, Smart City," in a conscious evocation of the "Safe Streets, Safe City" program that had been so successful in improving the quality of life in New York. By making construction to relieve overcrowding my number-one priority, the council and I forced Mayor Rudy and Assembly Speaker Silver to confront the issue. Both of those parties had their own ideas about how to raise money for school construction. Unfortunately, Governor Pataki and the state legislature were starving the city of funds, and with the city's finances not yet fully recovered from the low point of the early 1990s, the state's Financial Control Board began to make menacing noises about an impending fiscal crisis and the possibility of taking over the city's finances. Rudy felt he had no choice but to keep the income surtax—not as a fund for new schools, but merely to meet operating expenses. Luckily, the economic recovery of the 1990s was beginning to kick in, and by budget time we were able to keep alive our visionary idea of a $1.4 billion school reconstruction fund, with strong support from the city's editorial pages.

Two years later the effects of the great economic boom of the Clinton years made much more possible. In the spring of 1998 the City Council not only terminated the Safe Streets, Safe City income surtax as promised eight years earlier, but took the $1.2 billion that Mayor Giuliani had proposed to spend on moving Yankee Stadium from the Bronx to the West Side of Manhattan and spent it instead on the construction and maintenance of schools as well as the purchase of new textbooks. (Some textbooks in use referred to the Vietnam War as if it were still going on; the typing manual was from the 1950s!) One of the new schools to emerge from that building program was my personal favorite: the Frank Sinatra School of the Arts, a high school for young musicians and actors in Long Island City, the realization of a dream of the great Astoria-born singer Tony Bennett.

That same year my new chief of staff Bruce Bender suggested that the council could provide sufficient monies to cut in half tuition at city colleges. Bruce knew I had long dreamed of making higher education as affordable as it used to be when I attended Fordham. After Bruce explained his plan to me, I verified the cost with CUNY and our finance people, discussed it with the Steering Group and borough delegations, and came up with a budget amendment that awards a council scholarship of half tuition to any high school graduate who graduates with a B average or better, attends any of our seventeen public universities, and maintains that B average. The council later formally established the New York City Council Peter F. Vallone Academic Scholarship Program, which to date has awarded tens of thousands of scholarships. One only has to visit a CUNY campus to see the tremendous improvement in our city universities. A city student who enters high school now knows that an affordable higher education awaits anyone who does well. I can't think of a better incentive for our young people to stay in school and succeed in life.

In 2002 Mayor Bloomberg finally wrested more control for the city over its schools and virtually eliminated the Board of Education, replacing it with an advisory Department of Education. Accountability now lies squarely with the mayor, and testing indicates that some children are doing better. Not surprisingly, a group of legislators in Albany immediately sued the mayor, which shows yet again how much more the state capital cares for its own power than the welfare of the state's schoolchildren.

17

A Passing Feud and the Race for Governor

In the summer of 1991 Matilda Cuomo invited me and Tena to the Governor's Mansion in Albany. Maybe it was getting a glimpse that hot August day of the long-closed pool that had once refreshed Franklin Delano Roosevelt, but immediately after the visit I decided I would run for governor myself if and when Mario moved on. I had realized by then that the biggest problem in Albany was the failure of the executive and legislative branches to work together in an open process. The Democratic-controlled state assembly was only doing what was good for the Democrats, and the Republican-controlled state senate was only doing what was good for the Republicans. I wanted to place government over politics, as I had succeeded in doing in New York City. Besides which, I looked forward to reopening FDR's pool.

Unfortunately, Mario himself stood astride my path to the Governor's Mansion. When I visited him and Matilda that day, he was widely considered the front-running Democratic candidate for president of the United States. In those days William Jefferson Clinton was a largely unknown face from a back-country state and given little chance of pulling off his long-shot candidacy. For that matter, George Herbert Bush was still fresh from his successful prosecution of the first Iraq war. Few political commentators considered him vulnerable to defeat by whatever candidate the Democrats put up. Perhaps it was not surprising that in December Mario, after years of waffling, finally issued a "definitive" decision that he would *not* run for president the following November.

Mario's chances of retaining the governor's office after 1994 were not, however, brilliant, as I and countless other political leaders readily told him. After three terms and nearly twelve years in office, Mario would have served as long as any of New York State's governors except for Nelson Rockefeller, who was elected to a fourth term but did not finish it. Voters had tired of the constant squabbling between Mario and the legislature. Worse, the economic downturn that had so jinxed the Dinkins administration was bound to make it hard for Mario.

Mario was apparently undaunted, and as early as April of 1992, more than two years before the next gubernatorial election, he let it be known that he would indeed probably run for that fourth term. Many of us took this declaration as no more than a testing of the waters, and when Mario's poll numbers continued to decline and Bill Clinton was elected president, we hoped and predicted that the Democratic president would nominate Mario to the Supreme Court.

By the early 1990s I had under my belt a half dozen years' experience as majority leader and then Speaker of the City Council. During that time I had developed not only a wealth of city experience, but strong connections with political figures in Albany and Washington. New York was in many ways the most international of all the world's cities, and its regional economy of such significance that the symbolic stands we took on both national health issues (like smoking and campaign finance) and international issues (like apartheid) allowed us to blaze a trail for the nation as a whole. It did not seem a stretch to me to run for the only office which, in my mind, was even more important to New York City than the mayor's: governor of New York State.

On March 30, 1993, I met with Mario to discuss his plans and mine. As far as becoming a Supreme Court justice, Mario told me he did not like the idea of being "locked away . . . unable to speak out," although he would certainly appreciate the honor. He promised to let me know whether or not he was running for governor. I told him in return that I would definitely run for governor if he did not run, even though he had told me he was committed to support Lieutenant Governor Lundine as his candidate. I told him I was absolutely convinced I could win the Democratic primary in 1994 and beat any Republican opponent who might emerge. I also told him that my trips around the state had convinced me it would be almost impossible for him to win a fourth term—but he would make a great Supreme Court justice!

It was not to be. During our conversation Mario was interrupted by his secretary's buzzer several times. From the fragments of conversation I picked up and what I learned later, I am almost certain the brief interruption involved a call from President Clinton regarding the Supreme Court nomination. Mario, who was still thinking it over, did not take the call while I was present, and one week later he sent a letter to President Clinton asking not to be nominated. On the same day Senator Patrick Moynihan told me that I was "the only one who could govern the state" (in 1998 he would repeat his ringing endorsement of me all over the state, and actually campaign for me more than he did for himself). Confident of my capacity for reforming state government, but still perplexed by Mario's unpredictability, I decided to continue my preparations for a campaign and in May 1993 formed a fund-raising committee. As the new year 1994 began, Mario announced that, indeed, he would run for a fourth term as governor. It was too late to do anything but go ahead with my large fund-raising event scheduled for late January. Besides, Mario might change his mind again for all I knew! The gala dinner raised a million dollars for my campaign. I explained to the audience of four hundred that I would drop out of the race if Mario indeed continued with his plans to run. Mario himself, I told them, had just called to apologize that he could not come to the dinner because there was ice all over the wings of the governor's plane and the pilot had advised him it would be too dangerous to fly. "Mario," I said, "for once in your life, take a chance!"—a line that brought down the house.

In November, Mario did indeed lose his bid for a fourth term, to the relatively unknown Republican candidate George Pataki. Rudy Giuliani, who had bucked his own party to endorse Mario's bid for reelection, bemoaned what I had felt was inevitable: "How could Mario have lost?"

An unforeseen outcome of the 1993 municipal elections had provided me with an additional motivation to run for governor: the passage that year of a term limits referendum applicable to New York City alone. The term limits question arrived on the ballot through the efforts of a well-meaning multimillionaire named Ronald Lauder and his well-funded political action committee, New Yorkers for Term Limits. In the 1989 Republican primary for mayor, Mr. Lauder reported spending $13.7 million. He lost nevertheless by a 2-to-1 margin to Rudy Giuliani, and received less than 10,000 votes as the Conservative candidate in the general election the following November. Obviously disappointed, Lauder apparently decided that the only way to "get the rascals out of office" was to launch a nationwide term limits campaign. At the time this idea was popular with the Republican Party, since most of the " rascals" in office were Democrats.

The movement was blocked on the federal and most state levels as being unconstitutional, but not so in the great City of New York. New Yorkers for Term Limits spent millions of dollars to place the 1993 referendum on the ballot. Fifty-nine percent of those who voted on the measure (less than half of those who voted in the general election) favored it, and starting on January 1, 1994, no New York City elected official could spend more than two terms in office. Practically speaking, this meant that New York City's government would change over almost entirely starting in 2002 and every two terms thereafter.

Ron Lauder believes conscientiously that career politicians are bad for government. Any student of the way politics worked in Albany in the 1990s, where three men held all the power and let no one else have a say, might come to a similar conclusion. A legitimate argument can indeed be made along these lines in the case of the mayor and other city executives, who wield considerable budgetary power and can count on extensive media coverage. (Besides which, few citywide executives plan to stay in office for more than eight years.) Unfortunately, when term limits are applied to legislators, their effect is to destroy the balance of government, since legislators usually only gain real power through the seniority they accumulate over the years. Term limitations of not more than two terms in any six-year period actually existed for Congress under the Articles of Confederation. They proved a dismal failure, and were wisely discarded by the current U.S. Constitution. The answer to removing nonresponsive elected officials is twofold: 1) Vote them out when they come up for reelection; and 2) Institute a sensible campaign finance law that provides for matching public funds, to encourage competition.

In an attempt to avert the complete turnover in the City Council forced by passage of the 1993 ballot question, the council put its own referendum on the ballot in 1996. It would have provided for staggered terms with a twelve-year maximum, avoiding a mass exodus at the end of 2001. Ron Lauder had indicated to me that he would accept such a graduated termination, instead of an abrupt one. But no, he and his minions once again spent millions to defeat our measure, launching an advertising campaign that accused me of "trying to pull a scam" on the people of New York. Practically no one with whom I had a chance to discuss the issue at length disagreed with me (except Ron Lauder himself). My arguments did not translate easily into thirty-second television ads, however. Also, we had limited money, since it was difficult to raise funds for what struck many as an act of self-perpetuation. Of course, the mayor had no interest in supporting our campaign, since an inexperienced legislature would be that much easier for him to "manage," if not manipulate. Although a *New York Times* editorial came out in support of our ballot measure, the reasoning it employed in arriving at its conclusion was so tortuous that readers might well have presumed it was an argument against the proposal.

By 3 P.M. on Election Day, November 5, 1996, I sensed our term limits proposition would go down to defeat. At least it was by a 6-point margin this time, as opposed to the 19-point margin three years earlier. I was not surprised I had not been able to beat a $3 million campaign with a $1 million one, but I believed then, and believe now, that a long-term project of educating the voters to better understand the function of their legislators will eventually turn the tide.

As early as 1989 some of my political advisors had tried to persuade me to run for mayor in the event Ed Koch stepped down. From almost the first days of the Giuliani administration Ed Koch had been pushing me to take up the gauntlet and challenge Rudy. Ed resented the criticisms Rudy kept leveling at previous Democratic administrations. With his radio show and ready access to the media Ed kept the running feud between them in the public eye. By 1996 I had been the second most powerful person in New York City for nearly a decade. It seemed logical to Ed that the next stop in my political career should be the Mayor's Office. I was certain, however, that I did not want to run against Rudy Giuliani. As I told Ed, "Rudy and I have our fights, but we also have a good working relationship and I like the guy. Why would I want to break that all up by running against him"

"How could you like the guy?" Ed would say to me.

"Look Ed," I'd reply, "I'm thinking instead of running for governor in 1998."

"You've got my support," Ed told me.

Ed Koch was not the only one looking to me to challenge Rudy Giuliani when he came up for reelection in 1997. Senator Alphonse ("The Fonz") D'Amato, like Ed a bitter antagonist of Rudy's, came to see me in early 1997 during a hearing we were holding on the Swiss banks' defrauding of Holocaust victims during World War II. He told me that Rudy would definitely run for Moynihan's Senate seat in 2000, and that I should de-fund Mark Green's office, like Rudy wanted me to, so that I'd have a clear shot at winning the mayor's race. The Fonz was outrageously funny, if not with the most polished manners. He made me laugh, but his powers of political prediction were questionable: he had not only been certain that Cuomo was not going to run for a fourth term as governor, but also implied that I could easily beat his own protégé, George Pataki, if I decided to run.

With my name being bandied about by New York's political headliners, it's not surprising that the press often asked me about my plans for seeking higher office. While I did not publicly rule out ever running for mayor, I was frank about two factors that gave me pause. One was that I could not run for the council and for mayor at the same time. The other was the public's expectation that the mayor be on call twenty-four-hours a day, the local media's constant attention, and the corrosive effect this had on family life. I knew that I could not be successful unless I could go home and be nourished by my family. I wasn't certain whether this city would allow that. Being governor in a place like Albany was a different matter.

In the end I decided to stick with my earlier ambition to run for governor, and former council member and Manhattan borough president Ruth Messinger was the 1997 Democratic mayoral candidate. I thought well of Ruth because she had always worked responsibly toward a budget agreement. With Rudy's strong negatives, especially among minority voters, it looked at first as if Ruth had at least a chance of pulling off an upset. Unfortunately, her race became complicated when she was forced into a runoff against Al Sharpton, which hurt the turnout for her among African-American voters. Given these circumstances and the generally rosy state of the city's economy, Ruth did not do that badly in retaining all but four of the same assembly districts that voted for Dinkins in a much closer race four years before.

Al D'Amato's political handicapping of my election chances against George Pataki may have been off base, but someone in the Pataki campaign was taking no chances about me. In July 1997, twenty-four hours after Bernie Mendik, the chairman of the New York City Real Estate Board, and his wife each contributed $25,000 for my Democratic gubernatorial primary campaign, Bernie called me to say he had to take the money back. A Republican strategist had made it crystal clear to him—and all members of the Real Estate Board—that they were not to donate to my campaign, even if was only for the primary and not the general election campaign. This was a severe disappointment, since four years earlier Bernie had chaired the fund-raising event I had held in anticipation of a 1994 run to succeed Mario Cuomo. I felt sorry for Bernie and returned his checks. I knew that every big developer needs the cooperation of Albany to do business at all in New York City.

That kind of behind-the-scenes hardball politics was only half the story behind Pataki's successful reelection bid. The other half was a national economy improving throughout 1996 and 1997, especially in New York City if not nearly enough upstate. That favorable economic picture allowed Pataki to claim credit for rising fortunes and to sprinkle favors to important political constituencies in return for their political fealty. With those kinds of factors weighing on his decision, Carl McCall, the Democrat I most respected and feared as a primary opponent, announced that he would not run against Pataki in the 1998 election (though he would do so in 2002). My brother-in-law Tony and I were in Atlantic City when we heard that Carl had withdrawn. We danced around the bench on the boardwalk! I would have hated to run against a good friend for whom I originally campaigned (and to whom I gave $30,000 from my own campaign funds when he first ran for comptroller). Immediately Tony and I went to the phones and started to call Carl's people and ask them to transfer their support to me.

In September, December, and February of 1997 and into 1998, Democratic leaders met three times in an effort to form some kind of united front. If we could not coalesce around one candidate for governor (and I was the natural front-runner once McCall dropped out), at least we hoped to frame an agreement that would commit the principal candidates to back whoever ultimately won the Democratic nomination. This was always important in New York State with its history of "spoiler" independent parties (Liberal, Conservative, Right-to-Life), and particularly important this year because of the expected Democratic candidacy of Pataki's own renegade lieutenant governor, Betsy McCaughey Ross. My friend Tom Manton of Queens and some downstate leaders were the main organizers of these meetings, at which it quickly became apparent how much leftover resentment still lingered upstate about Mario Cuomo's refusal to step down earlier. To say that they were not looking forward to running in 1998 with yet another Italian guy from Queens is an understatement. My friendship with Mario was back in full bloom, and when we had lunch during this period he even joked that if I thought it would help me, he would gladly endorse Pataki.

After the defeat of Mario in 1994, Shelly Silver had become the Democrat who wielded the most power within the party statewide. At a lunch I had with him in an effort to promote my own candidacy, he told me he was seriously considering running for governor himself. I thought he was kidding. As time went on I realized he was serious. Shelly may have been the most powerful Democrat, but his negatives upstate were nearly as high as Mario's. Over the next year and a half of my active campaigning he did everything possible to make sure I did not become the candidate of the party. The rap Shelly used against me was that I was a "regional candidate." How, he asked, could I win if I had never run a race outside of Astoria?

It seemed not to matter to Shelley that in Astoria alone I represented more people than Shelly did from his assembly district; or that my first run for office, in which the final outcome had to be determined by the courts, was a U.S. congressional race in three boroughs; or that as City Council Speaker I represented an entire city that accounted for nearly half of the state's population.

Once he thought better of his own scheme to run for governor, Shelly toyed for months with the candidacy of Betsy Ross, the Republican-turned-Democrat, because of her husband Wilbur Ross's personal fortune and her knack for making headlines. Apparently the fact that he had once ridiculed the one-time lieutenant governor by wiggling his hips tastselessly in supposed imitation of her made no difference to him now. Shelly even liked to belittle me and my Astoria roots by pretending that my two male opponents in the Democratic primary—Brooklyn DA Joe Hynes and Nassau County Executive James Larocca—represented "larger" constituencies.

However disappointing I found Shelly Silver's hostility to my candidacy, I was not about to abandon my efforts on his account. I would not, however, play the usual game: I would not trade political favors for the sake of being elected and I would not engage in negative campaigning against the other primary candidates, despite the opportunity to do so, particularly against a relatively silly candidate like Betsy Ross. As for raising the funds necessary to wage a serious campaign against Pataki during this economic boom, it was a nearly impossible task without the unqualified support of major political figures like Shelly Silver. Shelly, however, would not pick up the phone to help me. I choked on my pride and spent as much time as I could bear trying to raise close to $2 million for the governor's race by January 9, 1998, the last day to report monies raised for campaigns. That figure, trumpeted by media publicity, would be seen as a barometer of my chances of success.

In addition to all my responsibilities as Speaker during the first six months of election year 1998, I made several international trips of the kind expected by any gubernatorial candidate, to Ireland and Israel. When my seven-day-a-week schedule threatened to burn me out, I was reminded by President Clinton's travails, in the breaking Monica Lewinsky scandal, of the perils of running for public office.

On March 9, 1998, the day before I was planning to declare for governor, I received a real wake-up call from Kevin McCabe. Kevin was leaving as my chief of staff in order to become my campaign manager. I had told him not to flatter me, but to tell me the whole truth about my chances of winning. We had taken a poll, and the results were bad news.

"I hate to tell you this," Kevin put it bluntly, "but there's no way you can win. Why don't you save your money and pull the plug now?"

"Are you kidding? I'm not a quitter. I want to get my platform out there; I want to expose what's going on in Albany and change the relationship between the state and the city; I want to represent a united Democratic Party."

"Okay, boss, just wanted to make sure you knew."

On March 10, knowing full well that my chances of winning were a very long shot, I declared my candidacy for governor on the steps of City Hall. In my speech I accused Governor Pataki of distraction and drift as New York's upstate economy stagnated and schools and health care worsened. New York's economy might be heading in the right direction at last, but it was still lagging behind the rest of the nation. I promised to use the Governor's Office "as the seat of leadership and accountability for the state, not as an incubator for overheated personal ambition and oval-shaped flights of fancy."

While I attempted to focus my political message upon the negligence in Albany, a different sort of conflict between the mayor and me was brewing. I felt it was necessary to clarify some of the unresolved balance-of-power issues left over from our first budget standoff in the fall of 1994. I still believed it was a bad idea to leave the mayor with the sole power to estimate revenue and thus give him the independent power to change the budget in midyear if revenue projections changed. In November, after Rudy had been reelected by a wide margin, I said to him, "While we're both here, why don't we work together on some of these issues? We could establish a charter revision commission to address the balance-of-power issue, and propose mechanisms for resolving it." Rudy indicated both privately and publicly that he was opposed to my idea, but I decided to go ahead with it in the council, and scheduled hearings about it.

At about the same time Rudy began to skip or cancel our weekly meetings. At first I was mystified, but in late February, just as the council started to hold hearings on our charter commission plan, he announced that he was forming his *own* charter commission. I was enraged, and let him know it. I wanted to salvage our relationship, but politics kept interfering. Because of the very large crowd that had formed on the steps of City Hall the day I announced my gubernatorial candidacy, Rudy had been forced to enter the building via the side entrance, and was not happy about it. A day later he came out with a new set of rules and regulations that would make it impossible to gather a crowd on the steps of City Hall. I pointed out to him that the more he criticized me and "my crowd," the more favorable play I received in the press. This seemed to make sense to him. Within days Rudy and I, agreeing it would be highly impractical to have two separate charter commissions going at the same time, agreed to drop both commission plans and instead establish a joint task force to explore recommendations to be presented to some future charter commission.

Six weeks later however, Rudy appointed his own charter commission anyway—but for reasons that had less to do with the governance of the city and more to do with his passion for the New York Yankees. Myself, I've always been more of a Mets than a Yankees fan, since I'm an underdog kind of guy. Rudy, however, so loves the Yankees that when he talks about them he takes on the aura of a starstruck twelve-year-old. In his State of the City message of January 1998, he had laid out an enthusiastic vision of the expansion of the Javits Convention Center and the transformation of the entire West Side of Manhattan—not to mention increased revenues pouring into the city's treasury. This would come about, he said, by moving Yankee Stadium from the Bronx to near the heart of Midtown. As the outlines of his proposed budget emerged that spring, he made clear that he wanted to use the expiring safe streets' surtax on the expense side of the budget to jump-start his plan to move Yankee Stadium, for which he also put $1.2 billion in the capital expense budget.

Now, I have never underestimated the importance of major sports teams to New York City. A dozen years earlier, one of the first things I had done when elected majority leader was establish a city sports commission. One purpose of the commission was to encourage our children to participate in sports and to help fulfill my vision of a full gymnasium in every school in New York. A second purpose was to eventually bring the Olympic Games to New York, which thanks again to Speaker Silver we lost for 2012. And finally, I wanted to keep our professional sports teams in the city. We had already lost two baseball teams, the Dodgers and the Giants, and football's Giants and Jets; I was genuinely concerned we might lose the Yankees and the Mets. At this time Ed Koch was mayor. Although I loved the guy, he knew absolutely nothing about sports and couldn't care less about it. One of the prominent members of the new sports commission was Bill Fugazy, the owner of the big limousine company. I got him to have lunch with me and George Steinbrenner, the owner of the Yankees, to hear Steinbrenner's complaints about Yankee Stadium and to agree to put money into the stadium to fix it up. At the time I assured Steinbrenner, as I also assured Fred Wilpon of the Mets, that whatever Ed Koch said or did, the council would look after their interests.

Now, ten years later, Steinbrenner was again making noises about leaving the Bronx because of his dissatisfaction with the stadium there. Although Steinbrenner was coy about whether he would actually follow through on his threat, or even under what conditions he might stay, Giuliani knew perfectly well that the Yankee owner would jump at the prospect of moving Yankee Stadium from the Bronx to Manhattan. Rudy also knew that if he could somehow convince me and the council to back his scheme, the opposition expected from disappointed Bronx residents and overcrowded Manhattanites might be overcome.

Consensus building, however, was not Rudy's forte. He tended to rely on the overwhelming force of his own personality. I had already let Rudy know that I thought he was misguided in his enthusiasm for moving the Yankees out of the Bronx. To help him understand that my reluctance was neither arbitrary nor personal, I offered to hold a citywide referendum and let the city's voters decide: he would be free to use the persuasive powers of the mayor's soapbox.

Rudy, sensing how hard it was going to be to sell his idea to the general public, was not amenable to my referendum idea. He offered other inducements to make me change positions: support for our promise to return the income tax surtax that had allowed us to institute Safe Streets, Safe City; an offer to lead a campaign to end term limits for council members. Both offers were great, but not as part of a deal.

At the end of April our dispute over alternate tax-cut plans and the stadium became unpleasant. Giuliani wanted a modest temporary cut in the income tax. I wanted to permanently end the surtax we had instituted eight years earlier. "We made a commitment to New Yorkers to hire five thousand more cops and rebuild our criminal justice system," I declared in a public statement. "We did that, not Mayor Giuliani. Now it's time to keep our commitment to the taxpayers." A couple of days later Rudy let it be known that, just to make sure that the City Council proposal for a referendum never happened, he was going to appoint a charter commission for the purpose of creating a city government question for the November ballot. Doing so would block our referendum because, by law, no other question or referendum could appear on the ballot at the same time a charter question was being offered voters.

On the first of May, during preliminary budget talks I was holding with Rudy, his staff, and mine, the subject of the stadium inevitably intruded. He made a final effort to win my support. The conversation went something like this:

"Look," he said to me, "you're running for governor. If you win, this is our last chance to make history. You know you could do this, if you wanted to. You control the council."

"No, Rudy," I replied, "I don't control them."

"Come on, you do."

"Rudy, I bring them in, I talk to them, I don't just order them around. And Rudy, I've been honest with you all along. I don't believe in moving Yankee Stadium to Manhattan. I was stuck on the West Side last night for twenty minutes just trying to get past Madison Square Garden. Can you imagine what playing eighty-one regular season home games on the West Side would do? The area couldn't take it without an entirely new transportation system. West Siders would sue until hell freezes over."

"What are you saying?"

"I don't think it's the right thing to do. I just read in the newspaper that Bronx County is now listed as the most improved county in the nation. How would it look if we moved the showcase stadium of the world from there to Manhattan?"

"We'll bring them by boat from New Jersey. Eventually we'll extend the Number 7 train."

"'Eventually' doesn't work, you'll destroy the West Side."

"Everybody leave the room," Giuliani said.

With just the two of us left, Rudy said some unpleasant words that did not sit well with me. I responded forcefully. Had our staffs been there, they might have thought a schoolyard brawl was about to break out. After taking a deep breath, I told Rudy as coolly and calmly as I could that although I was opposed to his idea of moving the Yankees, I would not kill "his baby," but go in good faith to my fellow council members, present his case to them, tell them "the mayor wants this," and, even if I vote no, a majority rules.

In fact, I could not find one council member who was in favor of Rudy's stadium idea, not even a Republican. This left me with no choice but to inform Rudy that the council was going to take the $1.2

billion set aside in his budget for the stadium and put it into school construction.

From that moment on, the Yankee Stadium question infected not just the political scene but every aspect of city governance. The mayor and Yankee owner Steinbrenner accused me of wanting to put the Yankee Stadium referendum question on the November ballot in order to boost city election turnout and increase my chances of winning the race against Governor Pataki. Rudy refused to meet with me again. All conversations took place only between our staffs. Rudy was saying, basically, no negotiations, take it or leave it. Rumors flew that Deputy Mayor Randy Mastro had said in a meeting with my chief of staff Bruce Bender that the mayor would "bring the council to their knees"; the media lapped up the drama of the confrontation.

For the first time in history the council was forced to adopt its own budget. When the mayor vetoed it, we overrode his veto and also vetoed the budget he had submitted, preventing him from spending any money we had not approved. For the first time ever the City Council had said definitively to the chief executive of New York City, "NO!" No wonder the *New York Times* christened us "The House That Roared"; that *Newsday* ran a cartoon depicting me as "a thorn" in Rudy's side and the *New York Observer* caricatured Rudy as Captain Bligh thrown off a huge sailing vessel—the *Budget Surplus Bounty*—by a mutinous City Council.

My campaign for governor continued even as the Yankee Stadium melodrama played itself out in New York's media circus. In May Betsy McCaughey Ross, to my consternation, successfully used her husband's large bankroll to win the Liberal Party's nomination—giving her a place on the November ballot whether or not she became the Democratic nominee. In response, my campaign manager Kevin McCabe and I helped form a new grassroots party to be supported by multiple small donors. Our hope was that this Working Families Party, as we called it, could eventually supplant the Liberal Party and the unprincipled maneuvering of its bosses to become the legitimate liberal platform for New York State candidates. (To our gratification, this strategy has worked.)

On May 28, 1998, Assembly Speaker Silver orchestrated the state Democratic convention in such a way that I would be denied the 50 percent vote I needed to become the official candidate and possibly avert a September primary fight. During an artificially prolonged roll call of delegates, he organized a horse trade of Ross's supporters that pushed Joe Hynes over the 25 percent threshold. This not only guaranteed Hynes a spot on the primary ballot, but had the domino effect of losing me some delegates who would otherwise have supported me.

Whatever Shelly's plan for my demise, it turned out to be a good thing I did not win at the state convention, because failing there meant I had to organize a petition drive to get on the ballot in every county. That in turn meant I had to establish organizations in those counties, which would prove crucial in the upcoming primary.

During the summer of the primary campaign I traveled extensively throughout New York State and tried to keep the political coverage focused on my eventual opponent, Governor Pataki, rather than on the other Democratic candidates or my feud with Rudy Giuliani. The effort proved difficult, since Pataki had adopted a "Rose Garden" strategy of acting gubernatorial, ignoring his opponents, and even ignoring the campaign itself. Throughout the summer he flitted across the nation in an attempt to boost his credentials with Republicans in other states. In my speeches I complained to him about his absence: "Governor, we have problems. You're out of state. You're out of touch. You have to come back and address those problems." But the national economy was chugging along, and Pataki had no political interest in bringing attention to the very real problems for which many voters, unfocused on the race, were not holding him responsible. Meanwhile the labor unions largely shifted into neutral. Most indicated they would sign on with the eventual winner of the primary, but were reluctant to be vocal in challenging a governor they expected to win reelection. Pataki had played a shrewd game, making severe cuts in programs favored by organized labor early in his term, and later, as the economy and tax revenues increased, conceding more to labor in an effort to win their support.

At the end of August Thomas Golisano, founder of the payroll company Paychex and candidate of the Independence Party, began a major, self-financed anti-Pataki advertising campaign. Golisano had won 4 percent of the gubernatorial vote in the 1994 campaign, and had considerable wealth to draw upon. He was outraged at Pataki's liberal spending policies, targeted as they were to bring him maximum advantage come November. (Golisano also confessed to me that every time he ran, his business increased from 10 to 20 percent.)

Also in August, I began to pull way ahead of Betsy Ross in the polls. Statewide name recognition had given her a lead early in the race, but since its roots lay more in notoriety than in solid achievement, the lead quickly faded. More notoriety soon followed as she and her husband engaged in a public debate about how much of his money he was going to spend on her campaign. At one point he had promised as much as $10 million. In early September, as he realized how little chance she had of winning the primary, he withdrew more than half of the $4 million he had actually put in. Ms. Ross then tried to salvage her campaign by making a series of random, uninformed, and contradictory attacks on me. It did not help her. On September 15, I pulled in 56 percent of the vote, nearly three times as much as she did at 21 percent (Joe Hynes got 15 percent and James Larocca 8 percent). At last, I was a statewide winner.

My prospects for the general election did not look good, however. In my diary, I noted that "Pataki has you two to one in the polls. . . . He also has twelve million dollars to your less than one. But if you have God and your family, what does it matter who is against you?" As things turned out, winning the statewide democratic primary for governor would be the biggest election victory of my life.

The Yankee Stadium dispute continued throughout the summer and into the fall gubernatorial campaign. Rudy refused to spend anything for council budget items that did not agree with those in his budget, and proceeded to hand-select a charter commission with no clear mandate other than blocking the council's referendum. The mayor maintained he was "forced" to do this by my misuse of council powers. In response the council sued the mayor not only on account of illegally freezing our appropriations, but over his phony commission, designed not really to revise the city charter, but simply as a political diversion.

As far as Pataki was concerned, Rudy's stadium idea had never been a favorite. Anxious to diminish city turnout and thus my margin of victory there, and knowing that opponents of a West Side stadium were expected to vote overwhelmingly in my favor, Pataki made an oracular pronouncement about the Yankees shortly after I won the primary, mentioning that he favored the Yankees staying in the Bronx, but would not totally rule out the idea of a West Side stadium, although he saw many good reasons for not doing so. By gently undercutting Rudy on the stadium, Pataki hoped to pull the rug out from under the council's argument for holding the referendum.

In court rulings regarding Giuliani's charter commission and our referendum, the council won a decision from one state judge, but was overturned by another. We then filed an appeal and brought our concerns to the federal Justice Department as a possible Voting Rights Act violation. But time ran out on us.

It also ran out on the Giuliani & Steinbrenner vision of a Manhattan stadium. By the end of September Bronx borough president Fernando Ferrer had released his plan for the city to refurbish Yankee Stadium as a way of keeping the Yankees in the Bronx. Steinbrenner announced that he would not say anything about the Yankees' plans until after the baseball season and the general election were over.

My prospects for winning that election had not improved since Kevin McCabe first warned me in March about the likely outcome. A day after I won the Democratic primary, Pataki went flying around the region he had neglected for years, upstate New York. The highlight of his public tour was an appearance in Buffalo to accept the embrace and endorsement of the city's Democratic mayor, the very man who had been one of my biggest early backers. I felt this betrayal as a real stab in the back. (Although Ed Koch also said he would endorse me and then endorsed Pataki instead, I felt differently about him because I believed it when he said he had made an inadvertent double promise.) Losing the backing of upstaters who should have been my allies was discouraging—even if I understood that they were anxious not to alienate a governor who might kill off state assistance they vitally needed.

I had already spent a lot of money by the time of the primary. I had not worried too much about this, since the minute you win the primary, especially by a significant margin as I had, you usually get a jump in donations and an influx of funds from the national party. Not this year. For several weeks before the primary date, polls had shown me far ahead of my three rivals. Nonetheless, the Democratic Senatorial Campaign Committee scheduled, for the Monday immediately preceding the primary, a $5,000-per-head fund-raiser at the hottest play in town, *The Lion King.* When I learned about this I realized that such an event would empty the pockets of Democratic donors at the very moment I needed them most. I called my friend Senator Bob Kerrey, the chair of the committee, who politely told me that he was sure the scheduling was a mistake but that he was no longer chair. I should call the new chair, Senator Robert Torricelli of New Jersey, to clear up matters. When I called Torricelli, he told me it was my problem, not his, and refused to lift a finger to change it. Our heated conversation ended when I told him, "Thanks, Senator, for nothing!"

And nothing is what I received from the national party. (In the middle of an intense campaign for reelection in 2002, Torricelli was forced to resign from the Senate because of ethical lapses which he was alleged to have "covered up.") Disregard from the Democratic National Committee, and the continuing disaffection of Shelly Silver, meant that the only money I received in the general election came from telephone calls I personally made. Getting "free" coverage from the media was equally difficult. In 1994, Pataki had called Mario Cuomo "gutless" for not debating. Yet in 1998 he refused to commit to a single one-on-one debate with me. "I know that you've made speeches in California, in Iowa, in New Hampshire, and in a couple of other states," I taunted him. "I challenge you, Governor, to debate right here in New York State . . . in Buffalo."

And so it went for most of the campaign. Polls showed the likelihood of Pataki swamping me in the general election and possibly even carrying New York City, even though New York State was ranked forty-seventh of all the states in job creation. I had offered substantive proposals for a statewide health insurance program and statewide campaign finance legislation modeled on what we did for the city as well as a strong plan for boosting education in the city and elsewhere. My theme was "New York First!" I believed that New York should have been "first in education" in the nation and in the economy—yet a mainstay of New York's upstate economy, Eastman Kodak, was slowly dying. Why wasn't New York doing more to promote its own products? I asked.

Meanwhile, on a national level, the Republicans continued to shamelessly grandstand about President Clinton and Monica Lewinsky, and on the local level the feud between the City Council and Rudy Giuliani that began with Rudy's Yankee Stadium scheme escalated as he withheld city payments for programs dear to the council members who had opposed him. The hopelessness of my efforts seemed underlined a couple of days before the election when the driver of an out-of-town photographer's van who was following our campaign caravan, and was unable to interpret New York City stoplights, rear-ended my car. My injuries were little more than a sore back, but I had to spend a valuable day of campaign time in the hospital getting fitted with an electronic stimulator so I could campaign the following day.

On Election Day I did indeed lose statewide by a large margin, but contrary to prediction we carried the city by nearly 2 to 1. "So how does it feel to be 'Governor of the City of New York'?" I wrote the next day in my diary. There were a few consoling factors. Although we lost, our margin of loss was narrower than those of Mario Cuomo's opponents in his successful reelection campaigns. And none of the Democratic candidates in the state were hurt because of my loss. In fact, two major posts—the U.S. Senate race and the state attorney general position—switched out of Republican hands and into Democratic ones.

By the end of my campaign for governor I had traveled to all sixty-two of New York's counties, and I now know why it was christened the "Empire State." It is enormous in size and in beauty. I had to fly to Vermont and take a ferry across beautiful Lake Champlain in order to meet supporters in Plattsburgh, New York. I cannot describe the serenity and peaceful joy of standing on that ferry—it was as close to standing in the presence of our Creator as I have ever been.

As I traveled around New York State I learned that, for all the hundreds of supporters I met in person, there were hundreds of thousands who could only be reached through local radio and television stations. This had proved crucial in my defeat. In New York City, you could travel to several affairs in a few minutes and meet hundreds of people at one time. In the state you had to spend hours to meet just a few dozen voters. Time and swift transportation became my greatest obstacles. The millionaire independent candidate Thomas Golisano skimmed off much of the upstate Italian vote that might otherwise have gone to me, and although I was able to raise what was once the respectable sum of $7 million, I was outspent by over $30 million by the Republicans and by another $14 million by Golisano. The importance of money in winning an election in this state is scandalous.

Six weeks after my campaign for governor ended in defeat, I hosted my annual brunch for state legislators in Albany, despite an intense northeaster that nearly blocked me from coming. During the same visit I held my usual one-on-one meetings with my recent opponent Governor Pataki as well as Speaker Silver and Albany's other political leaders. In my tête-à-tête with Majority Leader Michael Bragman I was stunned to hear his apology "for staying silent as Shelly derailed your campaign."

A little more than a year later Mike openly challenged Shelly Silver in a bid to replace him as assembly Speaker. There was heavy resentment among Democratic legislators in Albany about the close-fisted methods Shelly used to exercise near absolute control, and Mike probably would have been successful if he had been more politically adept in carrying out his revolt. Instead, he failed to contact me or other potentially sympathetic allies who might have helped rally support. He also announced the rebellion on a Friday (giving Shelly all of Saturday and Sunday to regroup, make promises, and win back crucial support). As the new week began, Bragman's insurgency faltered and even Carl McCall, whose upcoming campaign for governor Shelly Silver had already begun to undermine, made peace with the Speaker. In the end, Shelly made a few gestures toward less autocracy, and Mike Bragman lost his leadership positions and left the assembly. I have heard tell that to this day Shelly Silver believes I was the hidden power behind Mike Bragman's rebellion. All I can say is that if I had been, the result would have been different.

18

Reconciliation and Religion

The day after I lost my race for governor, Rudy Giuliani saw me smiling and laughing with a few of my colleagues in the center hallway of City Hall. From the corner of my eye I saw him signal me to come into his office. There, he complimented me for running a good race and avoiding negative campaigning. But one thing he could not understand: Why wasn't I crushed by my defeat? He had just left "the other guy," and Governor Pataki looked miserable. How did I explain that?

I said, "Mr. Mayor, there are some things far more important than winning or losing a race. I have no regrets because I did the best I could. I never would have forgiven myself if I didn't try, or if I'd run a divisive, negative race. Far more important to me is my relationship with God, my family, and the things that really count in life, like the privilege of serving this city, and working with you to make this city the best in the world." We embraced, apologized for the argument that had divided us the past six months, and shared cigars and champagne he took from his cabinet. From that moment on we never again had a dispute that we could not amicably settle. Even today we remain close personal friends.

Rudy and I never again discussed his unsuccessful attempt to move the Yankees to Manhattan. Rudy also soon agreed to release all but $20 million of the $150 million the council had approved which he had refused to spend. A few months later, Steinbrenner expressed public interest in a plan developed in consultation with Charlie Rangel and Freddy Ferrer to keep the Yankees in the Bronx by revitalizing the stadium and the neighborhood around it. I'm happy to report that this project, having long since gained Rudy's approval, is now on the drawing boards (as is a brand-new stadium in Queens for my own favorite New York Mets). Rudy Giuliani became "America's Mayor" because he learned so well, put the right people in the right places during the city's darkest hours, and stifled nearly all criticism with his effective leadership.

It was not easy for Rudy Giuliani to overcome his instincts as a prosecutor. There may be no clearer example of this than the way he reacted to the tragic death of the young West African street peddler Amadou Diallo. Twenty-two-year-old Diallo was an immigrant from Guinea who had been in this country for about two years. In the very early morning of February 4, 1999, four young white officers from the city's Street Crime Units were working the streets in Diallo's neighborhood, the Soundview area of the Bronx. When they glimpsed Diallo they thought he bore a strong resemblance to an artist's sketch of a rapist believed to be operating in the area. The four officers confronted him in the vestibule of his Bronx apartment. They apparently believed he was reaching for a weapon when he moved his hands. Forty-one shots were fired, nineteen of which struck the young man, who died immediately. After police searched and identified the body they found he bore no relation to the rapist, had no criminal record, and was unarmed. The *New York Times* carried this early, unofficial version of the officers' story of what happened:

> The officers . . . were said to have approached Mr. Diallo as he arrived at the vestibule of his building about 12:35 A.M. on Thursday. They had seen him acting in some "suspicious" way. . . . He failed to comply when the officers asked him to do something. . . . There may have been a language problem. Mr. Diallo spoke English, but slowly and with a stutter. The officers opened fire when they thought he reached for a gun, a person familiar with their account said, although Mr. Diallo carried only a wallet and a beeper. It was unclear which officer fired first, but all joined in firing once it started.

Here was a clear instance of police overreaction. However incomprehensibly a suspect is acting, you don't need to shoot him forty-one times. I am usually generous in making allowances for police officers under pressure. Even here I could not and would not say that what the cops had done was criminal. But I knew it was *wrong*, and I said so. It never should have happened. That Amadou Diallo was an innocent victim made the tragic result even more poignant.

Unfortunately, Mayor Giuliani was slow to understand the significance of the Diallo case. Rudy had become so used to the exaggerated claims of police brutality used by some publicity-seeking activists, that once again he fell into his accustomed role as defender of the police. True, he expressed sorrow about young Diallo's killing, and offered condolences to the family. But he could not avoid using the same platform to offer a spirited defense of his administration's policies against the critics who for several years had been increasingly vocal in their complaints about police misconduct and disrespect, especially toward minorities.

His usual remark in such instances was something like "It was absolutely justified, based on the preliminary investigation," or "We have to wait for the facts to emerge." Indeed, most of the time I agreed with Rudy. With one major exception: I believed the police were no less fallible than the rest of government, and that they too should have a check upon their exercise of authority. For this reason I had been instrumental in seeing that civilian members were appointed to the Civilian Complaint Review Board in 1986, and that after the "Police Riot" of 1992 the review board be completely overhauled to become fully independent, with investigative powers. For the same reason, I had been instrumental in passing legislation in 1994 establishing an Independent Police Investigative Board (IPIB) for the purpose of looking into charges of corruption. I knew that the police, like any group, sometimes rallied around their own kind, even covering up misconduct and crimes when they felt threatened by the outside. An independent forum like the IPIB was meant to provide a permanent governmental body that could be approached by truth-tellers who might otherwise be intimidated by their fellow officers (the way the Knapp Commission of 1970–72 took testimony from police detective Frank Serpico).

I was disappointed when Rudy, who felt the IPIB would undercut morale in the police department, successfully challenged it in the state courts as an intrusion into executive authority. A couple of years later, a revolting example of the sort of police cover-up the IPIB was meant to prevent occurred when a Haitian immigrant named Abner Louima was savagely tortured in a Brooklyn police station. When the wall of silence protecting the miscreant cops finally cracked, Mayor Rudy and his police commissioner Howard Safir were appropriately outraged. Nevertheless, Rudy again vetoed another attempt by the City Council to reestablish the IPIB along lines more to the court's liking. Although this legislation was also eventually overturned, it did force Giuliani to establish his own Mayor's Commission to Combat Police Corruption.

The trial of the officers involved in the torture of Abner Louima was still going on when the Amadou Diallo case arose, and naturally enough, the sensitivities of the city's minority communities were aroused accordingly. So were those of the mayor, anxious to depict the torture of Louima as the case of a few rotten apples and not, as his critics charged, symptomatic of a larger pattern of police misconduct. Thus, when Giuliani quoted a statistical decline in the use of weapons by the police, his critics pointed to a sharp rise in formal complaints of police misconduct. And while Giuliani defended his Street Crimes Unit as a vital force behind an unquestioned decline in crime in the city, even some prosecutors noted that the group's assignment to root out crimes before they happened left them vulnerable to charges of unlawful search and seizure.

While Rudy concentrated on rebutting his political critics, he paid insufficient attention to the bitterness brewing in the city's minority communities, which erupted within days of Mr. Diallo's death. At protests organized by the Reverend Al Sharpton, Mayor Giuliani was assailed as insensitive and uncaring, and rebuked for not visiting Mr. Diallo's relatives. One Senegalese summed up much of the crowds' sentiment when he said, "When people shoot cops, he is there, but when cops shoot people he doesn't show up." The protesters called for the immediate arrest of the four "renegade" policemen on murder charges. While Rudy quickly attempted to set up a meeting with the parents of the dead man, who flew into New York from Africa and Australia and arranged for the Reverend Sharpton to become their spokesperson, they at first declined to meet with him. Rudy appropriately refused to call for the arrest of the officers, pending legal proceedings—but was too matter-of-fact about it. I had a firsthand sense of the frustration and distress felt by much of the city's minority population. Most members of the City Council's Hispanic and Minority Caucus were extremely angry at Rudy, feeling that in his book the cops could never do wrong, no matter what.

Rudy's defensiveness rekindled old resentments. A task force appointed two years earlier by the mayor himself to review police-community relations in the wake of the Abner Louima case reassembled and declared that its recommendations for revised police procedures—many previously rejected by the Giuliani administration—should be resurrected in the aftermath of the Diallo shooting. A month after the shooting, the African-American community was still up in arms against the mayor. Cardinal O'Connor attempted to broker a reconciliation by holding a meeting of those on all sides. At this meeting the director of the Archdiocese's Office of Black Ministry recounted that he was often stopped by white police officers, even while dressed as a priest, for no clear reason other than his dark complexion. "Clearly, we have problems," the cardinal was quoted in an interview in the *New York Times.* "We have to get at those problems."

Although Rudy and Commissioner Safir attended an Interfaith service sponsored by some African and African-American leaders, other leaders and Al Sharpton refocused their protest campaign into one of civil disobedience. They staged a series of sit-ins at police headquarters meant to disrupt business as usual until formal charges were brought against the four officers. Sharpton's clever tactics and Rudy's intemperate response (he decried the sit-ins as "a publicity stunt," and derided the city press for being "sucked" into them) solidified the city's African-American political leadership in opposition to the mayor—even Congressman Rangel and former mayor David Dinkins let themselves be arrested at police headquarters.

Dialogue was more important to me than protest. While the sit-ins continued and the cameras rolled at City Hall, I set up a special council committee for police-community relations. The committee and I traveled to every borough and held open discussions involving that borough's police commander, the local precincts, and the community. To me, the police officers' violent response to Amadou Diallo reflected a lack of training. I consistently condemned it, without calling it a crime. I also scheduled general hearings on the same subject for City Hall, but kept running into resistance from Commissioner Safir over the ground rules for his testimony. It was vastly important to me to help bring about a dialogue between the council's minority leaders and the mayor. I also wanted him to finally meet with former council member Virginia Fields, who had succeeded Ruth Messinger as Manhattan borough president and who had been refused a meeting with Giuliani for over a year.

Seeing Dinkins and Rangel join Al Sharpton had so enraged Rudy that when I first proposed the idea of meeting Fields and the council members he talked about them as "rabble-rousers." "No, Rudy," I said, "they're elected officials." He reluctantly agreed to a meeting, but only under strict ground rules. Meanwhile negotiations continued with the police commissioner's office about his appearance at our council hearings, which began the following Monday. As Monday approached Rudy told me that Commissioner Safir was in Los Angeles and would not be back in time for the hearings. When I pressed him as to why not, he said that Safir had been invited to attend the Academy Awards.

"What?" I babbled in disbelief to Rudy. "Your police commissioner is vacationing at the Oscars while people are getting arrested at Police Headquarters? Do you want my council members to stay in the hearing room listening to Safir or go join Sharpton on the steps out there? He has got to get back here!"

On the Sunday night before the scheduled hearings, viewers who tuned into the Oscars caught several shots of Howard Safir dressed in his tuxedo. As we later discovered, the Oscar trip had been arranged for Safir by the president of Revlon, Inc., and Safir's original plans called for him to return to New York on Revlon's corporate jet during business hours Monday, conveniently skipping the hearings at which he had been so reluctant to appear. I spent a nervous Sunday night and early Monday morning waiting to see whether the commissioner would show up as Rudy promised he would. Indeed, Safir bought himself a ticket on the red-eye flight in order to arrive at my office 9:30 Monday morning. He testified at ten. A few weeks later, stories emerged about Safir's using police department detectives at his daughter's wedding and to investigate a woman against whom he and his wife were bringing a lawsuit. Clearly, Commissioner Safir was not the most able spokesperson for reconciliation in a bitterly divided city. Luckily the hearings went fairly smoothly, as did meetings between the mayor and borough president Fields, and the mayor and the minority council members. Soon, to Rudy's credit, the administration accepted the political realities and changed course.

A year later, the four police officers who shot Amadou Diallo were acquitted of all charges. Many leaders thought the verdicts unfair; I myself did not criticize the verdicts but urged that the police continue building better relationships with local communities. I put $20 million into the budget to improve the interracial training of police officers, in the hope we could avoid this ever happening again.

Meanwhile, I narrowly avoided being tripped up by the Reverend Sharpton some six weeks after the sit-ins ended at Police Headquarters. Early in the morning on May 19, 1999, my communications director came in to ask me, "Did you make an appointment with Al Sharpton?"

"Would I have a meeting and not tell you?" I asked. "Of course not."

He then explained that in the press daybook, the schedule of major press conferences and other public events put out daily by the wire services, I was listed that day as having a scheduled appointment with Al Sharpton. I vaguely remembered that some time earlier the press had blown up a story about Giuliani refusing to meet with the Reverend Al. Smelling something similar in the works, and noticing the small accumulation of cameramen that had already gathered outside my office, we quickly decided to improvise.

At exactly that moment, Al Sharpton came sauntering in. "Hello, Al, how you doing, good to see you!" I greeted him warmly, offered him a seat, and sat down beside him. "What can I do for you?"

Al quickly got up, looked over all the pictures on my walls (there are a great number), and started making small talk.

"Is there something I can do for you?" I repeated.

He said something like, "Oh, no, I just came by to pay my respects."

To which I responded, "That's nice of you, any time you like."

And every time I've seen Al since then, he's given me a nice big hug.

Over my life I have learned that our Creator likes surprises and the unexpected. In February of 1994, my secretary informed me that Mother Teresa was on the phone and wanted to speak to me. I figured it was a practical joke and hesitantly picked up the phone. To my utter amazement it really was Mother Theresa. She asked if my chief of staff and I could meet her at mass early the next morning "to go over a few things." Of course, we dropped everything and met her in her East Harlem convent the next morning at seven.

When mass was over, she signaled us to accompany her to a small room behind the chapel. It became quickly apparent not only that she knew the name of my recently-appointed chief of staff Kevin McCabe who became my campaign manager four years later—but that he was one of those amazing Irish politicians who seems connected to everybody, especially the Kennedys and the Clintons. "Mr. McCabe," she said to him, "I understand you have good contacts in Washington, and I would like you to arrange a meeting with the First Lady Mrs. Clinton so that I can discuss with her the building of a home for unwed mothers and mothers who are planning abortions."

She went on to explain that she had built more than four hundred such homes throughout the world, and paid all the medical expenses. If the unwed mother of a child chose, she could put her baby up for adoption to a loving couple of whatever faith or persuasion was desired. Needless to say, Kevin arranged the meeting with Hillary, and the home was built in Washington, D.C. Before leaving, Mother Teresa gave Kevin and me a blessed medal (which I still carry with me), grabbed my hand, and said, "The motto I chose for my order is 'Whatsoever you do to the least of my brethren, you do it for me'" (Matthew 25:45). For emphasis she took the fingers of my hand and one after the other squeezed each individually as she repeated the five words—"YOU—DO—IT—FOR—ME!" A decade later, I still feel the electrifying touch of her hand.

We met with her on several occasions thereafter, and each time it was an unforgettable and beautiful experience. On one occasion she held my hand and said, "Mr. Speaker, I need help in Vietnam—" when her assistant politely cut her off. "Mother, he is the Speaker of the City of New York, not Mr. Gingrich of the United States Congress."

"Oh yes . . ." Mother Teresa replied. "Mr. Speaker, I need three parking spaces in front of this convent."

"Well, Mother," I said, "*that* I could help you with!"

During one week after both Cardinal O'Connor and I sprinted up to the Bronx on five minutes' notice to see some of Mother Theresa's nuns take vows, the cardinal made a friendly crack about me and her in front of 1,500 people at the Waldorf. It came at a time when there was a lot of talk around town about my political ambitions. "Somebody tell Peter," the cardinal declared, "that Mother Theresa does not vote."

Pope John Paul II beatified Mother Theresa some time ago and I have no doubt that she will be declared a saint in the near future. As for Cardinal O'Connor, the only thing I can say is that I loved the guy. When he died in May of 2000 I wrote in my diary: "Touched your soul for good . . . true servant of God . . . a giant in life and will continue." Besides all that, the cardinal knew exactly how to use his unique brand of humor. I'll never forget him quipping at a 1994 New York Police Department Holy Name mass, "If I see Peter Vallone one more time that would make three times in three days, and I'll have to make him a monsignor."

That does not mean that our relationship was always completely smooth—as indeed relationships between lawmakers and religious leaders probably never should be. In 1997 and 1998 the City Council was considering various versions of a domestic partnership bill that would extend to non-married couples, both gay and straight, some of the legal and civil protections enjoyed by married ones. My position had always been, and remained, that while I would not endorse the gay lifestyle, I would also never endorse discrimination against gay men and women, and in June 1997 I indeed turned down a bill that I believed went too far toward endorsing a gay lifestyle. In 1998, however, Mayor Giuliani introduced, I endorsed, and the council passed a Domestic Partnership Bill that I believed hit the right balance.

The cardinal, however, spoke out against all versions of these bills, both from the pulpit and in private discussions with me, feeling they were contrary to the church's teaching on the sanctity of marriage. When I had breakfast with him in 1997 and he brought up his opposition to extending rights to homosexual and unmarried couples, I changed the subject to persecution of Christians in the Sudan. The result: eight months later the council, with the public encouragement of Cardinal O'Connor, passed legislation establishing the principle that New York City would divest itself of any investments in countries that persecuted for religious reasons.

The other area over which Cardinal O'Connor and I had disagreements revolved around abortion. The question of abortion has always disturbed me deeply. I am very much pro-life in the largest sense, and I told both Cardinal O'Connor and Bishop Daily in Brooklyn that I cannot accept that a woman who cannot deliver a fetus in the early stages without dying must die; no one on the face of this earth can tell me to choose a fetus over my wife. This sort of thing actually happens. I also cannot necessarily expect that a woman who becomes pregnant through rape or because she is a victim of incest will carry a child to term. If I am willing to make such exceptions in good conscience—as a practicing Catholic and not just on my own, but with the advice of my confessor—then who am I to say that you cannot make an exception? I believe that everyone has to make a choice, and that choice is between you and your God. I believe in good conscience that condemnation is up to God, not me. On the other hand, I don't think abortion should be used as a form of birth control, which it is now, with about half as many babies being aborted in the world as are born. And I certainly don't agree with partial abortion.

The Cardinal's response to me was, "We just can't let the perception out there be that you are pro-choice. We have to find another way."

I told Cardinal O'Connor, Bishop Daily, and my staff that my preference would be to say that I was "pro-conscience," and avoid being caught between the political labels of "pro-life" or "pro-choice."

No one seemed to agree with me. Bishop Daily argued that I could not just say "pro-conscience"; that I had to say "correct conscience" because it was not an entirely subjective question. I would reply, "I'm not in the business of condemnation. I leave that to God. I took an oath to obey and enforce the law to the best of my ability." Meanwhile during political campaigns my staff argued that I had to keep things simple, that I should accept the "pro-choice" label, and that to do anything more complicated would be political suicide.

This was an agonizing decision for me and to this day I still wrestle with it. I would prefer to use "pro-conscience" or "pro-life" (in the larger sense) if I could be assured of not being completely misinterpreted, because by saying I'm "pro-choice" I believe I have bought a little bit into the celebration of abortion. If asked today, I simply say my choice is for life, and leave the rest to you, your conscience, and your Creator.

Some other controversies from the Giuliani years that supposedly had something to do with religion should really never have even become public issues. The brouhaha over the Brooklyn Museum show that featured the painting of a black Madonna with a breast made of elephant dung and surrounded by cutouts from pornographic magazines is one example. A fortnight before the exhibit opened in October of 1999, Rudy went on a rampage, threatening to withdraw the city's subsidy to the museum unless they withdrew the show, and accusing the artist and curators of "Catholic-bashing."

Both Rudy and I found the idea of dung on Our Lady's portrait deeply offensive. Nonetheless, government should never be Big Brother attempting to impose its morals, likes, or dislikes on a museum, which should be free to exhibit what it likes, within the limits of decency. In this case the British artist of Nigerian background described himself as a churchgoing Roman Catholic. I told Rudy he could not out-Catholic me on this question, and that he was going to create a monster if he continued to publicize the event. I told him it was unconstitutional to stop the funding because he didn't like a particular painting. You can't censor art, I told him—but that doesn't mean you have to go see it.

"Or fund it," he would say.

"We're not funding the picture," I would say, "we're funding the museum."

"What's the difference?"

"You're forcing them to do what you like."

In off-the-record negotiations with museum officials we even discussed ways of meeting Rudy's objection to the city's appearing to subsidize "blasphemous" art. For whatever reason, city officials leaked word of the discussions and Rudy escalated his attacks on the city's "effete" cultural elite.

Then, something truly unfortunate was narrowly averted. For a few days, Rudy's intimidating words had a disastrous effect on the leadership of many of the city's leading cultural institutions. Knowing Rudy's unfortunate tendency to treat some who disagreed with him as enemies and afraid of having their own funds cut, these leaders said nothing. As Rudy continued with his press campaign against the Brooklyn Museum, I warned that acceding to the mayor's wishes would set a precedent for this mayor or any future mayor to cut off funding for any institution that displeased him. I hoped the city's cultural leaders would immediately rally around me. Yet in several emergency meetings of the Cultural Institutions Group (representing the art organizations that received city funds), my representatives were forced to make First Amendment arguments to some of the very people who should have been spearheading its defense. Luckily, the silence was soon broken, a united stand was formed in defense of the Brooklyn Museum, and the only negative fallout from Rudy's one-man "decency" campaign were the mammoth attendance figures for an offensive and tasteless exhibition.

My close aide and counsel Richard Weinberg tells an interesting anecdote about deliberations that occurred at a Lincoln Center board meeting that took place as the Brooklyn Museum fight was beginning. Mayor Giuliani had just begun legal proceedings to de-fund the museum and rescind its corporate charter. The City Council, in alliance with some but by no means a majority of the city's cultural organizations, had started a countersuit. Among the city's cultural boards, that of Lincoln Center may be the one that boasts the "heaviest hitters," the city's most powerful players. Among the members at that time were Michael Bloomberg, Beverly Sills, Nat Leventhal, Parks Commissioner Henry Stern, former executive director of the Metropolitan Opera Schuyler Chapin, and others. Rich Weinberg sat on the board as an ex officio member representing me as the Speaker of the City Council. (Rudy's deputy mayor Randy Mastro usually attended as the mayor's ex officio, although he was not present at the meeting in question.)

After cocktails at noon, during which people were shaking their heads over the Brooklyn Museum case, the meeting began. Henry Stern said that Rudy was right in his stance on the Brooklyn Museum show and recommended that the Lincoln Center Board adopt a position supporting the mayor. Everyone was squirming. They had hoped to escape the issue by staying neutral, but Henry, by pushing the envelope, was forcing them to think harder.

The last thing Rich wanted was to be controversial. He, like me, tried to be a facilitator, not an agitator. What Henry Stern had proposed, however, and the embarrassed silence around him, forced him to raise his hand. Nat Leventhal then asked Beverly Sills to recognize Richard, who said:

"I was not going to say anything, but since Henry Stern has spoken, I feel I have an obligation to point out the facts. First, there's nothing in the state constitution or the city charter that authorizes the mayor to be the city's cultural czar. When the City Council enacts the budget and puts money into an organization, that money is to be spent by that organization. The mayor can only put a hold on money when there's a fiscal crisis. Most significantly, think about who might be next. At this very moment, a theater in Lincoln Center is showing a foreign film that includes a lesbian love scene between two nuns. Say the mayor decides to hold back the funds for Lincoln Center until you decide to withdraw it?"

The tenor of the meeting completely changed. At the end of it Mike Bloomberg came up to Rich and told him he wanted to support Peter Vallone's stand on this issue by sending a check. The only thing was, he wanted to make the check out to the Council Political Action Committee, and not to the Vallone mayoral campaign committee. When Rich looked at him quizzically, Mike explained why, and when Rich saw me alone in City Hall a little while later he told me in private: "I have some good news, I have some bad news, and I have some worse news."

"What's the good news?"

Rich told me the story of the meeting, how the tenor had shifted, and that we had earned the financial support of Mike Bloomberg in the process.

"Great," I said. "What's the bad news?"

"He's not giving it to you for your mayoral campaign."

"Why not? That's exactly what I need it for."

"Well, you see, that's the worse news—Bloomberg's running."

19

The Mayoral Race That Wasn't

In my eleventh State of the City address as Speaker of the New York City Council, delivered on January 11, 2000, I tried to emphasize one of my favorite themes: It is better to lead with love, not fear:

> Welcome to the first "State of the City" address of the New Millennium. . . .
>
> The twenty-first century has arrived. Within a few years, the landscape of New York City will have changed its government—and its people.
>
> Those who have long been classified as "minorities" soon will be the new majority in New York City. We have always been a world-class city, one that thrived on immigration. But now we are truly becoming a city of the world—the whole world. Where once five languages might be heard every day, today it is more like seventy-five. Every race, every religion, every color and hue under the rainbow—is now represented here. John Rocker can live wherever he wants. I wouldn't want to be anywhere else.
>
> New York is entering uncharted territory. But I for one look forward to it. . . . Because I know this city will emerge stronger, more dynamic, with more vitality, and with the bonds between us stronger than ever before. . . .
>
> I believe that what the people of New York want in this new era is a city where we care about each other once again. Where we feel a connection to one another—as individuals, and as communities living side by side in the most diverse metropolis on this planet.
>
> We want New York to continue to be the safest big city in the nation. But we also want all New Yorkers, in *every* community, to feel that those who keep the peace are on *our* side—that they respect us, whatever our color or origin.
>
> We want our city to continue to be a place that generates great wealth. But we want it to be a place that

continues to open the doors of opportunity for all, poor and middle class as well as rich.

We want our city to be competitive. But we also want it to display compassion—*genuine* compassion. The sign on the Statue of Liberty says, "Give me your tired, your poor, your huddled masses yearning to breathe free." It does *not* say, "Get a job—or get lost." We want to attack the causes of homelessness—*not* attack homeless people.

And we are looking for leaders—*true* leaders.

Leaders who are not afraid to ask the opinion of others.

Leaders who do not think it is a sign of weakness to build a consensus.

Leaders who listen, who understand that the experience of others is sometimes very different from our own.

Leaders who, when a terrible tragedy strikes, and one community among us is in great pain, reach out to that community in an effort to heal the breach and bind the wounds.

Leaders who, when they govern in a democracy with the consent of the people, do so from a seat of government that is *open* to the people.

That's where true leadership begins. But it doesn't end there. Leadership means action. Pragmatic action. Collective action. And, in the twenty-first century, in the uncharted new era that awaits this city, I believe there is no better model of leadership than what you and I achieved in this body in the 1990s.

I went on to lay out an ambitious, forward-looking agenda whose number-one priority was education (including abolition of the Board of Education, which happened two years later). Other significant initiatives involved senior citizens, housing, transportation, and public health. I had reasons for being optimistic about the future. The race for mayor that so many had been urging on me for years finally seemed to have a logic and rationale of its own. In 2001 Mayor Giuliani and two-thirds of the City Council would be forced by the term limits law to give up their positions. I was convinced New York City needed an experienced hand at the helm to guide the transition into the New Millennium and I was certain I could provide that leadership. With that in mind, I brought down the house at the end of my speech by introducing Mark Green—the Public Advocate who, like me, was running for mayor—as my "compromise candidate for school chancellor."

Mark Green was not the only other prominent Democrat who would be competing against me for the top city post. While Mark was a favorite of Manhattan's elite, Bronx borough president Fernando Ferrer had an unassailable record as champion of the city's minority populations. The real problem candidate for me, however, was my friend and fellow Queens Democrat, former state assemblyman and current New York City comptroller Alan Hevesi. Like me, Alan had been a favorite of Donald Manes, and by this point his connections with Queens political leaders were as strong or stronger than my own.

The surprise candidate of the 2001 mayoral campaign, however, was billionaire Democrat Michael Bloomberg. In 1996, three years before his conversation with my aide and counsel Rich Weinberg at Lincoln Center, he had donated $5,000 to my Council Political Action Committee to help fight term limits. A year later, shortly after Ruth Messinger's unsuccessful effort to unseat Rudy Giuliani and during the first stages of my campaign for governor, I was surprised to hear that Mike Bloomberg would be amenable to meeting with me. On December 4, 1997, we had a cup of coffee together in his offices. During our chat he asked me what I thought about his chances of winning if he ran for mayor in the Democratic primary.

"None," I told him. "There will be a lot of liberals, like Ferrer and Mark Green." At that point I was not even thinking that I myself would be a candidate for mayor in 2001. "As a Republican, though," I went on to tell him, "you'd have quite a shot, because in the Republican Party money means a lot, they don't have the grass roots." The thing that impressed me the most about Mike's way of doing business was that he did not separate himself from his top people. In fact, he did not even have a private office, but one with glass all around, so that everyone could look in on him. Some time later he invited me to attend one of the Randall's Island picnics he staged in a big tent for his employees. When I got there and noticed how many non-employees were there besides me, I knew for sure that he was indeed going to run for office.

I had kicked off the fund-raising for my mayoral campaign in December of 1999 with a gala sixty-fifth birthday party featuring musicians Tony Bennett and Wynton Marsalis, actors Ossie Davis and Paul

Sorvino, and comedian Pat Cooper. Celebration and joy were to be the watchwords of my upcoming campaign. As I wrote in my diary: "*Joy* must be mark of your campaign for mayor . . . because that's why He came (and that's the most important campaign of all)." I wanted to make sure I didn't take myself, or the possibility of losing, too seriously—and compromise myself in the process.

As the year 2000 opened, for example, many of the city unions approached me with a huge wish list that primarily involved increasing their pension funds. Granting these kinds of requests would eventually bankrupt the city. Since Albany would ultimately have to weigh in on most of these questions, my political advisors pointed out that I could easily gain the unions' favor (and support in the upcoming mayor's race) by passing a "home rule," while simultaneously signaling the mayor to tell the governor to kill what we just passed. I told my staff they could keep the mayoralty if that was the price I'd have to pay. I was not about to do something I knew to be wrong, for the unions or anyone.

Attitudes like this may not have helped my efforts to become mayor, but they did win me praise from Rudy Giuliani, recorded in my diary on December 31, 2000: "You're the only politician who never lied to me!" I realized that same New Year's Eve that although I had raised over ten million dollars over the preceding four years, I could not stand raising money. While I enthusiastically anticipated moving into Gracie Mansion in 2002, I also looked forward to never running for office again.

Mayor Giuliani was facing his own electoral uncertainties in the New Millennium. On the one hand he was doing as much as he could as a Republican to promote my candidacy (on March 15, 2000, he asked me, "What can I do to get Hevesi out and you in as mayor?") On the other, his own all-but-certain campaign to become the Republican U.S. senatorial candidate against presumed Democratic candidate Hillary Clinton was foundering because of illness and domestic difficulties. In late April Rudy announced that he had prostate cancer, the disease that had killed his father. While my heart and prayers went out to him, I warned his potential temporary legal successor, Mark Green, not to "pull an Al Haig," like President Reagan's onetime secretary of state had, and prematurely declare himself "in charge."

Two weeks later, when Rudy announced that he was seeking a separation from his wife, the former television reporter and actress Donna Hanover, and made public his liaison with another woman, an uproar ensued. Immediately the dirty laundry of a soured personal relationship became grist for the media's sensationalism. It was a painful reminder of the political storm that had engulfed President Clinton a couple of years earlier. Five days later, a transformed Rudy dropped out of the Senate race, affirming that he would devote his energies to being mayor, fighting cancer, and bringing peace to his private life. During this very public personal crisis, Rudy went through a private hell. But he emerged from it a transformed and even stronger individual.

Coincidental to Rudy's travails I had my second Oval Office meeting with President Clinton. Luckily no cameras were on hand when I, expecting the president to take his place behind or near his desk, began to sit down in what I presumed was the guest's chair only to discover that Bill was already sitting there! Our discussion then turned into an hour-long bonding about Cardinal O'Connor, abortion, power plants, the U.S. navy base in Vieques, Puerto Rico, and Hillary's plan to run for Senate in New York.

Emboldened by such solid political connections, I was delighted a few months later to shake hands with prominent political consultant David Garth on what promised to be an agreement for him to work on my mayoral campaign. Even as we shook hands, however, I was skeptical we'd ever end up working together. Indeed, later he went with the Bloomberg campaign for a $25,000 monthly retainer. By the end of the year I had raised nearly three million dollars, but it was still almost two million behind Hevesi's war chest, well below Mark Green's, and barely below Freddy Ferrer's.

The state of the city, and particularly the need to drastically reduce class size and improve the educational performance of the city's students, was still more important to me than raising money ever could be. In January 2001 I again laid out my vision for the city's future. Still, it rankled me that Hevesi was able to broadcast enough TV ads in late March to boost his poll results by five points, and that my Queens county leader, Tom Manton, called in early May, shortly before I announced, to tell me that the Queens organization "always had a commitment to Hevesi." When I told Ed Koch about my disappointment, his ebullient response was: "Manton, Schmanton—you got me, Ed Koch!"

On May 31, I formally declared for mayor in front of my elementary school alma mater, PS 122 in Astoria—one block from my home and from the apartment house where I was born. In July my media campaign guru David Doak finally succeeded in getting some creative political advertising onto the city's TV screens—although my favorite one, showing former Mayor Koch presiding over People's Court, banging his gavel and holding three mayoral contenders "Out of Order!" while at the same time pointing to me as the only qualified candidate, was never filmed. In mid-July, during a primary season in which almost all of the city's unions were staying neutral, I got the biggest boost of my campaign when District Council 37, the city's largest municipal employee union, gave me their endorsement. In late August I received ringing endorsements from the *Daily News* ("combines competence and character") and the *New York Post* ("a man of integrity and honor"), as well as *Crain's New York Business* and the Patrolman's Benevolent Association.

I was dogged, however, not only by being forced to compete with Alan Hevesi for the same core voters, but by polls that overstated support for Green and Ferrer by failing to sufficiently factor in expected turnout. Nevertheless, as the September 11 primary approached, my campaign polling began to register a distinct surge in my favor. Nonetheless, everyone considered the race too close and unpredictable to call. As if to show just how fickle the city electorate might be, the weather on September 10 alternated between full sun, clouds, and a sudden downpour. All my chances for success in the race depended on turnout. At an Irish fair on Coney Island that day I tried to dramatize my need for them to come out to vote. "Nine-one-one . . . September 11 . . ." I exhorted my audience of supporters, oblivious of course of the cruel irony my words would later acquire: "It may not be an emergency for you, but it's an emergency for me."

When the polls opened at 6 A.M. the following day, I was first on line to vote in my own election district. I was brimming with enthusiasm and met equally enthusiastic volunteers who accompanied me to Bayside, Queens, where I hoped my presence would help mobilize my voters. I visited various sites and drove onto Grand Central Parkway at about 8:30 A.M. We were headed for the headquarters of DC 37, located on Barclay Street, two blocks from the World Trade Center, where several hundred volunteers were making telephone calls on my behalf and a mini-rally was waiting to greet me.

At about 8:45 A.M., while we were still on the parkway, my bodyguard and driver noticed a puff of black smoke rising suddenly from one of the towers. "Boss," he said to me, "I think a plane just crashed into the WTC." The smoke was clearly visible. At about the same time my brother-in-law Anthony Constantinople called me on my car phone from his office at 123 William Street. From there he had an unobstructed view of the ongoing horror. He confirmed our fears. I told my driver to divert the car to campaign headquarters in Astoria and told Tony to get everyone out of Barclay Street and our City Hall staff offices, right across the street from the crash.

I instructed my staff to call off the campaign and get out of Manhattan. It seemed most important at the moment to stay out of the rescuers' way. Those who wanted to help were to meet me in Astoria. From there I would try to contact the mayor to see how we might be helpful. The second crash proved beyond doubt that both were the work of terrorists. Tony called again to say he saw many people jump out of the windows as he was leaving. Soon after both towers collapsed.

Back at Astoria headquarters we stripped our vehicles of all campaign signs and materials. Then we gathered up all the sandwiches and water stored there for campaign workers during the day and a victory party later that evening, and headed for the Queensborough Bridge, which we figured people would be crossing on foot.

It was incredible! Hundreds of thousands of New Yorkers were walking across the 59th Street Bridge from Manhattan into Queens. Many were covered with ashes from the fallout. I want to emphasize that they were walking, not running, and none were panicked. It was more like a march of anger. As they thanked us for the water and asked for directions, they wanted to know who was responsible. They wanted to make sure the evildoers were brought to justice.

Before the day was over at least a hundred of my campaign volunteers came to help give out water and directions to weary and thirsty walkers. The flow of refugees and the refilling of the large water bottles from stores on the Queens side never stopped. I gave my credit card to an aide with instructions to buy all the bottled water and plastic cups he and others could find anywhere in Queens. Despite the horror of the day, I felt it was the best way I had ever spent a Primary Day. As the day finally wound down and I got back my credit card, I asked the young aide how much he had charged on it—a good deal, I imagined, since we'd never once run out of water. "No charges at all," he replied. "The volunteers all chipped in out of their own pockets."

These were the finest hours for many New Yorkers, none more so than the three thousand martyrs for freedom, led by the finest and bravest uniformed forces in the world. For I believe that, like the brave firefighters, police, Port Authority, and emergency service personnel who rushed into the burning inferno and up the stairs holding out their hands to save so many thousands, God too was waiting with outstretched hands for those who could not be rescued, and lifted them to a far better place. As scripture proclaims, "No greater love hath a man than he who lays down his life for his friends" (John 15:13).

No other city could have survived the catastrophe of 9/11 the way New York City has. And no other mayor could have performed better than Rudy Giuliani. He was the right man at the right time to lead us out of the dark sadness of Ground Zero. Any and all disagreements or difficulties he and I had during his administration pale in comparison to this record of achievement.

I cannot describe adequately how impressed I was as I watched him handle the crisis. The scene at City Hall on September 12 was worse than anything Hollywood could ever conjure up. Rudy brought out the best in all of us. At that very first meeting after 9/11 he asked me if the council would free up budgetary money earmarked for other purposes. I immediately told him it would be done and the vote would be unanimous. City Hall was still covered with a thick layer of white dust and ashes, so I convened the council for September 13 in the New York Public Library. The mere mention of Mayor Giuliani's name brought every single council member to a standing ovation.

Rudy deserved every moment of that ovation. I sat across from him as he gathered his handpicked commissioners and listened to their reports one by one. He was calm, decisive, and encouraging. Even as it became clear that there would be no survivors, Rudy knew how important it was to make survival and recovery the first priority, all the while advising anxious families to prepare for the worst. There were no dry eyes among us as we listened to the health commissioner describe body parts and explain how experts would have to rely on DNA to identify lost loved ones. The unsung men and women who so lovingly and patiently gathered the human remains in the midst of this war zone were true heroes.

Fragments of the aftermath come back to haunt me: the wife who caused me to break down in tears at the Armory as I was talking to anxious families when she explained, "If he's dead, I know he's all right"; the funeral service for Mychal Judge, a Franciscan priest, New York Fire Department chaplain and good friend whose last words to me a few weeks before he died in the Trade Center inferno were: "I pray for you to become mayor"; the sense of rebirth I felt when I saw with astonishment what New York City's unbelievable emergency services could do in twenty-four hours to salvage the unsalvageable. Here was proof, had I ever needed it, that the Big Apple would bounce back better than ever. It was also confirmation that the aborted primary election, rescheduled by Governor Pataki for the second Tuesday hence, paled in significance to the battle of good versus evil represented by the terrorist leveling of the World Trade Center.

Two days before the rescheduled primary I attended prayer services for the victims at Yankee Stadium; a poll released that day showed Freddy Ferrer gaining 35 percent of the Democratic vote, Mark Green 32 percent, yours truly 20 percent, and Alan Hevesi 12 percent. The next day I attended a prayer service for Father Mychal at St. Francis of Assisi in Manhattan. A close friend to both me and Rudy, he had sacrificed his own life to save another's. The mayor and I broke down during the service. It was impossible to get into a campaigning frame of mind during those very sad days.

On Primary Day the vote results were almost identical to those predicted by the poll two days earlier. While I had indeed bested Alan Hevesi, I had come in third, and only the first two finishers were entitled to take part in the runoff necessitated by no candidate winning more than 40 percent of the vote.

At least one Peter Vallone would probably stay in City Hall, however. That same September 25 my son Peter Jr. won the Democratic primary by a 2-to-1 margin. He had secured our party's nomination to take my place in the New York City Council. I was delighted for Peter. I was also disappointed. Not because I lost the election, but because I could not undo the irretrievable loss of life that had occurred that first Primary Day: September 11, 2001, a day that will live in infamy, anger, and sorrow ever more.

Afterword

10/5/01: See Cross at Site . . . made out of fallen steel beams.

10/11/01: *Runoff:* Green (52%) over Ferrer (48%). Endorse Mark.

10/12/01: Robles gets City Clerk!

10/28/01: Bloomberg closes gap w. Green. . . . *Now* people are sorry you're not on the ballot!

11/6/01: Election Day: *Peter wins* 10,000 to 5,000 *and* Bloomberg beats Green by 20,000 to 30,000 votes. All said, "You should have been mayor" . . . as God wills.

12/19/01: LAST DAY of your running *Stated Meeting* of City Council in City Hall.

12/21/01: Mayor Giuliani swears in Richard Weinberg as criminal court judge.

12/31/01: Reggie and Alice, two longtime detectives assigned to my security, help clean off top of desk.

A decade before making the diary entries above, I made an entry of quite a different nature. It was September 14, 1990. With the City Council suddenly at the center of everything significant happening in New York City, I had become very powerful and I was beginning to lose patience with people coming in to see me with what seemed to me minor problems. But that day I wrote in my notebook: "Corruption comes in many forms—remember Eddie." This was a shorthand way of reminding myself of an incident with a client that made a deep impression on me.

It happened while I was still a lawyer at Weinberg & Jacobowitz, when I still used one room of my apartment in Astoria as a local office so I could save clients the long trip out to Far Rockaway. One day I got a call from a guy who said he had to see me right away. It turned out he worked for the railroad that shipped Hafnia Hams, and he had arranged to steal an $80,000 load of the hams and unload them at bargain prices. He came to see me at my home and said: "All I want to do is surrender. The detectives are after me and they'll beat the hell out of me unless I give them money.

I say that's totally illegal. Please, let me surrender, but not to the Queens district attorney. Take me to Manhattan instead."

This was by far the biggest criminal case I had had to date. I called my father, who explained to me to that I needed to arrange for protective custody and I should indeed bring my client in to Manhattan. The next morning I called the Manhattan DA's office and said I wanted to surrender a client who was receiving threats from New York City police detectives. I was told to bring him in to the first assistant DA. I brought Eddie with me to his office. As we walked in, two tough-looking detectives were standing there. Immediately Eddie began to tremble.

The assistant DA, who was a tough guy and clearly very busy, gestured in an intimidating way. "Yeah? What the hell do you want?"

I started to explain why my client was afraid to be booked in Queens, and he angrily cut me off, declaring, "Can't you see I'm busy?" He ordered me and poor Eddie out of his sight.

The detectives grabbed my guy and hustled him out of the office. "Where are you taking him?" I protested to the "too busy" DA. Eddie would be arraigned tomorrow morning in Queens, I was told.

I followed Eddie and the detectives as far as I could, until he was thrown into their car. "Take care of Eddie—and make sure he doesn't get hurt," I warned them.

The next morning I showed up in court in Queens and found Eddie beaten black and blue. I stood up and started to appeal to the judge, "Your honor, please, look at my client's condition—" but Eddie grabbed me and said, "They did nothing to me. I just tripped and fell down the stairs. I want to plead guilty." Eddie no longer trusted me and there was nothing I could do to protect the poor fellow.

Many years later I had reason to run into that particular assistant DA, who had gone on to become a state supreme court judge. I recalled the incident to him. He explained that at the time he had been dealing with several important murder cases and considered Eddie's story nothing more than the fantasy of a petty criminal. What detectives were going to beat up a small-time thief on account of a few hams? Of course, it hadn't helped matters that I was just a cub attorney. Thanks to Eddie, I have tried never to be "too busy" to listen to anyone's tale of woe, and helped whenever I could.

In all my years of public service, the most flagrant example of sheer politics triumphing over good government was the 1999 repeal by Albany of the so-called commuter tax. This tax should have been more properly called a "user fee" for nonresidents who worked in the city. When it existed, it amounted to a daily fee half the price of a subway token. Ed Koch was absolutely right when he called the repeal "the greatest betrayal of New York City since Benedict Arnold." Which brings us to the "Albany Question" and the story of how a special election for state senator in Rockland County cost the greatest city in the world more than half a billion dollars in annual revenue.

The facts are simple enough. The Republican incumbent senator from that district resigned his seat when Governor Pataki appointed him to a state job. The May 1999 special election for the seat he had vacated pitted a Republican assemblyman against the Democratic chairman of the Rockland County legislature. The stakes were particularly high because the Republicans had a shaky majority in the senate and feared they might lose control of that house for the first time in decades. The Republican candidate pledged that he would vote to repeal the commuter tax—a particularly appealing pledge in that suburban county. Unsurprisingly, the Democratic candidate then felt he had to do likewise. This was good politics, since no commuter likes a tax. But it was also bad government because the city is the economic engine that drives the state and its commuter-dominated suburbs, and anything you do that damages the city's revenues ultimately comes back to haunt the state and suburbs.

During my recent campaign for governor in all sixty-two counties of the state, I had not heard a single person complain about this commuter fee. Unfortunately, political control and patronage were more important than the well-being of New York City. Joseph Bruno, the Republican leader of the Republican-controlled senate, arranged for the state senate to repeal the commuter tax shortly before the election, in an effort to give a clear advantage to his candidate. Surprised and disappointed, Mayor Giuliani and I traveled to Albany to express our dismay to Mr. Bruno, who told us not to worry. A bill passed by one house alone was not unusual. Surely the Democratic leader of the assembly, Sheldon Silver, would do nothing to hurt the city, some of whose voters he represented. We went to see Mr. Silver, as well as the governor, to caution them against participating in this game of chicken which would do irreparable harm to the city. No good. In Albany, political control is far more important than good government. Shelly sensed that his man in Rockland had a chance—why not let New York City pay for it? So the Democratic assembly passed this mad law, and the governor happily signed it.

Rudy and I sued the state, contending that the state had decimated the city's budget without even asking for our input in the form of a "home rule." We had had to provide such a legislative measure decades ago in order to have the commuter tax established—surely we would need to be consulted before the state reversed the process? The state's court of appeals ruled, however, that home rule was whatever the state said it was. Since then the city has lost billions of dollars.

At the time of its passage, Speaker Silver claimed the repeal was for the "greater benefit" of the state, and that both the council and Mayor Giuliani had planned to cut taxes. It was true we wanted cuts for residents and owners of city businesses who were already the most highly taxed American citizens. Their tax bill, however, would not be lessened one cent by this repeal. Furthermore, the repeal became legal only after it was extended to commuters from New Jersey and Connecticut. The ultimate effect was to provide more tax relief to out-of-staters than upstaters. No wonder that many of the bill's supporters later acknowledged that the repeal had been hastily conceived, with no hearings, little debate, and adopted for no good reason other than an attempt to gain partisan advantage.

When Michael Bloomberg took office three and a half months after September 11, 2001, both Washington and Albany made sympathetic noises about the city's plight. The president pledged $22 billion of aid and came to Ground Zero to show solidarity. You would think that Messrs. Bruno, Silver, and Pataki would at least have restored the commuter tax. When San Francisco was hit by an earthquake, the State of California came to its immediate relief with a special statewide surcharge earmarked for the city, and San Francisco did not even have to ask!

But no. Four years have passed and New York City still does not have all the money promised from President Bush and Congress, not to mention the commuter tax. Our "friends" in Albany maintain that New York is just another city in financial trouble, as if *we* were responsible for 9/11, not Al Qaeda. Generously, they gave us permission to raise yet again the city's sales and personal income tax to cover the deficit. You don't have to be a genius to cover a deficit by raising taxes, but you have to be an idiot to think that was all the state could do to help. When the state legislature at last tried to help a little by agreeing to pay a portion of the city's interest debt, the governor not only vetoed this token, but actually sued to stop it from being implemented.

How ironic that almost anyone running for office in both the state and the nation comes to the City of New York to ask New Yorkers to donate to their campaigns—yet so few use their power and influence to help in its time of need. One way of getting the attention of at least a state representative seeking donations might be to ask whether he or she would co-sponsor a bill to restore the commuter use fee. Its loss is only one part of a larger pattern of financial discrimination by which the city is being shortchanged hundreds of millions—from an unjust Medicaid burden of $3.5 billion to an unfair distribution of educational funding (declared unconstitutional by the state's highest court, yet still not remedied). Maybe it is time to talk about secession. My son Peter Jr. has introduced such a bill to the City Council. How else is a city of eight million supposed to get its fair share? Right now New York City gives Washington and Albany billions more than it gets back. It may take decades before this issue is resolved. But then, it also took decades to get rid of the all-powerful Board of Estimate.

Most voters vote in favor of term limits because they know some elected official they would like to get rid of. You now know some of the officials I would like to see out of office: the gang in Albany who voted to punish New York City by repealing the commuter tax. Yet I still think term limits are a terrible idea. Their effects on New York City will only grow worse in the years to come. I'm afraid that it will take a good deal of education and heartaches for the electorate to come to its senses, as our forefathers did, and outlaw term limits for the representative branch of government. The "seasoning" of a legislator comes only with experience. Term limits wreak havoc on a legislature because no one can really know the ability of a colleague only recently met. As Speaker, I could have introduced a bill and passed a law to repeal term limits. I did not because even if upheld by the highest court, New Yorkers for Term Limits would have immediately initiated a new referendum that for all I know would have limited the term of office to *one* term, and the council would have been accused of defying the voters' wishes.

I decided the better way was to raise enough money to finance a real voter education project on the issue, get sufficient institutional and financial support to answer any media blitz, and bring a new referendum to the public to change the current limitations. Educating the voters will take time and perseverance, but it is the best and only answer.

Meanwhile, my solution for making changes in the legislative branch, whether federal, state, or municipal, lies not in mindless wholesale removal but in a campaign finance system that provides for healthy competition.

The virtues of campaign finance were vividly illustrated in the 2001 mayoral primary. All four democratic candidates spent the same amount of money, and Mark Green eked out a victory. True, the ultimate winner, Mike Bloomberg, spent almost $100 million—more than all of the Democrats spent together on both the primary and general election. Still, he barely won the general election. The election was as close as it was only because of the campaign financing law passed by the City Council I had led. Today, you no longer have to be a millionaire or a billionaire to run for office in New York City. You do, however, have to enjoy party support and build up name recognition along the way if you do not have deep financial pockets. There is nothing wrong with using your own money for public purposes, but there is something wrong when money is the only thing that counts.

Many well-intentioned people support "nonpartisan elections" for citywide office, thinking that the current party system prevents qualified candidates from winning a primary or a general election. Recently I had a conversation with a member of Mayor Bloomberg's charter commission who supported the idea. I asked him, "How could you support nonpartisan elections when you know that you would be turning this country over to an aristocracy?"

He answered, "Peter, you of all people should understand. You would be mayor now if your Democratic primary had been open to all the voters!"

"Even if that were true," I replied, "I would never have been a Democratic candidate for mayor if I hadn't started out in my local political club and 'worked the vineyards' with their support."

The average person needs a party to win an election. Only an independently wealthy one can afford to "buy" one.

APPENDIX

How to Run for Office

During my run for mayor and Peter Jr.'s run to succeed to my Astoria seat in the City Council I heard him say, while being interviewed on television, "I'm running for public office in the same tradition of honesty and integrity as my father and grandfather." At that moment I was as proud as I had felt when my dad was elected a judge. Neither Dad nor I could ask for anything more.

I hope that younger citizens who don't have the same kind of family tradition as we Vallones may have been inspired to run for office by reading this book. For those who are tempted to try, I offer the following pointers.

Most aspiring candidates for office join the political party of their choice and become the party's candidate. The easiest way to do this is to join a local political club or committee and meet its leaders, members, and elected officials. You will probably find yourself being welcomed with open arms. Most people interested in their government are cordial and community conscious, if for no other reason than they want you, your family, and friends to vote for their candidates. You will be asked to serve on various committees and to meet with and help their candidates for the next election.

The excitement of a political campaign quickly becomes contagious. You may begin to realize that you can make a difference. Participate in meetings, speak out on issues that affect you and everyone else: police protection, sanitation, clean streets and sidewalks, homelessness, the schools, the quality of life. Besides the local political club, seek out neighborhood civic associations, community and school groups, and religious institutions and become better known in your community. It's also wise to meet with the publishers of the local newspapers and try to get a letter to the editor published along with your photograph—a picture is still worth a thousand words. It comes down to establishing credibility and making friends with people who will volunteer their precious time to go out and get valid signatures that will place your name on the ballot.

Familiarize yourself with the number of signatures needed for the office you are seeking. In New York, Section 6-136 of the Election Law mandates that you collect either 5 percent of the party members in the given constituency, or a maximum of 900 signatures for New York City Council;

500 for State Assembly; 1,000 for State Senate; 1,250 for U.S. Congress; 4,000 for borough president; 7,500 for mayor, public advocate, or comptroller; 15,000 for governor, state comptroller, or attorney general. These numbers must be from registered party members or they will not count. Many would-be candidates have been removed from the ballot the hard way when their signatures were successfully challenged in court. In general, it's wise to get at least twice as many signatures as needed, then check that those gathered are indeed registered members of the party. A good organization will first pay for and obtain from the Board of Elections a list containing the names and addresses of party members and go door to door to obtain signatures.

In New York City, where the Democratic Party dominates, the "maximum" numbers are usually required for it and the Republican Party. This is not true, however, for the other parties, for which the 5 percent rule becomes operative. For example, the Conservative, Right to Life, Working Families, or any other party may have only 100 registered voters in a given council or assembly district. In such a case only five valid signatures would get you on the ballot in that district. You might even make it to the November election with that number—although minor parties rarely win elections alone. Their practical value usually arises when a Democratic or Republican candidate seeks multiple-party endorsement.

If more than one candidate for the same office obtains the necessary signatures and survives court challenges, a primary follows in which all registered party members now have the right to vote. It is a sad fact that only about 20 percent of registered voters come out to vote on Primary Day, one of the most important decision days for all Americans.

The road to victory is bumpier than what I describe above if you are an insurgent challenging a regular party organization, but it's not impossible. You will not have the advantage of having people in place to gather the necessary signatures. You and your friends will have to go out and do the job yourselves, or you will have to hire people to do it for you. Assuming you are not independently wealthy, as many candidates seem to be today, you will have to round up enough volunteers. I have found that if you start at the local office level it is far easier to become a successful insurgent because enthusiastic members of the family and friends of the candidate are worth a lot more than paid people who are just doing a job and lack any vigor. You will also need a campaign manager who is familiar with election law. Also, be prepared to retain a lawyer to defend your petitions and signatures because the regular organization or a well-funded candidate opposing you will surely attack them in court. This gets back to the unpleasant business of raising money to pay the lawyer and print the petitions, mailings, and campaign literature you will need to wage a campaign. An insurgent in New York City has the tremendous advantage in the matching funds provided by the campaign finance law, which enables her or him to create a level playing field with other candidates and/or the incumbent.

The legal age to run for office on the local level is 18, the same year you earn the right to vote. It is different, however, for other state and federal offices. You have to be at least 25 years old to run for Congress (and be a citizen for seven years), and at least 30 to run for the U.S. Senate (and a citizen for no less than nine years). If you want to be president, forget about it unless you were born a citizen of the United States, are at least 35, and have lived in the United States for a minimum of fourteen years. In New York State the governor and lieutenant governor have to be at least 30, and a citizen and resident of the state for at least five years. State legislators have to be citizens and residents for no less than five years and must have lived in the election district for the preceding twelve months, except in a redistricting year, when only a county residence during the entire preceding year is required.

You can easily see why there are so many court challenges, but balance and fairness is necessary in a democracy, as is the rule of law.

The most important thing to remember if you want to serve is that you simply cannot lose if you keep your priorities straight: God, country, and family. Simply: doing the right thing is far more important than winning or losing an election.

INDEX